M000239293

# UNIONIZING THE IVORY TOWER

# UNIONIZING THE IVORY TOWER

## Cornell Workers' Fifteen-Year Fight for Justice and a Living Wage

**Al Davidoff**

**ILR PRESS**

**AN IMPRINT OF CORNELL UNIVERSITY PRESS**

**ITHACA AND LONDON**

Copyright © 2023 by Cornell University

All rights reserved. Except for brief quotations in a review, this book, or parts thereof, must not be reproduced in any form without permission in writing from the publisher. For information, address Cornell University Press, Sage House, 512 East State Street, Ithaca, New York 14850. Visit our website at cornellpress.cornell.edu.

First published 2023 by Cornell University Press

Library of Congress Cataloging-in-Publication Data

Names: Davidoff, Al, author.

Title: Unionizing the ivory tower : Cornell workers' fifteen-year fight for justice and a living wage / Al Davidoff.

Description: Ithaca : ILR Press, an imprint of Cornell University Press, 2023.

Identifiers: LCCN 2022056552 (print) | LCCN 2022056553 (ebook) | ISBN 9781501769801 (hardcover) | ISBN 9781501771552 (paperback) | ISBN 9781501769818 (pdf) | ISBN 9781501769825 (epub)

Subjects: LCSH: International Union, United Automobile, Aerospace, and Agricultural Implement Workers of America. Local 2300 (Ithaca, N.Y.)—History—20th century. | Cornell University—Employees—Labor unions—Organizing. | Universities and colleges—Employees—Labor unions—Organizing—New York (State)—Ithaca. | Collective bargaining—College employees—New York (State)—Ithaca.

Classification: LCC LD1346.7 .D38 2023 (print) | LCC LD1346.7 (ebook) | DDC 331.8809747/71—dc23/eng/20230118

LC record available at https://lccn.loc.gov/2022056552

LC ebook record available at https://lccn.loc.gov/2022056553

This book is a memoir and constitutes the expressions of the author's views, perspectives, opinions, and personal interpretations of events and interactions recounted. Some readers might find some of the language used offensive. The author recalls the conversations and events as his opinions and commentary in the context of academic engagement surrounding both his impressions at the time of the events recited, or upon later reflection on the experiences shared.

*This book is dedicated to three amazing women: Cathy Valentino, a Cornell duplicating machine operator who had the guts to spark a working-class rebellion; Emily Apgar, a custodian who organized coworkers day and night for years; and Barbara Rahke, a clerical worker from Boston and UAW organizer who outsmarted Ivy League bosses and taught us to believe we had all that we needed to win.*

**Pain shared is halved, power shared is doubled.**

—Adapted from Chinese, Swedish, and Native American proverbs

**There is no greater purpose than to struggle with utmost love and determination for our betrayed hopes and dangerous dreams.**

—Eduardo Galeano, Uruguayan writer

# Contents

# Preface

This book is about one union and my experience helping organize and then build that union during the 1980s and 1990s. The US labor movement's numerical decline and struggle for its identity were already under way when we began our fight. In the years since, the issues raised in the following chapters have only become more salient for labor's future.

Labor has now gotten to the point, in 2022, where less than seven percent of private-sector workers are unionized. Seven percent! That's lower than before the passage of labor's "Magna Carta," the National Labor Relations Act in 1935.

Labor's decline is due to four factors: the brutal and unchecked opposition of employers; an American culture that consistently devalues collective action in general and trade unions in particular; the growing use by businesses of part-time, temporary, and contract workers—typically harder to organize than a stable workforce; and the structural transformation of the world and US economies since the 1970s that has severely diminished major unionized industries. Capitalism's unchecked search for more and more profit severely eroded organized labor's base and made bold, creative action even more necessary.

These plagues did not all come from outside forces, employers, or capitalism. We in organized labor also faltered and failed ourselves in critical ways. Nationally, too much of organized labor's energy has focused on protecting those declining numbers still unionized and not enough on being the voice, advocate, and mobilizing vehicle for the working class. This has led to a lack of vigorous, creative organizing, linked to important energized social movements like the women's, immigrant rights, and racial justice movements.

There are sparks of change lighting up labor's dreams. A great deal of those hopes depends on young people, who are fed up and want voice and agency in their work lives. A resurgent grassroots labor movement will face the same fundamental questions we faced. There are not only external challenges confronting us. A dynamic, growing labor movement will be challenged to make critical workplace-level decisions about how to build healthy unions.

These challenges don't just play out at the headquarters of national unions or the AFL-CIO, but also in the struggle to build effective unions in every local, and in every shop. Do workers own their union at the most relevant level, their workplace? Is there one leader, or are there dozens? Conservative, nonstrategic business unionism, as it is called, treats the members as manipulable customers and not as a wise and capable collective force. This struggle at the heart of the labor movement, for the identity, the soul of our unions, was with us from day one of this story. These challenges were there in the organizing drive and came crashing down on us just as we were struggling with what it meant to be a healthy local union. The decline and complacency of too much of the American labor movement was the nagging background score, never far from my mind as I, much to my surprise, found myself wondering how to be a union leader.

# UNIONIZING THE IVORY TOWER

# Introduction

I was sixteen.

I had my learner's permit but no insurance, and I needed the car for a short drive across town. My father stared straight at my chin with those always fearful eyes and said, "If you run into some little old lady, we could lose everything."

What stuck with me about that moment was that we always had enough but that he repeatedly reminded us how close to some invisible, harrowing edge we were. That moment wasn't about an imaginary little old lady and a sixteen-year-old driver without insurance. It was about how hardship, how growing up as a refugee's son in the Great Depression, as my father did, can burn a gray-tinted lens over the bearer's eyes, and how nothing, not even decades of middle-class success, can make the world a safe and secure place.

The World War II Battle of the Bulge left him with lots of medals, shrapnel in his hand, and a "frozen" foot, but it also compounded his sense of precarity. He was politically very liberal, the offspring of a Jewish working-class immigrant father, but he was a personal and parental conservative. We lived below his means: practical and cautious. I wore hand-me-downs, and new clothes came from Woolworth's basement.

He wanted to believe in things—those were *his* roots. His dad was buried in a socialist Workmen's Circle grave and proudly claimed, like millions, to have met Eugene V. Debs. But my dad's response to hard times was to keep most beliefs about justice and political ideology private. Instead he focused on the requirements of survival and security.

The only time he ever truly rolled the dice was marrying my mom, a gentile, a shiksa from Scotland, *oy vey*! He broke with his Jewish culture and faith for true love. He risked losing friends and family for true love.

My mom planted in me the sense that justice was a practical thing, applicable to our daily relationships, not something grand or ideological. Reddish hair, stubborn, a fiery impatience. She had a tough, and what at times felt like an hourly, sense of right and wrong.

I grew up thinking she was a simple housewife and that my dad was a complex man, a great thinker. But it was my mom who, by example, taught me to stand up and to speak out. It was our righteous mom who shoved soap in my mouth when ten-year-old me mocked a kid with cerebral palsy. It was Mom who cried for Kennedy *and* King.

When it came to choosing a college, I knew it would be wise to avoid math and science and focus on social studies and writing. Not too far from home, and not expensive, were the other considerations. Cornell University in Ithaca, New York, was only a three-hour drive southeast from our middle-class Buffalo suburb of Tonawanda. But Cornell was a million miles culturally from my hometown, populated mostly by Polish and Italian industrial workers making a solid living. At Cornell many students came from wealth and multiple generations of college grads. The majority of my friends' parents had no college education, but Tonawanda's union jobs meant most of my peers did enter higher ed.

Cornell had twenty thousand students, fifteen hundred faculty, and thirty-five hundred staff, working across seven colleges on 745 beautiful rural acres. The nonstudent population of Ithaca was only around twenty thousand, so Cornell dominated every aspect of community life. I was part of the smallest college, six hundred of us studying history, economics, and organizational behavior at the College of Industrial Labor Relations. ILR is one of Cornell's statutory colleges, which meant tuition was less than half that of the private schools like Engineering or Arts and Sciences.

I came to Cornell as a seventeen-year-old student in 1976, and after a freshman year of hitting the books and falling in love I became a student rabble-rouser. It was easy; my dad had quietly raised me to analyze, to think independently, albeit cautiously. My mom had loudly challenged me to know right from wrong and do something about the wrong. Years later, when my dad asked me with a twinkle in his eye how I became such a loudmouth troublemaker, I told him he had given me the privilege of never knowing hunger or war. That he and Mom had given me the gift of a secure childhood. I told him I felt the freedom to follow what I care about most.

Student, staff, and faculty activists were trying to get the university to divest from South Africa. The first demonstration I ever participated in was a student and faculty rally during the board of trustees meeting at Cornell's world-famous, I. M. Pei–designed Johnson Art Museum. There were maybe five hundred protesters chanting and eventually blocking the doors so the trustees couldn't leave to get to their banquet. Our radical leader, Marty, was charismatic, an acned whirling dervish of positive energy and good humor. He realized that the blockade could fail because we had not covered the obscure rear escape at the loading dock. He asked for volunteers, and I raised my hand. "OK, you, what's your name? Al, take about twenty-five people, and don't let them out!"

None of us wanted to leave the mass action, the speeches, the rowdiness, but we did. As fate would have it, the trustees were trying to escape out the back, so we played a pivotal role in sustaining the action. It was a valuable lesson for my teenage self that I would soon be applying as both a student and later as a worker activist. Every job matters. You can lead from behind and away from the spotlight.

We were trying to get the university to boycott the union-buster textile giant and sheet and towel maker J. P. Stevens. (As promiscuous college radicals we loved the slogan "Don't sleep with J. P. Stevens!") We were trying to win tenure for a brilliant, radical labor historian, Roger Keeran. He won the student vote for Excellence in Teaching three years in a row and published a critically acclaimed history book, but that was not enough to overcome discomfort from peers about "his communist politics."

None of these early struggles were fully successful, but I got a lot more than an Ivy League bachelor of science degree thanks to those good fights. I learned how to be an activist, how to write a flyer, how to build a coalition, how to speak through my nervousness in front of groups, and how to be a team leader. I got elected president of the student government.

We were the first student group in a decade to take things over. We occupied the senior vice president's office, with him hostage for four hours (until we became more bored than he). We marched in and took over an entire faculty meeting. We even had a high-tech takeover, tying up every phone line of every top administrator for two straight days.

My first direct experience with workers organizing came thanks to my good friend Rudy Porter. Rudy came from a union family. His dad was the secretary-treasurer of the AFT, the American Federation of Teachers. He was a fellow student labor activist but with none of the naïve-around-the-edges, newer-found radicalism most of us were growing through.

A group of about forty Cornell staff worked operating three utility plants on campus. The heating plant, chilled-water, and water-filtration operations kept the hundreds of buildings warm in the long winters and cool in the short summers and with running water. These were mostly high-skilled jobs, and the workers had just quietly voted for the Operating Engineers Union. Bargaining had started, and Rudy made a connection to Ron Bess, the union rep out of Local 71–71A in Rochester, who had agreed Rudy could sit in and observe. I was jealous as hell and begged my buddy to ask Ron if I could sit in too. Rudy has a calming effect and reassured Ron I would be quiet as a mouse, and if they got into a fight and wanted student support, I could be a big help. I was in!

I nervously met Ron and the intimidatingly grizzly blue-collar bargaining team. Top HR honcho Cecil Murphy was bargaining for management. Their team came in, and Ron introduced me as a student observer from the ILR School, basically suggesting this was a learning opportunity for one of Cornell's own. Management began whispering to one another. Before any bargaining took place, management demanded a caucus and to see Ron in a private sidebar outside.

I hadn't a clue what was happening but in the meantime began getting to know the worker negotiators: Casey, a sweet, shiny bald-headed leader; Les Niles, a sardonic and wily ringleader; and— But then Bess came back minutes later and announced that management had a problem with my being there. "They know who you are, Al. You must be some big thorn in their side, cuz they want you out." Ron asked if Rudy and I could step out while their team decided what to do.

This was a nightmare. I was mortified. Instead of helping this small, brave group taking on this giant employer, I had caused them grief and stopped the bargaining cold. I felt like I'd probably screwed things up for Rudy too. I wanted to slink back to my dorm.

Ron called us back into the union team caucus. Niles spoke before Ron could get a word out. "We had to give up a week's vacation, but you can stay," he deadpanned. For about two seconds, I felt like my dog had died. But then the whole group started laughing. Niles added, "Well, you don't look like much, and I don't know who the fuck you are or what you can do, but those assholes are afraid of you, so welcome to the team." Bess smiled and said, "Management can't tell us who is on our team." The smile disappeared, he stared right into my eyes and slowly, enunciating each word, added, "But don't say anything."

It was only forty workers, but Cornell was not going to let them succeed and set a positive example for thousands of unorganized workers. Bargaining went nowhere, and as winter approached, the workers, united, went out on strike.

Running those plants required very specific skills, and Cornell struggled to replace the thirty-eight guys and two women. On top of that it was nine degrees out, and that put added strain on the heating system. But Cornell was trying to send a message. They erected a huge gate, with barbed wire, and prison-style floodlights around the heating plant, "to prevent sabotage."

Rudy and I rallied student activists to picket with the workers, and then decided to try to put more pressure on the antiquated heating and water system.

Very late one night we worked our way through a few dozen buildings, leaving water faucets running full blast and doors propped open to the frigid night.

The workers got a decent contract after a twelve-day strike. They eliminated merit pay and won 40 percent wage increases over three, high-inflation years. The money was good, but Cornell hadn't given so much as to make other workers jealous. Cornell had sent a powerful warning message: you will have to strike to get anything, and we will treat you like criminals when you do.

About a year later, when larger and more diverse numbers of workers began challenging Cornell, I went directly to Cathy Valentino, the Neuman Lab duplicating machine operator who was sparking things and offered to help out in any way. I'd make copies, hand out flyers, whatever the fledgling ACE (Active Concerned Employees) group asked me to do. I had worked odd jobs throughout college, and I had grown up in a working-class middle-class suburb of Buffalo surrounded by autoworkers and steelworkers. The poor "lowlifes" of those neighborhoods were the teachers, who earned half what the rivetheads were bringing home. I'd been studying labor relations for three years and become a student activist. Here was something important, fragile, and real, beginning to happen all around me.

My suburban youth did not include fully witnessing the indignity and the deprivation that low-wage service-sector workers were suffering until I met the folks who cleaned my dorm, cooked my meals, and fixed the furniture broken at our wild parties.

My activism and emerging radical politics led me to want a life fighting in and for the labor movement. I also was deeply moved by the courage, and what even in my youth I realized was the openhearted naïveté of ACE's fledgling effort. They were a tiny collective David, with no slingshot or strategy and a hundred years and ways that Ivy Goliath had been kicking their ass. I felt useful and accepted by these local folks. They were more like the working-class families I grew up with and less like the students that were now my activist family. I needed money to pay some college expenses, and I wanted to be as big a part of the organizing drive as possible, so I applied for a job as a custodian during my senior year.

Much to my shock, I was hired right away. Now I had to figure out how to punch in at 7:25 a.m., work until 3:55 p.m., and still get by as a full-time student. I visited my profs, explained what I was doing, and then never showed up for class again. I would read the summaries and write the papers. I made dean's list for the first time.

I learned three important lessons: Not having any time makes you focus on what counts. Second, underneath the century-old Ivy was an academic system that often rewarded regurgitation over independent thought. Third, having some profs who secretly supported the organizing drive meant I was being cut some serious slack. My favorite professor told me, "I'll think of your custodial work as independent study."

Being a custodian *and* a union organizer—that's where making the grade was to be more of a challenge.

Part I

# BECOMING THE UNION

# 1

# MOPHEAD

It did not surprise me to hear that West Campus was the dregs of all the university workplaces. I had been a contributing West Campus dreg myself, having lived there as a freshman. The cluster of dorms had the deserved reputation of being a wild, drunken world of eighteen-year-olds experimenting with booze, drugs, sex, and general destructive debauchery.

It was one thing to be a card-carrying wild young puking fool and quite another to be the janitor who cleaned it up every day. The first morning at punch-in I arrived at the "line," which for some reason was connected to the freshman laundry room. Twenty-three custodians lined up, heads hung down, bodies slouched over. About half men and half women—more like zombies.

Cliff, the main boss of the area, approached me. He had interviewed me. I had lied, telling him my girlfriend was working on a PhD and that I would be around for four more years. He muttered encouragingly, "That's twice as long as most last here."

He welcomed me and introduced me to a tiny old woman, saying, "Martha Wiicki, this is your new partner. His name is Al Davidoff. Can you show him how things work at U-Hall Five?"

She barely turned around, never making eye contact with me or Cliff, and then grunted, "You mean things *work* at U-Hall Five? Coulda fooled me."

Cliff responded, "Martha's one of our very best workers here. She'll be able to show you the ropes."

"Cliff, open your eyes." Martha sneered up at him. "Look at these losers. You think being one of the best is supposed to make me feel good? Shit, bring back that Mr. Lemon you took away from me—that'll make old Martha feel good."

Cliff slouched off toward the safety of his office. Martha muttered, "I oughta give him some rope."

I asked Martha, "Who's Mr. Lemon?"

"He's the only friend I got," Martha said, suddenly staring straight into my face. "And old Cliffie boy took him away."

Martha's face was wizened beyond her years, but her eyes blazed She also seemed to tilt over. As the line finally began to move forward with the clunk of time cards being punched, Martha shuffled, never lifting her feet. She was a cross between a bulldog and ET.

As I got closer to the time clock, I realized that the arrogance of a college senior wasn't going to be a handicap. It was simply irrelevant who I was. If I was on that line, maybe I was just another loser.

When I looked across the room at the freshman boys and girls chatting and doing their laundry only three yards away from our line, I saw how they saw us. We were strange animals in some circus. We were the freak show on parade every morning from about 7:15 until the *clunk*, *clunk*, *clunk* of the machine sent us off to clean up after them. After a few months I came to realize there was a twisted kind of strength in numbers here too. It was the only time each day we weren't invisible to the students.

I was Martha's seventeenth partner in thirteen years.

"One killed himself," she began. "Two of 'em were drunks like my husband, two of 'em still work here but couldn't stand me, and the rest are on welfare or just disappeared. The only one of 'em worth his salt just got promoted to some other job on campus."

"Is that Mr. Lemon?" I asked.

Martha cackled and sniffled and then coughed until I thought she might toss up a major organ.

"That's the cancer," she said to me. "Now don't you feel like a bad little boy for bothering poor old Martha?"

We walked side by side, Martha shuffling, head straight down, me awkwardly trying to walk slowly enough to match her pace. "Walk this way," I said to myself. I followed her into the dorm and down to the basement loading dock area.

She turned to me, and her eyes, ringed with red, practically leapt up into my face. "If you last a month, which I don't think you will, come remind me, and I'll introduce you to Mr. Lemon. He's my secret boyfriend. Till then keep off of my floors, and I'll keep off of yours. Now get!" Martha shooed me out of her break room and into mine. So much for what my profs would call "the mentoring experience."

I couldn't get over how invisible I was to the students. I felt like Dracula. In my custodial coffin all day and then emerging as an experienced, Big Man On Campus in the evening. How frustrating to spend four years getting to be somebody and then have these freshman nobodies treating me like the dorm garbage I now was responsible for.

I would be cleaning the women's bathroom and showers with the doors propped open and my cart blocking the entrance. Some of the freshman women would push my cart aside and come in and take a shower behind some flimsy curtain with me scrubbing floors just five feet away. They would emerge from their rooms in T-shirts and panties and come flitting by me as if I was the broom I was holding. No man, just mop.

I had entered a world that was slowly swallowing me up. I smelled different, like cleaning chemicals with their sickly sweet cherry scents masking toxic substances. We were not supposed to get any of this crap on our hands, but all the custodians covered themselves in it day after day. Nobody wore the gloves. Eau de "Scrub-All."

Some of the custodians would clean shit out of toilets, piss out of urinals, and puke off the floors with their bare hands. It was as if hands were no longer human things but covered with some plastic layer. It was an acknowledgment of a futility, of a worthlessness. Hands as rags, hands as sponges. Nostrils as vacuum filters. Backs as bending, lifting machines.

After only five weeks, I looked older and more haggard. I began going out with some of the men to a country bar and getting plastered two or three nights a week. I was irritable with my girlfriend. After three months I had trouble focusing on the union organizing during some breaks and lunches. I just wanted to sleep or escape or shut down.

I struggled to maintain some sense of my student identity and what I thought was dignity. I'd borrow tapes from the library of great speeches. I'd listen to Michael Harrington or Carl Sagan while bringing a row of six urinals to a gleaming polish. I made friends with a couple of students who would talk to me like a human being, inviting me into their room, a work rule taboo. I'd share their food, listen to their music, throw a Frisbee in the hall.

I found that I, like almost all the male custodians, could not care less about the cleanliness of the dorm. The women custodians, especially the older ones, still called themselves maids. They treated the job like an extension of what had been traditionally women's work: cleaning, washing, vacuuming a "home," with lots of children to look after.

Even Martha, who was as crusty and hard as any human being I'd ever known, took immense pride in her work and resented my mediocre efforts. She cared what the kids' "home" looked like.

## Men Will Be Boys

After about a month I experienced my first rite of passage when some of the male custodians invited me to meet them in their attic during break. I went over and found a scene I could only imagine perhaps got edited onto the cutting room floor of *One Flew over the Cuckoo's Nest.* There were five grown men. Real adults by my twenty-one-year-old standards, men with wives and kids and trailers.

The attic itself was massive, filled with empty trunks and luggage but also expensive bikes and stereo systems. If two students in a room each brought an amazing music system, one of the setups ended up in the attic. It looked like backstage at *The Price Is Right.* It was another harsh reminder that many students' storage leftovers were worth more than the family savings accounts of my coworkers.

The guys had two shopping carts and were playing a game of chicken, running the carts at each other as fast as possible and watching them collide and carom off into student storage or supplies all neatly organized in rows and piles.

They then began a game of "Attic Bombardment," which consisted of each of us grabbing two brand-new lightbulbs from the supply area and chasing each other around and throwing the bulbs. There were no real winners and losers, just mayhem, shattering glass, a lot of hooting.

Attic Bombardment rotated from dorm to dorm, with the "host" being stuck with cleaning up the mess.

As I headed to the elevator to return to my dorm, one of the custodians, Jeff, grabbed me and shouted to the others, "Let's put the new guy in the cage."

I shouted, "No fucking way" and wriggled free. As they surrounded me I said "No fucking way" again and reminded them I still had two months of probation left. They nodded at this somber revelation, for they all hated management.

They immediately turned on one particularly hapless looking fellow, Bill Fenner, a man who had gotten bombarded more than most, and dragged him off into a locked cage where students' bikes were kept in the winter.

Jeff Clark and Leo LaMontain locked him in, shut off the lights to the frighteningly cavernous attic, climbed in the elevator, and left.

I asked what the deal was. Wouldn't Cliffie boy wonder where Fenner was eventually? Wouldn't Bill get in big trouble?

Jeff replied, "Naw, this is his building. I'll go get him in half an hour or at least before punch-out, if I remember."

My closest friend among the crew was Leo LaMontain. He and his wife, Diane, both worked at Cornell as custodians. Leo was part of the bad boy band, but he also was openly eager to help build the union and work with me to talk to others. He was an alienated rebel through and through, but his frustrations were focused clearly on management. I went to dinner at Leo and Diane's many times, got to know their wonderful little kids, and conspired with the couple about fighting Cornell.

Leo had a funny ritual, where he would use our paltry thirty-minute lunch break, sprint to his car, blaze downtown to the Busy Bee, get a bunch of disgusting, half-cooked Texas hots, and speed back up the hill with lunch. I realized it wasn't about the cuisine; it was just another small way to feel momentarily free.

One time, Leo took off at lunch and got his hair cut somewhere. He got back twenty minutes late, and Cliff caught him. Leo was a solid worker, and Cliff didn't want to fire him. But Leo couldn't leave well enough alone. He told Cliff, "My hair grows on work time. I thought I should get it cut on work time."

## Squeezing Mr. Lemon

I returned from my first attic melee to find Martha uncharacteristically waiting for me. She tapped her foot in the hall.

"Out having fun with the boys, were you?" she asked.

"Some strange folks work here, Martha," I responded.

"Yeah, well, you'll fit in fine with those jokers. But if you want to get your showers clean you've got to come to old Martha."

I followed Martha into her room, where she dug down underneath a pile of paper towels in a garbage can and pulled out a yellow bottle.

"Wanna meet him?" she asked coyly.

"Wouldn't miss it for the world," I said.

"This is Mr. Lemon. I put a little of this into my bucket and mix it with a little of this." She pulled a bottle of ammonia off her cart and poured it in. A puff of eye-scalding smoke came swirling up.

"You use this on your floors, and they'll get white like mine," she whispered.

"But, Martha"—the noxious smell of this mixture was overpowering—"we're not supposed to mix ammonia with anything. It can burn your throat and screw up your lungs."

"Listen, little boy, I got cancer. You think I give one shit about serious health problems from breathing in this?" She took a spoon out of her coffee mug and used it to stir the bucket. She looked up at me, grinning. "Ahh, this is good stuff. Cleans out your lungs and your showers!"

I fled the fumes to her witchy cackle.

I asked boss Cliff if I could get some Mr. Lemon for my floors. He said, "Has Martha been filling your head about Mr. Lemon? Christ, we phased that stuff out about two years ago because it caused too many skin rashes. If she still has any, let me know. She was supposed to turn it all in."

"Naww, I just heard her talking about it."

Meanwhile the zoo parade continued. I tried to strike up conversations at punch-in, but nobody talked. At punch-out everybody whooshed out of the building like it was on fire. Some of the young men actually sprinted to their cars and roared away.

At a union organizing meeting I was told that no other workplace on campus had higher turnover. Big Kevin, as he was called by all, was the first casualty during my initial weeks in the West Campus gulag. Kevin was about six foot six, with an unkempt shock of black hair that drooped down over his eyes. He had some developmental disability, and his mom dropped him off in a van.

His rep was he worked hard, always smiled, and as long as nobody messed with his routine, he was fine. Management loved him. He was one of only a couple of male custodians who didn't spend half the day playing hide and seek with Cliff, peeking out behind curtains to see if the big boss was coming to their building.

Kevin also would wash Cliff's car every now and then. It would happen just before punch-out, so we would be slowly sauntering over to the main building and Kevin would smile and keep polishing the boss's car. It was my first taste of solidarity in the group. The men and the women all tried to tell Kevin he shouldn't do this, that it wasn't his job. But Kevin would just smile and say "I don't mind," over and over. Because all our raises were completely dependent on how Cliff felt about us, Kevin's car washing hit a deep chord of resentment. One way or another, we were all washing Cliff's car, kissing his ass, or getting little to no raises. There was a story about an attractive young custodian whom one of the bosses made passes at. She got a big raise her first year, then married somebody, and got zero the next. She transferred out.

If you saw Cliff coming, Jeff told me, "Grab a broom and start sweeping. Sometimes though he sneaks up on you, or doubles back, but most of the time you can catch him coming and then look like you're working."

I understood some of the alienation toward the work that the men felt. Not only were they being forced into this invisible, degraded role before these shiny, BMW-driving students, but it was seen as "women's work." They were being paid a wage that was unlivable. They were raised with the notion that they should provide for their families, and they couldn't. They were cleaning up shit and piss and puke every day. Giving less than your full self to a system that treated you as less than a full person was one way of fighting back. The union was introducing a much bigger way.

The other striking reality was, from a cleaning perspective, none of it mattered. You could bust your butt cleaning a lounge to spotless perfection, and fifteen minutes later some student would shake open a can of soda and spray it all over the floor chasing some other student. The building never stayed clean for more than a few hours. What was the use?

One day at punch-out a rumor began working up and down the line. Kevin had been fired. It was the kind of communications system you expected in the "yard" of a prison movie. Nobody looked up; everybody acted as if they didn't want to get caught talking to another human being.

I asked Jeff what happened to Kevin. He said, "I don't know. Let's ask Lucy, his coworker."

"I'm not talking about it, I don't know," she said, rather contradictorily.

We all punched out. In the parking lot—one of the only lots that Cornell had yet to consider charging employees to park in—a few of us stopped and compared notes. Finally, Fenner furtively said, "I heard it was something, y'know, something sexual."

"Bullshit," "No way," or "Go fuck yourself, Fenner," was the general reaction of the crowd. Fenner was not exactly the Moses of the group.

"Yeah, I overheard Cliffie boy say they had a sexual incident with Kevin," Fenner stated, crossing his arms for emphasis.

We all drifted off, shaking our heads. The next day an official version had somehow emerged. Kevin had been jerking off in his solo break room, and a student had abruptly opened the door. It seems Kevin was always afraid to lock the doors and then forget which was the right key. As word spread, fellow custodians mainly felt bad for Kevin. Our break rooms were our only refuge, to eat, read, doze, relax. We didn't go into the students' rooms, and they shouldn't come barging into ours.

The student had called her parents, who called some muckety-muck, and Kevin and his seven years of perfect attendance and outstanding car washing were history.

Cliff came out to the line the next morning after the gossip had reached a crescendo and said, "Kevin Blake was terminated two days ago. It's none of any of your damn business what the reasons were. Now stop spreading rumors. I don't want to hear Kevin's name mentioned again. He does not work for West Campus any longer."

"Was that his name, 'Blake'?" Fenner mused out loud.

"Bill, I just told you I want this subject dropped," Cliff said, staring down Fenner.

"But, Cliff, it's just I never heard him called anything but Kevin or Kevin the Retard before. Is he related to Tom Blake? My brother worked with a Tom Blake at Smith Corona."

"That's enough, Bill, unless you want to come into my office right now." Cliff was beet red.

Fenner seemed oblivious to the big boss. Jeff spoke to Fenner in a voice just audible enough for the line but not to Cliff. "Well, I guess that means there's a spot open now—maybe you could become 'Fenner the car washer.' Just remember to lock the door when you're flipping through your Penthouses."

Everybody laughed. Cliff glared at the line and then stormed back to his office.

## Oh Yeah, the Union

I assumed it would take many months to be accepted enough by my fellow custodians before I could do much union talking. I was resigned to lying low, adjusting to the job, and making friends. The union organizers knew this made sense but kept gently pushing me to assert some leadership in a work area with no union activists.

Whatever hang-ups I felt about being a student first and a worker second disappeared as I came to realize two truths. The men accepted me immediately, as long as I was no rat and played their crazy alienated games. The women would never truly accept me unless I cleaned like they did. Perhaps in some abstract sense I had a choice, but in fact I quickly shared the alienation and the rebelliousness of my fellow male custodians.

It was a strange but short step from defiantly trashing attics to pointing out that a union would be a force to fight with in tackling the degradingly low pay and the absence of opportunities for promotion. When it came time to signing UAW cards, all but two of the twelve men signed up right away.

It took two cleaning incidents before the women would open up enough to let me talk union with them. The first happened on a Monday. Mondays were twice as bad as any other day. The dorm would be totally trashed over a weekend of intense partying. There were Mondays when it took me two hours just to get the trash down to the loading dock.

As I entered the men's bathroom, I glanced back to see two students snickering in the hall. One, John, who had befriended me, yelled, "Look out, Al, it's not a pretty sight."

It never was, so I just walked in, my tape of an Upton Sinclair speech droning on. The bathroom was a war zone. Feces were smeared on the floor, and there were puddles of urine under all eight sinks. All of the four toilets had been jammed and overflowed with pieces of crap sprinkled on each stall floor.

I walked out, gagging from the stench. John came up to me and said, "Sorry, Al, you should not have to clean this up. It's disgusting. A couple guys did it. Make them clean it up."

I didn't know whether to laugh or cry. I didn't know what the rules were. I told my friend in a voice filled with tense humor, "You know what, John? I'm the only guy in this fucking dorm that won't need to take a piss or a shower or brush my teeth here. This isn't *my* bathroom, it's your fucking bathroom, and I'm not going to touch it. It's just one less thing for me to clean."

"Hey, man, sorry. I hope they catch the guys who did it," John spoke as he watched me roll my pathetic, three-wheeled supply cart to the elevator. I waved back, "Hey, I hope *you guys* catch the guys who did it, unless you like climbing two flights of stairs to put on your fucking Clearasil."

Art Watkins was my new immediate supervisor, the level below Cliff. Art was a wise old heavyset Black man. In the university's service and maintenance world of over one thousand workers, you could count the Black supervisors on one hand. Art had been through many jobs. He had headed the City's Youth Bureau twenty years ago and was a renowned local umpire. Art knew I goofed off like the other guys, but I showed up every morning, got the basics done, and kept out of trouble. That was good enough for Art.

White, conservative, Polish Martha had no use for any of the bosses but particularly despised Art. "You think I'm gonna take orders from that big monkey," she shouted to Cliff in front of half a dozen coworkers he had called together to "rap" about the new supervisor. Cliff ignored the racism and tried to explain that nobody had to take orders around West Campus, that we all needed to just work together.

"I work alone," Martha stated.

It struck me that Martha's apparent ignorant prejudice knew no bounds and was not particularly directed toward African Americans. One day we were staring out a lounge window together and a differently abled student, limping, "hunchbacked" (the medical term for such severe spinal curvature is kyphosis) with medium dark coloring walked past us. Martha turned to me, shaking her head, and casually observed, without apparent malice, "Must be a Jew."

Toward the middle of that Monday, Art found me and asked to visit the men's bathroom with me. I ushered him in for a tour. The only way I could ever tell Art was annoyed was when the toothpick in his mouth switched from side to side.

We exited the nauseating scene, both gasping for air. Art's pick wiggled back and forth, and then he looked me dead in the eyes. "Al, I'm telling you, you are not going to have to clean that up. This is way beyond your job. As far as I'm concerned this is vandalism, and those who did it need to be caught and made to clean it up."

"Damn straight, Art," I said, thanking him.

For two days the investigation went on. I felt safe from it all, a very innocent bystander. The head resident of the dorm interviewed various lager louts, but when I peeked in the bathroom at 8 a.m. Wednesday, it was still the same, only now it was much, much worse for the delay.

On Friday, Art came and found me first thing in the morning. He had a hang-dog expression. His eyes welled up a little. "Al, you know I'm new here. You know a lot of folks aren't too comfortable with a Black man bossing them. Well, I made a mistake. I shouldn't have told you you wouldn't have to clean that up. Even though it's totally unfair, they can't catch the kids that did it, and it's your job, buddy. I'm sorry."

"Oh, that's just great, Art. What a terrific lesson for these kids. The shit is totally dried onto the floor and the walls. I'll need a goddamn ice pick to get it off before I can even clean."

Martha heard the ruckus and came over. "I told you he was no good," she said to me, staring down Art.

"Martha, this came from higher up," Art replied. "Sorry, Al. Do the best you can. If you refuse to do it, we're both in deep shit, cuz we're both on probation."

Martha gave me all her best chemical combinations, and I went to work. I opened all the windows but still had to leave the bathroom every minute to gasp for air. I started with gloves and boots on. By the end of the first hour, I was scraping feces and puke and dried piss from the floor with my bare fingernails. I wouldn't look any of the students in the eye. I was furious and ashamed. I swore the students would pay.

From that day forward I cleaned their sink with the same sponge I cleaned their urinal with.

A knock came at my break room door just before that Friday punch-out. Martha came in and spread a big white doily over my beat-up old table.

"My youngest daughter makes these for me," she said. "I don't know what the hell she thinks I'm gonna do with eight goddamn white tablecloths." She shook her head and walked back out.

The next Monday I had lunch with Martha. We talked union. She said, "It's about time we did something around here. Cliffie boy don't know his ass from a hole in the ground, getting rid of all the good cleaning supplies, hiring some know-nothing like Art to do his dirty work. Hell, you know Alice, who's been here twenty years, was up for his job, but they didn't hire her. I guess cuz she's got too much common sense and no education, or maybe cuz she's a woman."

Martha signed a union card and agreed to set up a lunch meeting with the other women, Alice included. I could feel my organizer heart racing watching her put pen to card. Within a week, five of the eleven women had signed UAW cards. The antiunion campaign hadn't begun in earnest. It was organizing the way the original labor law intended: no coercion, no threats, no aggressive interference from management. It wouldn't last much longer.

Two weeks later I came in on another Monday. I was fifteen minutes late from oversleeping. I rushed to my building, where I found Art and Martha waiting for me. I knew it must be something serious, because the two of them didn't exactly "hang out" much.

Art spoke while Martha eyed the floor. "Very early this morning a girl on your floor slit her wrists. She did it in *your* shower area. I want you to wear these gloves and clean it up. Martha's offered to help you. You can imagine the girls are extremely upset. So I want you to take care of it first thing. Forget emptying trash, just clean the bathroom."

"What's her name, Art?" I asked.

"Nobody told me. Cliff just said a U-Hall Five girl on the second floor. They're trying to keep this quiet." Art turned to walk out. "Sorry, guys."

"When you're the janitor, nobody tells you shit." Martha started rolling her cart slowly to the elevator. "We can use my stuff, that is if we want to actually clean it up," she said and gave me a wink. Martha did her garbage and quickly joined me on my floor, in that awful bathroom, and worked alongside me till the job was done.

Two days later Martha brought me three more signed union cards.

## Graduating with Honors

By May I had to ask for my first day off. My parents were coming from their retirement home in Florida, to see their one and only student government president son graduate in the top fifth of his Ivy League class. They were coming to get a goddamn firsthand explanation of why I was turning down "real" job offers to continue to be a custodian.

In the graduation line, the dean had to hand me a special, inscribed wooden gavel. He hated my guts. We had taken over his office, exposed his lies, and I once wrote a column in the student newspaper describing an altercation that resulted when he had called me into his office to try to intimidate me from continuing a pugnacious tenure fight for a pro-labor prof. The corpulent dean never forgave me for childishly writing that "as the Dean leaned over, pressing his face into mine for emphasis I noticed his belly dragging along his shag rug."

With my parents in hearing range, the dean handed me the gavel and, with ear-piercing sarcasm, uttered, "Well, Al, we're *really* going to miss *you* around here." My mom, always quick-tempered around disrespect, said for all to hear, "What the hell is wrong with that guy?" as we walked away.

My parents didn't truly understand. They had raised me humbly but with the security to follow my desires, to choose my own path. They were OK with me not cashing in and going corporate. They just hadn't anticipated my graduate work being in urinal studies. My mother would simply shake her head and say, "I can't believe a place as wonderful as this would treat their workers so poorly. At least you'll finally learn something about keeping things clean!"

I knew I'd reached a kind of peace with my father when a few months later he asked me over the phone, "Couldn't you become some kind of head custodian?"

That summer, as the drudgery wore on, the union drive was on the brink of really taking off. I found some escape in "supervising" three summer-help students, a year or two younger than myself. They were paid a dollar an hour less than us full-time folks, but they were given free housing for the summer. I indulged myself by relating to these college peers. I found that most of them were less accepting of me than my mop-rat, attic-smashing comrades.

Custodian Jeff Clark asked me how my graduation was and then muttered, "Man, why are you working at this dump? The economy sure has gone to hell, I guess." But the summer student help just couldn't comprehend my choice. They seemed a bit freaked out that one of their own could stoop so low.

They kept looking at my forehead for scars.

One student was an exception. Jim was a bohemian character. He was a beat poet, piano-boogying, lazy-ass fiend and was quickly welcomed into the full-time male custodial rituals. Supervision was so loose in the summer that student help enjoyed water-balloon fights, and snoozes in the now vacant dorm.

Full-timers had even more elaborate escapes. I prided myself on working indoors during virtually all daylight hours and yet still achieving a crisp, golden tan. I would lock myself into a vacant student room and climb out the window into a huge drainage gutter. I sunk down low enough so that as long as nobody saw me get in or out, they could never spot me.

The metal was scorching hot, so I'd bring towels and pillows. It was like a giant metallic tanning salon. The only danger was falling asleep and missing punch-out. (It happened once; I told Art my watch broke.) Once Jim snuck into my "suite" and locked the windows from the inside. But I just went back to dozing and woke up to a safe, unlocked escape.

The summer meant tearing apart every room and cleaning it from top to bottom. We goofed off more, but the work was more intense. We had to physically separate bunk beds and haul hundreds of heavy mattresses down to the loading dock for storage. Back injuries were common. Some students left their rooms disgusting pigsties. More importantly, some students abandoned valuable goodies in their rooms. We "team cleaned," as Cliff called it, so two custodians would eagerly bust into a heretofore private room simultaneously hoping for treasure.

I recall old Fenner diving under the dusty bed to scoop up coins, coming up grinning with a filthy quarter. We found pot and pornography because the students didn't dare bring the stuff home. We found clothes and even old stereos. We'd split anywhere from fifty cents to a few bucks in change that had fallen behind dressers and beds. We worked very hard but were making an extra five to ten dollars a day.

The rule was that all found property belonged to Cornell University, but nobody enforced it. You'd see custodians backing their trucks up to the loading docks before punch-out, tossing hefty bags full of loot into the trunk. The only time you got in trouble was if some student called back asking for something they left, or if you were stupid enough to bring the goods with you to punch-out.

## Escape from the Planet of the APes

There were two times I almost got fired. The first time was with Jim. In the early summer, after cleaning all the rooms, the "APes" moved in. These were sixteen- and seventeen-year-old summer-school Advanced Placement students. Typically they were rich kids, mostly from Long Island, getting a taste of Ivy life, for a hefty price. I cleaned one of the all-girl summer dorms. These glamour girls spent so much time doing hair and makeup in front of the bathroom mirrors that I needed to adjust my cleaning schedule. They were nothing like the down-to-earth, working-class Italian and Polish girls I grew up with in Buffalo. They saw Jim and me as wild animals. All but a few steered completely clear of us.

Jim and I were moving the lounge piano up to the attic for storage when Jim began boogying away like a maniac. We opened the elevator doors at each floor (each women's floor) and invited any interested APes to join us in the elevator for some great music and silliness. After a few trips up and back, two of our favorite APes had agreed to "check out the attic" with us.

We brought blankets, beer, munchies, our own piano, and young Victor Borge. There we were with the elevator locked off so nobody could surprise us. We knew there was no way old, heavyset Art would climb four flights to find us. Jim was banging away on the ivories while I was lounging around on our blanket with the

APes. It was innocent, silly fun that was going nowhere but not exactly what we were getting paid three dollars an hour for.

Suddenly there was a horrible banging noise. At first we ignored it, assuming the attic was creaking and groaning. But it was too persistent, too rhythmic. There, locked in the stairwell, with his beady face crammed into the tiny six-by-six-inch window, was Cliff.

Busted!

I let him in while Jim tossed the beers. Cliff escorted the girls back to their rooms and told me to be in his office in one hour. I was sure I was fired. Here I had blown my role as union agitator just because I couldn't cope with being a custodian. I had to revel in my student status, I had to keep one leg in that privileged world, and now I was gone. I had hurt the organizing drive over flirting with some seventeen-year-olds that six months ago I wouldn't have glanced at.

Miraculously, Cliff chewed me out, handed me a hilarious written warning, and told me to behave myself. Cliff's own prudishness prevented him from naming what he imagined. He accused me of "doing whatever" in the attic with "unauthorized personnel" and focused the discipline on my not working during work hours. . . . Oh, yeah, that!

## The Empire Strikes Back

As the union drive heated up, bosses like Cliff were told their job was on the line if they didn't keep their people from signing up for the union. Of course, it was too late at West Campus, and for that matter half of the rest of the workplaces on campus. Bosses were the front lines of the antiunion campaign and were given intense indoctrination about the horrors of unionization. They were told they would lose all power to an angry, vengeful mob. This, of course, was among our wildest dreams at West Campus. A signed, binding contract providing a livable wage and benefits package would have been an acceptable outcome too, I guess.

Cliff figured out that 75 percent of his people had already signed up, so he decided he needed to work us all over and shake up the solidarity. Cliff told my buddy Leo to stop worrying so much about the union and to "do his job." Leo shot back, "You come watch me work. You'll always see my arms and legs moving, cleaning, mopping—but the whole time my body is working, my mind is thinking union, union, union."

After that failed intervention, Cliff empowered two of the vocal antiunion custodians. He let the meanest of the gang, Ken the curmudgeon, wander around to every building, supposedly "checking lightbulbs." This gave Ken the opportunity to trash the union to every worker every day, all day. Of course, we all saw him as an extension of Cliff. Just someone else to despise and hide from. The sudden favoritism that elevated Ken to wandering around freely was a reminder of an entire system of pay and treatment we were determined to overthrow.

As this strategy was getting nowhere, Cliff decided it was time to make an example of one of us. Me. Top management had figured out that the moderately annoying student hell-raiser they tried to toss from the operating engineers bargaining was now on the UAW Organizing Committee while being paid full-time by Cornell.

Out of nowhere Art started checking up on my work three or four times a day. Not only was the frequency of his visits abnormal, but the fact that he led me around by the nose pointing out my custodial shortcomings was unprecedented. He noted every stain, every dustball, and every speck of mold on a ten-year-old shower curtain in a new little notebook he was carrying.

I asked him what was up. All he said was, "Be careful, and work harder."

Martha warned me. "Look for pennies. If they're out to get you, they plant pennies in hidden areas you're supposed to clean. That way they know if you did those areas or not. They're too cheap to leave us nickels."

Sure enough, pennies started appearing in corners, under heaters, and under couches. Meanwhile Art kept finding more and more things wrong with my work. My comfortably mediocre work routine was lost. I started busting my ass. No matter how hard I cleaned, Art kept writing down my failings.

One of my student friends came up to me and said he saw something very strange. He said he saw a man in his thirties with thick glasses and a beard pouring a full can of Pepsi behind a couch in the second-floor lounge.

"Really tall, like maybe six foot two?" I asked.

"Yeah, and he looked nervous doing it," he replied.

"That's likely Cliff, my big boss," I informed the student.

The students took up a petition supporting me. They lied, saying I was a terrific cleaner, and always had been. Two days after the petition was submitted, Art came to me and said I was being moved to one of the older buildings. I would have no student allies there. I would work alone.

Martha gave me a survival kit. Included was another tablecloth, a Gold Magnum condom she had found, and a tiny bottle of Mr. Lemon. Her parting words were, "I knew you wouldn't last." She hobbled away, as if I'd failed her, but then turned around and said, "See you at the line tomorrow."

My harassment from Art only worsened. I'd figured out most of the penny-hiding places in my former building, but I was lost now.

I used to like Art. He had confided in me his sympathy for the union and had even passed on some of the dirt from the newly launched antiunion supervisor meetings. But during this month of abuse and scrutiny he clammed up and never spoke a word that wasn't a work criticism.

I confronted him repeatedly, begging him to let me know what was going on, what I could do. But he would just shake his head, twitch his toothpick, and mutter, "Just do your job."

Finally, one day he came to me with my performance appraisal. I had been dreading this moment. I knew they were setting me up, and this would document my unacceptable performance. Art handed me a copy and said, "You're doing a good job. Now make sure you copy this, and do not lose it."

For the first time in two months Art was smiling. "You see, Al, I just made a little mistake. I was supposed to show this to Cliff *before* giving it to you. And 'oops,' I forgot, and now you have a copy. Now you have an honest review of your work. Not management's edited view. They can't fire you now, unless you screw up big-time again. No little chickies in the attic anymore. And don't blame Cliff for all this bullshit"—he waved the notebook in the air—"cuz it came all the way from Day Hall." Day Hall was the administration building where all the big bosses worked.

"Jeez, Art, thanks. Now will you get off of my ass?" I joked.

"Not until they get off of mine, buddy. Now we never had this conversation, right? I just gave you the appraisal and read it over with you, nothing more."

"Got it. Thanks for sticking your neck out, Art."

"I got a pretty thick neck. Besides, I came here looking for a job, and I can leave here looking for a job. No big deal." Art got up, shook my hand, and walked out of my break room.

At the bar after the union meeting that night the UAW organizer, Barbara, told me that one out of ten workers gets fired during an organizing drive.

And one out of how many supervisors, I wondered.

Months later, after all the organizing, thousands of conversations and home visits, after all the HR-run antiunion meetings, all the literature back and forth, the articles in the press, and a "Vote No" editorial in the *Ithaca Journal*, came election day.

Workers from two hundred buildings, all over campus, had to choose whether to leave their areas and, under management's watchful glare, march to the voting place. From West Campus that meant a half-mile-long climb up a very steep hill. Healthy eighteen-year-old students moaned about the intense hike up Libe Slope.

As I continued my frantic scramble all over campus that day, making sure our supporters had gotten to vote, I paused at the top of that hill for a minute. Halfway up, struggling inch by inch, was Martha, her painful gait unmistakable. I saw some well-meaning student offer her help, and I heard the slap of Martha's muscley hand against his forearm. Her head shook fiercely, and the student sidled away fast, shell-shocked.

Martha was coming to vote for her union.

## Discussion Questions

- Davidoff brought his activism but also his privilege to his West Campus custodial role. How did he make that adjustment, and why was he able to be an effective organizing committee member there?
- Gender differences in workers' attitudes toward work and the union seem significant. Beyond West Campus, how might the union benefit from taking steps to respond to those different experiences and perspectives?
- The initial organizing conversations happened before a full-blown, HR-run antiunion campaign unfolded. Is it fair for management to engage in the tactics described at West Campus? Why were those efforts mostly ineffective?

2

# YES, YES, NO

"*Yes, Yes, No, Yes, No, No, No.*"

Charlie Donner called out each vote the same way he had done maybe a hundred different times before, in a hundred different meeting rooms, in a hundred different union representation elections. He looked a bit bored.

For me it was different. Each yes was a vindication of all I believed in, and the reward for almost two years of work. No, work isn't the right word. Work is something you do for forty hours a week. I'm talking about two years of life. Two years of intense effort all focused now on Charlie Donner, and his droning yeses and nos.

I concentrated all my energy on Charlie, hoping I could will a yes from his lips, and then another and another.

Maybe if we all did the same—and there were about a hundred of us packed in the ROTC room, military memorabilia on the walls—maybe the law of science and reason would crumble and we actually could make Charlie intone *yes*, make all those ballots be yes votes for the union. If Uri Geller, the famous psychic, could bend forks with the force of his will . . .

Charlie shouldn't have had to count those ballots. Faith, decency, justice, hard work—all should have won the day for the thousand poverty-stricken antiunion-campaign-besieged service and maintenance workers at Cornell University in Ithaca, New York.

Who cared more about the election? Did it mean more to us or them? We hundred custodians, cooks, animal attendants, dishwashers, mechanics (and the many others we represented)? Or the five stern, smug Cornell management people, decked out in their suits and ties, who were also there to observe the late-afternoon vote count. Shouldn't the intensity of collective hopes and dreams count?

"*No, No, No, Yes, Yes, No.*"

How long would it take to count a thousand ballots? Do all National Labor Relations Board people look and act like Charlie—quiet, mustached, glasses, nebbish looking? (I've since learned that pretty much they do.)

Charlie had really surprised us earlier. Maybe it was his revenge for all the boredom, repetition, and bureaucratic crap he was regularly forced to take, but at precisely 6:05 p.m., after twelve hours of people streaming into the ROTC room in Barton Hall on the Cornell campus in ones, twos, and threes, Charlie karate-chopped the ballot box. We hadn't expected it, and certainly hadn't expected it from him. It exploded the box open; some of the ballots even fell on the floor. Charlie appeared taken aback with what may have seemed even to him as an excessive show of force. He held the beaten box aloft for all to see, like a magician. I wondered if they learned the ritual in labor board school.

The vote count was not going well for us. He was counting in batches of fifty, and we lost the first three of four batches. Keeping track of the numbers, of all the yeses and nos, began to feel too overwhelming. My heart was pounding, and my head was swimming.

How far behind could we get and still win? I was frantic for some rationale for our slow start: the no voters were less committed; they drifted in to vote later than our dedicated union-hungry majority. And now their ballots were all at the top of the pile?

"*No, No, Yes, Yes, No, Yes.*"

It had been like this all day. Euphoria alternating with depression. The voting started at 6 a.m., later than many Cornell employees get to work. Even though the thousand eligible voters worked across a huge campus in three hundred different buildings, they all had to trek to the cavernous field house, Barton Hall, which housed the room where the voting took place. It was an ROTC training room, adorned with photos of youthful militarism, discipline, and obedience to authority. The decorations did not seem like a good omen for our ragtag group of subversive workers.

Two years of organizing came down to this one day. My job was to help make sure every yes vote from my time clock and four other clocks made it to Barton. Getting the vote out is not too hard. Unlike political elections in this country, turnout for union elections is high, usually 95 percent. For months the workforce, the "electorate," is activated and organized, by both labor and management, all with an eye to this one vote. If we had done our work well these last two years.

Martha Wiicki said we had. Not with words. Watching this white-haired, cancer-suffering, diminutive custodian, close to retirement, barely able to walk after years of menial, physical labor cleaning dorms, trudge up Libe Slope on her way to vote, I felt sure we would win. After years of low pay and even less respect, Martha and her coworkers were finally to have a choice.

There were many others like Martha that day. The union supporters walked with a livelier gait, often entering Barton in twos and threes. I knew who a lot of them were. Others I just imagined as yes votes, or tried to convince them through desperate, last-minute mental telepathy.

But there were downers too. People like squared-jawed, square-headed Ken Whittaker. People who had been cold when I tried to engage them in discussions of unionization. People who treated me like I had some exotic disease. I knew I hadn't reached them with the message of how this union would affect our lives for the better. It was depressing to see them head for Barton, more so when they refused even to make eye contact.

As I walked into Barton to cast my ballot, a strange fright gripped me. An irrational fear. Would I screw it up? Would I mark no instead of yes? Would I invalidate the ballot by scribbling some gibberish?

"*Yes, No, Yes, No, No.*"

Charlie Donner's drone continued. I looked at my watch. It was seven. How were we doing? I looked at Judy Scott for help. She was our UAW lawyer. She should know. Lawyer? This was a union lawyer? Young, beautiful, wearing dungarees and a UAW baseball cap, a brilliant lawyer, very visibly pregnant. No, she had lost track too, but she signaled with her hands that it was close.

I looked around. Somebody must know the score. But nobody did.

I spotted Cathy Valentino, wearing her UAW T-shirt. She had been with this from the beginning. Longer than anyone. I knew she would cut off her arm for a union victory. I also knew that hadn't always been the case.

## What Does Cathy Want?

I first met Cathy in April 1979. I was a student then, before I graduated to become a custodian. "More holes than pants," Cathy would say later about her first impression of me, remembering me for my tattered student uniform more than anything else.

Entering the one-person print shop in Cornell's Newman Lab for Nuclear Studies where she operated a duplicating machine was like entering a new world. It was a world of a blue- and white-collar, mostly rural, workforce. It was a world populated by people who felt strong ties to the university that employed them but felt cheated by the low pay, poor conditions, and lack of respect accorded them by management.

When I first met her, Cathy was helping articulate this frustration, helping to mold this anger into a force for change. Unionization never entered her mind in those days. Why should it have? She was a fifty-year-old mother and soon-to-be grandmother, a Republican town councilor from a rural area of central New York, someone as filled with illusions and negative images of unions as the rest of us.

But this sweet cherub-faced, white-haired, pint-sized woman was also charismatic, tough, confident, and outspoken. She didn't like being pushed around. She didn't like being lied to. She didn't like unfairness. She didn't like the way Big Red was treating its loyal, hardworking peons.

One key issue was wages. In the inflationary 1970s, wages had fallen farther and farther behind. Second, Cornell was intent on passing on to its low-paid workforce increasing health insurance costs. And third, Cornell was proposing to charge employees for parking. Like most Cornell employees, Cathy drove to work, parked in one of two large lots outside the huge campus, got on a bus that took her to the vicinity of Newman Lab, then walked the rest of the way. To make matters worse, Cathy and everyone else knew that faculty and top-level management were allotted parking privileges on campus. Cathy, like many others, resented now being told they had to pay Cornell for their hardship and second-class status.

Without any legitimate employee organization or forum to air grievances, anger was pent up. Pressure built.

Suddenly, in 1979, flyers began popping up all around campus:

ANGRY ABOUT THE PARKING FEE, LOW WAGES?

COME TO STONE HALL, ROOM 10

LET THE ADMINISTRATION KNOW HOW YOU FEEL

I remember seeing one of these flyers and noting that they were advertising a brown-bag lunch, one of a series organized by employee trustee George Peter. George was notorious for being a shill for management. George Peter saying, "Let the administration know how you feel"? It must have been some left-wing student group playing a joke. Maybe the Spartacists.

Well, I soon found out it wasn't the Spartacists. But it wasn't George Peter, either. It was Cathy. She had charmed George into letting her arrange and publicize a brown-bag lunch. With her duplicating machine she churned out a huge number of flyers.

The 150 people who showed up were more than ten times the number that had been coming to George's sedate affairs. The numbers blew everyone's mind. A new group, Active Concerned Employees (ACE), quickly formed.

ACE blew Cornell's mind too, and Cornell tried hard to quash it. Big time. It was a big-time mistake.

But Cathy was not easily intimidated. When they tried to prevent her from handing out leaflets at some of Cornell's own employee meetings on health insurance, she ignored them. When they threatened to arrest her after she put flyers announcing an ACE meeting on cars in the massive, outlying parking lots the workers used, she dared them to.

"*You're in good hands with Cornell.*" Our most effective flyer mimicked the popular Allstate Insurance advertising theme. Rather than those two cupped Allstate hands comfortably nestling and protecting everyone, Cornell's hands were like a sieve, protecting none of the frantic employees falling between the fingers or desperately holding on to a fingernail for dear life.

Cathy was gutsy. And getting angrier. This populist firebrand holed up in the skin of a Republican family woman was quite an enigma for me. It was only later, when I found out that her dad had briefly been a CIO organizer in the thirties, that it began to make sense. I don't think it ever made sense to Cornell.

It's tempting to try to imagine why those very bright boys in Day Hall, who long had run roughshod over the university's employees, felt so threatened by Cathy Valentino and ACE. The founders of ACE, including Cathy, had no intention of unionizing; they merely wanted an employee group that could talk to management. Management could easily have wooed, schmoozed, and co-opted the group. Instead, they resented even this teensy-weensy challenge to their authority and overreacted. Peons 1, Egotists 0!

As people realized that Cornell had so little respect for them that it was unwilling even to talk about their gripes, many went from disappointed to radicalized. But the majority were still not thinking in terms of unionization. In fact, without a union, ACE was doomed. ACE was about empowerment, but empowering workers means union. Management has to listen and negotiate with the union. It does not, however, have to respond constructively to a group of "active concerned employees." Ignore, yes; patronize, maybe; listen and negotiate—never!

And, indeed, ACE peaked and then began to wither. Rebuffed by management, it was not accomplishing anything. This zero-budget, shoestring collection of a few dozen workers simply couldn't face off against Cornell. Flickers of hope were beginning to return to cynicism. Many workers were angry with Cornell, but most were discouraged.

Enter Brendan Sexton. Brendan was the most impressive person I've ever known. He was a retired UAW labor leader. Balding, with wisps of hair going

**FIGURE 1.** Active Concerned Employees founder Cathy Valentino multitasks in front of her duplicating machine in Neuman Hall. Cathy sparked the labor campaign and fearlessly faced down antiunion pressures from Cornell. (Photo by Earl Dotter)

in every direction and gloriously warm eyes that were fading in use, Brendan moved slowly around campus, at times taking my arm when he wanted to speed up.

The year we organized ACE, Brendan was teaching at Cornell's ILR School. The ILR School has the distinction of being the most prestigious labor relations program in the country, albeit a place where most students end up in HR or management or law. There has always been a strong labor-oriented minority of students and faculty, and several key academics there strove to support us. What the school lacked was enough access to the top union practitioners, few of whom had the academic credentials or time to teach at an isolated Ivy League college. After much student agitation, while I made full use of my role as student government president during the 1980 school year, Brendan was hired as a labor leader in residence.

I became his teaching assistant for a course that students gleefully renamed "Booze with Brendan." Brendan would draw to campus close personal friends who were inspiring, high-level labor and civil rights leaders. They would spend a long afternoon engaging with Brendan and a room packed full of rapt students. Then as class ended, Brendan would provide beer and wine, and we'd all continue the increasingly lubricated conversation into the early evening and often through a dinner somewhere.

Brendan's impact on students was profound. He was as interested in the quietest student's perspective as the biggest national leaders he brought to us. We learned from him about listening hard to every person, and all shed some of our arrogance and Ivy bravado. But it was his relationship to ACE, to Cathy personally, and his deep, powerful ties to the UAW that pivoted our fledgling organizing efforts into a major, viable campaign.

I've introduced friends who ended up getting married, but no matchmaking I ever attempted was as fruitful as the one between Brendan and Cathy. Cornell has never been the same. Brendan helped put Cathy at ease about trade unions. He was a high school dropout who spent his whole life in the labor movement. He rose to become president of the UAW's largest local, Willow Run, with thirty thousand members; the UAW education director who designed the best union education program in the nation; UAW president Walter Reuther's right hand. He then wrote a book, and now was a Cornell professor. Yet this renaissance labor man, this brilliant orator, was kind, decent, and immensely interested in Cathy, and listened deeply to what she had to say. In the process he saw and understood what was happening to her and other workers. It's an organizing truism, "Relationship before Task." I can think of no better example than Cathy's great trust and love for Brendan and what fruits this bore.

Maybe it was that Brendan so much represented the opposite of what the media and culture portray trade union leaders to be. Maybe he just reminded Cathy of her dad, the brief, onetime CIO organizer. Maybe his insight and

**FIGURE 2.** Brendan Sexton, retired UAW education director and assistant to UAW president Walter Reuther, was a visiting professor at Cornell's ILR School. He became the link to the UAW. His warmth and wisdom built trust with key worker leaders. (Local 2300 newsletter)

experience really helped Cathy clarify what her own experience was telling her. Whatever it was, Cathy Valentino became a Union Woman.

The union idea, once planted, found fertile soil among the ACE leadership. Some had always covertly seen ACE as a precursor to a union. But most, like Cathy, were driven to the union idea by Cornell's hardball tactics and by their own inner drive for basic justice. We also knew we could not take on Cornell without some serious resources. We needed all sorts of help.

But just having the "union idea" is a far cry—and a big struggle—from the real thing. The struggle is called the organizing drive or, more usually, the ORGANIZING DRIVE.

An organizing drive is a war, filled with battles, heroes, villains, and victims, brilliant tactical moves and withering failures. In a one-horse town where an employer could brag, "We have more managers than the next largest company has workers," and where the university could refer to firing an employee as "sending them down the hill," taking on Big-Daddy-on-the-Hill was like jumping off a cliff in a leaky hot air balloon. For the service staff, at the bottom of the Ivy League ladder, to take on Cornell was David and Goliath all over again. The ACE activists were exhilarated and also terrified. Cornell didn't give us much, but what Big Red giveth, they sure could taketh away.

To form a union, the workforce must either get management to voluntarily "recognize" the union and accord it bargaining rights after seeing that a majority have signed union cards, or it must choose the union in an election. The companies that voluntarily accord bargaining rights are few and far between. So it's off to the battle and the ballot box we go.

But to have a union organizing drive you have to have a union. We already had "active concerned employees," but we needed a union. Not any union would do. We knew we had to choose a union carefully to help us organize and win an election. Our criteria were clear. We needed a union that would respect and listen to ACE and allow us some autonomy, that had experience in a university setting, and that would have staying power over a long, hard fight. It quickly became clear that we would actually need to interview different unions.

That was a trip. I still remember our interview with the United Food and Commercial Workers Union, represented by their Local 1, based in Utica, New York. Their president, Joe Talarico, turned out to be still in the 1950s. "We can help you organize 'dose girls,'" he kept repeating over and over, referring to the mostly female Cornell workforce. The "girls," however, were decidedly 1960s and 1970s. Poor Joe didn't stand a chance.

But "those guys," who were thought to have Mafia links, didn't take no for an answer. A few weeks after the interview I got a call from their organizer. "I'm going to be in town next week. Let's have lunch." Well, a $3.58 an hour custodian/student never turns down an offer for a free lunch.

After a few pleasantries and some choice mouthfuls from the wonderful Souvlaki House menu, the organizer got down to business: "What does Cathy want?"

I wondered why he didn't ask Cathy, but then realized that one of the "girls" probably needed some good old male guidance in such important matters. It didn't take me—young as I was—long to figure out that he was after a little wheeling and dealing, a little "arrangement" to make the UFCW more "appealing." I tried to make him understand that all Cathy really wanted was a successful organizing drive, and not any staff position or anything else for herself.

I kept repeating versions of "Cathy wants to win; she wants a union here that can take on Cornell and that people can relate to. That's what she wants."

He was persistent, though. Organizers usually are. Seeing that Cathy was a lost cause, he turned his attention to me. Now this was getting really interesting. "It must be pretty expensive going to school here." *No shit, Sherlock*, I thought.

"Our union has a scholarship program we might be able to help you with," he said, looking hard into my eyes.

Well, where were you three years ago? Now I was about done with school, and between my folks and working as a custodian, I was getting by. After I told him that, I could see his heart wasn't in it anymore. He left me and turned his attention to the baklava.

We also interviewed New York State United Teachers. They were polished and professional but placed a strange amount of emphasis on all the consumer discounts NYSUT had bargained for its members. While getting 20 percent off on the purchase of a refrigerator was a good thing, they seemed to underestimate how raw a fight we would be in.

The largest union locally was the Machinists. They had a few thousand members, making solid union wages at several local factories. Their leader was well-respected and progressive. It was also a plus that many of our Cornell coworkers had family in the local IAM. But the IAM local "Lodge" was no match for Cornell. We just didn't see the scale of national commitment we thought necessary for a thirty-five-hundred-person campaign against a billion-dollar behemoth. We also worried that their lack of more white-collar identity would hurt us with techs and especially clericals.

Our experience with the UAW was wholly different. Brendan played a big role here. Who else could have assembled—right in Cathy's living room—the most powerful collection of UAW leaders to meet with unorganized rank-and-file workers since the days of Walter Reuther! Regional director Ed Gray and Martin Gerber, a top national VP who oversaw organizing, were the biggest big shots other than Brendan. More than power was involved. They were sincere;

they were familiar with the university setting; and their lead organizer was fresh from a major victory at Boston University. Barbara Rahke instantly impressed us. She knew our world. We also liked the UAW's emphasis on local autonomy. More than anything, we trusted Brendan. They met our criteria. We were off.

Cathy announced via hundreds of campus flyers in January 1980 that ACE had "invited" the UAW to help us organize, and that the UAW had accepted.

## "Must Be a Good Eater"

Organizing is no picnic. For almost two years, in addition to my full-time job as a Cornell custodian, I spent an average of three hours a day talking union with other workers—listening, cajoling, convincing. I wasn't alone, of course. Hundreds of workers were involved in organizing their fellow workers. Emily Apgar was the best.

By the time she reached Cornell, in her fifties, Emily had already led an incredibly hard life. Born on a farm, she fled her abusive alcoholic father and became a sort of vagabond waitress, moving all around the country. Two of her husbands—I think she was married three times—were also alcoholic and abusive. I remember her telling me that she was sure that one in particular would have killed her, if she hadn't left.

Emily was striking in a physical sense. Tall, skinny, bulbous nose, pockmarked face, a chain smoker. For me, though, what was incredible were her hands and forearms: strong, tough, sinewy. Below the elbow, she could have been mistaken for a linebacker. She wasn't. She was a woman whose life had been devoted to lifting trays of dishes and cleaning the buildings and homes of others, including now the retired president of Cornell. She worked full time at Cornell, 6 a.m. to 2:30 p.m., then cleaned private homes another four afternoons a week after that.

The one attraction working at Cornell held out for her was retirement benefits. But working at Cornell became, according to Emily, like being in some kind of Siberian gulag. The constant fear of being fired for whatever irked a supervisor or a manager; the "merit" system that allowed a few ass kissers to get good raises; the low wages that forced her to work two other jobs cleaning the homes of the Cornell aristocracy. "It's just unreal here," she'd say, "like some kind of chain gang. Every day I fear for my job."

Despite all this, she was slow to get involved in the union at Cornell. But she kept hearing about the organizing that had started and the risks that people were taking. She was in awe of her coworkers' courage but scared to death herself.

Then she began to hear the truth about retirement benefits. The paltry sums that people got, people who had worked at Cornell much longer than she had;

people who had given fifteen, twenty, twenty-five years working for the "Big Red Bear" and who were trying to live on pensions of thirty dollars a week. Because the pension was based on a percentage of your income, if you were a well-paid manager or professor, you got a decent retirement; but the poorest folks got terrible, unlivable pensions. Somehow, somewhere, at some point, she snapped. She became a union activist. The loss of hope for a decent retirement unlocked those leg irons, and Emily became the most successful, committed organizer we had. She had spent a lifetime working her fingers to the bone, running from lousy bosses and lousier husbands. Now she was too old to run. Emily was taking a stand.

Over the course of a year, Emily devoted every fifteen-minute break, every half hour lunch, every bus ride from B Lot to her time clock, and much of her weekends, to the organizing drive. No matter how tired she was, or how cold and snowy it was outside, she took that time to traipse across campus to talk to as many custodians in as many buildings she could get to. She talked union constantly. At the "clock" where workers punched out, on the bus going home, while shopping on the weekend—it was always the same.

Some poor oblivious coworker would be squeezing cantaloupes at the P&C market and Em would sidle up. "Y'can't tell by just squeezin' 'em; gotta sniff 'em like this." Sniff, sniff. "Can you believe the prices? I don't know how you young ones with kids get by on a Cornell paycheck. I'm barely makin' it just paying for myself. That's why this union is so darn important. I'll see you at the meeting this Tuesday night, won't I? Won't I? Good, here, take this melon. It's the best one for sure. See ya Tuesday."

She talked to her fellow gulag inmates and listened to them as they shared their stories about their poverty, about the arbitrariness of their employer, and the insulting retirement benefits. But she also talked union. Though she had no prior union experience, she quickly came to understand how the union was the workers' only chance out of Siberia, their only chance to achieve respect and better working conditions. It wouldn't come quickly, and it wouldn't come easily, but the union could empower the workers to make a difference.

Emily was one with the workers, and they knew it. She was genuine and had immense credibility, as well as energy and commitment. "Larry," she would say to a fellow custodian during one of her visits during break, "I know you don't want to hear it, but I'm here to talk sense with you about this union. If I have to knock some intelligence into you before I leave, I'm going to do it. Now I've only got ten minutes, and then I have to get my scrawny little butt back to my building, but I want you to pay attention. Don't be stupid about this. We've got to do this union thing."

The results were amazing. Emily would regularly come to our weekly organizing committee meetings with three, four, or five signed cards—cards signed by workers signifying their desire to be represented by the UAW. I would have maybe one or two. The next week she would have eight or nine; I might have three. No one signed up more Cornell employees than Emily.

And few could get us singing like Emily. This was Emily's ode to the Cornell personnel director, and our chief antagonist, Cecil Murphy (to the tune of "If You're Happy and You Know It Clap Your Hands"):

> Here's to you, Cecil Murphy, here's to you.
> Here's to you, Cecil Murphy, here's to you.
> Well, you think you're upper class, but your just a horse's ass,
> Here's to you, Cecil Murphy, here's to you.

It became our theme song.

Meeting and talking with people one-on-one during lunch and other breaks was an important part of the organizing drive. But as a tool for convincing large numbers of workers, it was very limited. For one thing, many workers were uncomfortable talking union at work, even during break time. It was the same *fear* that permeated everything about our Cornell lives. The wrong supervisor or wrong coworker hears you talking union, and . . .

Another problem was the time limitation. You can't really have much of a meaningful discussion during a fifteen-minute break, or even during a half hour devoted to lunch.

Home visits were the best way to deal with these problems. They took place on the worker's own turf, far from the watchful eyes of management. Workers often

**FIGURE 3.** Emily Apgar was a custodian at Cornell, punching in at Bailey Hall at 6:00 a.m. every day. She signed up more workers for the union than any single member of the organizing committee and served on multiple bargaining teams. She also wrote a very popular home improvement column in the *Bear Facts* called Emily's Helpful Hints. (Local 2300 newsletter)

felt honored to be visited, and not a little surprised that the strangers could even find their often out-of-the-way mobile homes or small rural farmhouses. These in-depth discussions were one of our most important tactics. Workers were comfortable, and we learned to listen more than talk and draw out hopes, dreams, experiences, and fears. We had time to inoculate against the coming antiunion campaign, the details of which Barbara Rahke predicted and taught us about with uncanny accuracy. In living rooms, we had time to assess and recruit leaders, to clarify names on staff lists, to hear what the rumor mill was putting out. We tried to have two or three teams out every night during the drive.

Rank-and-file organizers like me were always impressed at how gracious our hosts were during these surprise home visits. I had dozens of beers and many meals at the well-kept but ramshackle homes of Cornell's poorest workers.

I still remember my first home visit. I was very nervous about going, unannounced, to a total stranger's home, knocking on the door and just starting to talk union. I went that first time with John Earle. John was only in his late twenties, but with two kids and the facial lines of someone much older. As the twenty-minute drive out to the middle of nowhere progressed I got more and more nervous. I wanted John to run through with me what our "rap" was—what should we say, who would go first, what our host would be like—but John was more interested in chatting about his beekeeping business, not to mention a dozen other topics. I kept trying to get the talk back to the "rap." "What are you so worried about?" he said. "We'll just go and see what happens." I didn't want to seem like I was some kind of wimp, and his confidence was reassuring, so after a while I just shut up. But I *was* scared. We finally reached the house, went up to the porch, and knocked on the door. At that point I sort of noticed that John had stepped back one giant step. I looked at him, and his face was ashen. "You . . . you . . . start. You . . . you do it," he stammered. I thought he was either going to puke or run back to the car. He did neither. I managed to nervously introduce both of us, and said we were hoping to talk with so-and-so for a few minutes about the union organizing. Before we knew it, we were inside, the TV was turned off, and John, I, the worker, and his whole family were talking excitedly.

I often wondered what John would have done if he had been with me the night I knocked on the door of a Cornell worker's house and was greeted by a guy with a shotgun telling us to "get out." Norma Rae might have done it differently, but I got out of there—fast.

My usual partner on these home visits was Emily; sometimes it was Cathy. We always sent two rank-and-file organizers and tried to pair a man and a woman. If it were two men, and the worker we were visiting was a woman, we could elicit a condition called "male pattern badassness." The husband would get very uncomfortable with two men talking to his wife. The same could happen if we sent two women to a man.

Home visits were eye-openers. Cornell employees often lived way the hell out in "God's country," on dirt tracks, sometimes two or three counties away from Cornell. We had quite a time finding some of these places. The poverty was intense. Seeing the children, many times in raggedy clothes; the trailers patched together; the limited food on the table—it was my first experience of brutal Appalachian poverty. On the way home, Emily would repeat over and over, "This is just unreal." Even for someone who knew poverty, like Emily, conditions were indeed appalling. They only fueled our determination and made the unsuccessful interactions all the more frustrating. I recall one fellow telling me, "Cornell's taking pretty good care of me so far." No teeth, wind blowing through a busted-up trailer, a fifteen-year-old car, and two kids in torn, oversize T-shirts. God bless Big Red.

Emily was tremendous on these home visits. Warm, comfortable, genuine. Once we were visiting a couple—two custodians—and they had a young baby. Emily just went right over, picked the baby up, put him over her shoulder, ooh-ing and aah-ing all the way. Well, the baby wasn't as taken with Emily as she was with him, and just vomited all over her. Emily didn't miss a beat. Warm as ever, "Oh, that's OK. Must be a good eater." I loved her.

One group of workers that presented a special challenge were the forty or so developmentally disabled people in the bargaining unit. Representing almost 4 percent of the workforce, they were a constituency of fellow workers that could not and should not be ignored. While they presented some special challenges for management, Cornell took full advantage of the fact that they were vulnerable, under management's thumb, and accepted the low pay, questionable assignments, and poor conditions without resistance.

We decided that in this case it was critical that we reach their families, as well as the workers themselves. Most did live with parents or other family members. So we started to visit these families, and were surprised to find that family members, rather than seeing Cornell as a saint for providing their developmentally disabled adult child with a job, really focused on Cornell's insensitivity and poor treatment of these workers. They saw the union as a protection and as a source of help. Thus fortified, we made special preparations to assist these people to vote: a van to pick them up on election day and special training to familiarize them with the ballot.

The organizing campaign went beyond home visits and one-on-one dialogues. We had to do everything we could to combat the negative images management was promoting, all of which reinforced our society's generally negative perception of unions. This often meant being both bold and creative.

I remember one event well. During the late 1970s, Cornell began a program of holding "self help" workshops for the custodians and other employees. They were an offshoot of the decade-long emphasis on "me-ness," and Cornell's way of promoting a new, modern style of employee relations. Workshop topics ranged across everything from dealing with stress to safe winter driving. They were the sort of thing that the wild bunch of outcast, alienated custodians I hung out with scoffed at and never went to.

During the organizing drive, however, I began to look at these workshops as an opportunity and not as a target for ridicule. They were the kind of event that might sometimes bring together workers from all across campus. As a dormitory custodian based on West Campus, I normally had little regular contact with custodians from the three other dormitory areas, so the workshops had a definite attraction.

The one I remember was a diet workshop, which naturally attracted a good sampling of the most overweight "residence life" custodians. It focused on the role of sugar and salt. I wasn't a pound overweight, but I went anyway. Sitting with a couple of other custodians I recognized from the organizing drive, I immediately saw my chance. The lively young nutritionist leading the workshop wasn't having much success energizing this group of somber custodial heavyweights, so she lit up when I raised my hand.

"Isn't stress reduction also important," I asked innocently.

"Yes."

"What about stress that's caused on the job?"

"Yes, that's a definite factor and can be linked to weight gain. Workplaces are major causes of stress."

This was going better than expected. "Wouldn't having more of a say in what goes on at work reduce stress? Couldn't having a union do that?" This was a bit of a shocker, since at that point in the organizing drive no one said the u-word in front of management, and we all saw supervisors present at the workshop.

There was a pause, and then our newly discovered, obviously liberal, friend of labor went on about how positive unions could be. Of course, we nodded agreement, holding our glee in well, while the supervisors and antiunion custodians just muttered under their breath.

Our little coup is not the only reason I remember this workshop. I have not salted my food since.

People—those who weren't involved in the organizing drive—have the hardest time believing that the organizing drive was almost wholly a rank-and-file effort. It was the service and maintenance workers who ran the campaign and did the organizing. For eighteen months our organizing committee met weekly to run the drive. Usually there were about thirty of us there. It was our organizing drive, and we made the key decisions. Big decisions like whether to allow the rapidly organizing service workers to vote before clericals or techs, and when to petition the NLRB for a vote, signifying that we were ready. And smaller decisions—like should we hold that rally at the downtown Commons or somewhere else; or what sort of literature did we need; or how should we deal with the lies that management was pushing. Barbara guided and advised us, but she made it clear that this was our fight and our union.

The risks of organizing the drive this way—letting largely unlettered custodians, maintenance mechanics, food service workers, animal attendants, and groundskeepers mount and run the organizing drive against a $2 billion university/corporation—were outweighed by the benefits. It was *our* organizing drive, and because of this more people were drawn to it, and people worked harder. The antiunion lies fell flat because workers understood they were creating an organization they controlled.

Brendan shared an anecdote with us, and I'll never forget it. One evening, as a twenty-year-old organizer just starting out with the Steelworkers in the 1920s, he was helping prepare for a meeting with the rank and file. Dutifully, he got to the

**FIGURE 4.** Jim Royce was a longtime Cornell bus driver and member of the organizing committee. He talked union with hundreds of his riders and was a stalwart union leader despite a virulently antiunion boss. His son and daughter-in-law married during the drive in matching UAW T-shirts. (Photo by Earl Dotter)

meeting hall early to clean up and set out the chairs in the proper arrangement for everyone.

"What are you doing?" asked one of the older organizers.

"Getting the chairs set up for everyone."

"Don't do it. Let the workers do it themselves. They will have more ownership over the meeting."

The democratic tenor of our campaign had a lot to do with Barbara Rahke.

Barbara was only in her early thirties when the UAW sent her to Ithaca to work with us and coordinate the organizing drive. A secretary at Boston University, she had been a leader in a successful clerical organizing drive there. Barbara brought the philosophy that the rank-and-file workers needed to be the leaders and the organizing drive, democratic. If we weren't democratic now, she said, how could we hope to have a democratic union down the road after we won?

She did more than this. She really listened and learned from the workers, made everyone feel special, and could get people excited and involved. She had a great nose for spotting workers with leadership potential and a great touch in persuading them to move into these roles. It was Barbara who went the extra mile to make sure Emily blossomed into a great leader. When you left a meeting with Barbara, two things were a given. You felt reinvigorated, and you had more work to do.

Barbara also was a brilliant tactician who had a great intuitive sense of what needed doing at any time, and who could "see around corners"—predict what management was going to do before they did it. It was as if she had a tap on Cecil's phone.

## Breaking Up Is Hard to Do

The fledgling internal democracy of our OC—our organizing committee—was sorely tested with a huge and complicated decision after about six months of organizing.

When ACE began, any worker at Cornell could join in. We were small, but there was occupational diversity that included clericals, technicians, service and maintenance, and even a few folks who may have been vaguely managerial. As we made the decision to unionize, the group became clearly made up of only non-managerial-level staff. Our organizing committee ranged from thirty to forty folks who would attend weekly meetings and twice that many who were actively talking to coworkers.

We built close personal relationships over those early months, thrilled at the idea of one big union for over thirty-five hundred campus workers. There were some class differences within the group. Service staff were generally more rural and less educated. Our unit was about half women but had a more traditional blue-collar feel to it. The clericals were 90 percent women, often working directly for faculty or in the libraries. The techs worked in the dozens of labs around campus, many at the Ag school, but also the Veterinary and Engineering colleges, not exactly bastions of academic liberalism.

Techs and clericals had far less of a collective work environment. They tended to work directly for "important" people—professors and white-collar management. While the techs and clericals experienced the same low wage structures and mediocre benefits, they were a few rungs above the lower-paid service staff. While suffering their own unique forms of disrespect, techs and clericals held a higher level of campus status.

Clericals faced a culture of sexism and sexual harassment often from powerful, largely autonomous faculty, and were often treated as invisible. There was a classic story of a student coming into the entry space of his professor's office where the secretary's desk was. He looked her right in the face and impatiently said, "Isn't anybody here?" The sexist culture and working-class history of most clericals led to the kind of low self-esteem that made the idea of "standing up" to their boss, an "important" person they worked near all day, both terrifying and "inappropriate."

Several of the most active union supporters among the clericals came from strong political backgrounds. Their interest in organizing was as a worker who wanted fair treatment, better pay and benefits, but also from a women's movement perspective of equity and inclusion. Organizing among clericals was tough. With service and maintenance, the structures of our work were mostly collective. We physically worked together on grounds crews and in dining halls. We punched time clocks together twice every day. We had natural leaders, and unions, while not a big part of local culture, did exist in major factories among other blue-collar workforces. Clericals were isolated. Too many found the idea of the UAW too alien, and some found being clumped together with service and maintenance a bit beneath their identity, if not beneath their actual treatment from Cornell.

Techs were a funny bunch. Many were science types, not naturally liberal, a bit nerdy, typically with college degrees. They were often directly managed by professors who could really make or break not just their raise that year, but their future careers. Their funding was also often based on grants, so they felt more precarious. Many of their jobs were so specialized that they had little room for advancement or transfers. Not only were they underpaid and subject to all sorts of crazy behavior from stressed-out professors untrained to manage staff, but many also had to contend with working with hazardous chemicals and unsafe equipment.

We had terrific leaders among the techs and clericals. Folks like Jim Rundle, who went on to a long career in the labor movement, and John Edelman, who probably signed up more techs than any single person. The clericals had leaders like Carol Lane and Colette Walls, brilliant, funny, driven organizers. Carol became a full-time organizer for the UAW. She was the clerical version of Emily Apgar, working class through and through, disarmingly bold, genuine, with incredible emotional intelligence and persistent as hell. She moved dozens of clericals from doubters to supporters.

What became clear quickly was that we had three campaigns with three different dynamics. Service and maintenance was bringing in cards in chunks, ten to twenty every week. We had whole time clocks moving together, minus a few stragglers and ass-kissers. Clericals and techs were progressing much more slowly. There was very little ability to get collective momentum, folks were too isolated, the cultures too resistant.

Our OC meetings remained collective. Barbara treated us as the real decision-makers for this campaign, even though every dime was coming from the UAW. As a group of newly dedicated and inspired organizers we came to have close friendships and tons of mutual respect. We shared drinks, family get-togethers, and even formed a musical group called the Singing Bears, with some talented OC musicians, to perform labor songs at local events.

But gradually it was becoming clear that we were headed toward a difficult crossroads. Service and maintenance was closing in on 50 percent signed up, and clericals and techs were around 10–15 percent. Even if you averaged us out as one big group, the numbers were way too low to go to a vote and expect to win. We needed to see if we could push service and maintenance up to around 65–70 percent support, and if clericals and techs couldn't move dramatically toward a majority as well. Reluctantly, we had to consider a split, allowing service and maintenance to go ahead separately.

Organizing drives have a life of their own. One of management's most effective tactics is to force delay. They know slowing down the organization gives them more time to scare folks, to get rid of leaders; and if it drags on too long, workers get a sense of futility. The atmosphere is so stressful that having a reasonably quick, fair election gives workers a much better chance of not being torn apart or becoming exhausted. Service and maintenance leaders talked a bit among ourselves. Cathy, Emily, and I spoke and agreed that we preferred to all organize together, but that clericals and techs were moving so slowly we couldn't wait for six months to a year for them to catch up. Our service/maintenance coworkers were scared, they were getting harassed for wearing buttons, and they expected a vote sooner rather than later. But there was also the worry that without the others, Cornell might not respect service/maintenance enough to bargain a good contract. We had our own self-esteem issues.

When the decision meeting took place, the organizing committee, clericals, techs, and service/maintenance together, gathered in the big meeting room at the Ramada Inn downtown. There were maybe forty-five of us seated around a big rectangle. Barbara laid out the cold facts. The UAW was committed to organizing the entire campus. The numbers on cards spoke for themselves. There were some clericals who expressed that they would feel abandoned and that they "could never win" without being part of the more pro-union group. The people in that room had worked together a long time, and every person who spoke expressed mixed feelings.

Two issues carried the decision. Everyone saw the service/maintenance workers as the most downtrodden and exploited. Nobody wanted to reduce our chances of making change. There was also a sense that we could win, and that victory would send a powerful, inspiring message to the campus. We voted, and almost everyone agreed to "allow" service/maintenance to petition for an election first. Some clerical and technical folks were so upset that they scaled back their participation, but only a few dropped out entirely. Many of the strongest clerical and tech leaders redoubled their organizing, not only pushing forward within their own group, but helping with the service staff in their buildings. We *all* needed service and maintenance to win for anyone to win.

## To Love the Union, You Must Hate Cornell?

While we were beating the bushes to get cards signed, management was not exactly napping. Cecil Murphy (*Well, you think you're upper class, but you're just a horse's ass*) was their point man, and their main strategy was captive audience meetings.

Whatever the theories about democratic choice, an organizing drive is never a contest between equals. Management always has disproportionate power and resources, and the union is always the underdog. It's always David vs. Goliath.

A captive audience meeting is one example of management's power in an organizing drive. It is a meeting set and orchestrated by management. Because it takes place on company time, attendance is typically mandatory, and back talk or dissension forcefully discouraged. The workers are thus literally a captive audience, and management has a great opportunity to do a good deal of brainwashing. There are no legal limits as to how long these meetings can last, how often they are held, or which workers go to which antiunion meetings and which pro-union workers might be excluded altogether.

During the organizing drive there were over a hundred such meetings. The Cornell workforce was broken down into groups of twenty to thirty, and Cecil went around to each like a rock band on tour. He'd do forty identical "gigs" over a two-week period. The themes he emphasized were not very different from those that are standard operating procedure in any management effort to thwart a union organizing drive, and Barbara had us well prepared.

## One: "We Are One Big Happy Family"

I still remember the glitzy slide show they put together for us. It was literally cobbled from the one they used for student recruitment. Yes, for the first time ever we lowly custodians were the students' equals—all of us were being fed the same propaganda. We saw through it, but for many, especially the older workers, it still made an impression. The glorious Cornell we saw in the show touched a chord. It played heavily on Cornell's long role in the Ithaca area, and the pride and affection many workers felt for Cornell and their work. The implication that "to love the union, you must hate Cornell" really hit home to workers who spent a lifetime at the university, and much outside time rooting for Cornell's athletic teams. Cornell played on this theme in the antiunion button it created. It was simple and simply brilliant. All it said was "I ♥ CU." We know we couldn't win a majority on bitterness alone, that there were genuine feelings of pride many workers felt to be a part of this glorious university. Our equally brilliant comeback slogan was, "A Great Union for a Great University."

**FIGURE 5.** "A Great Union for a Great University" was our union's response to Cornell's effort to challenge pro-union staff's loyalty to the university. The "I ♥ CU" button Cornell produced was shrewd strategy. Many workers were critical of Cornell but also felt pride working there. We wouldn't win a union vote if our coworkers thought we hated Big Red. (Local 2300 newsletter)

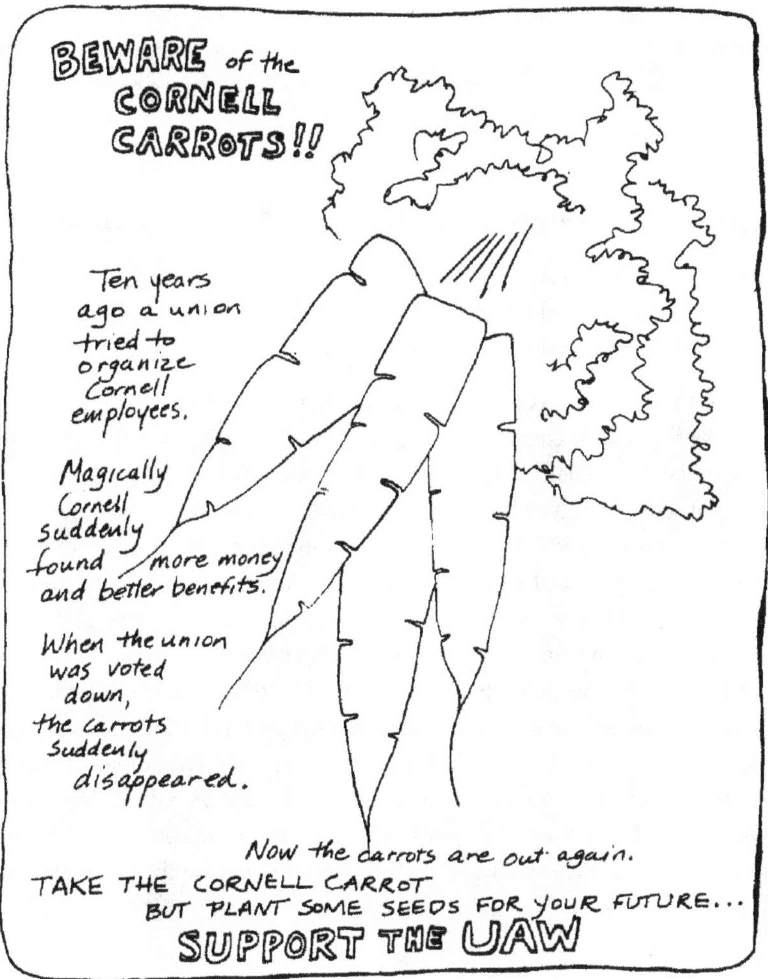


**FIGURE 6.** Many workers contributed original graphics and cartoons to the organizing drive. During the campaign Cornell made many promises but suggested their hands would be tied if the union won. This graphic and the phrase "beware the carrots" became an easily understood response. (Local 2300 newsletter)

## Two: "Things Are Really Not So Bad, and without a Union We Will Make Things Even Better"

Using real and spurious data, Cornell tried to convince people that no matter how bad off they thought they were, they were really better off than many others in the local community or those at other Ivy League institutions, and that the "good" benefit package made up for lousy wages. Cornell, moreover, was committed to making things even better if only we workers would vote no and give management a chance to work together with us to make it happen.

## Three: "The Union Is an Outside Third Party"

"The union, headquartered in Detroit . . ."
"The union, headquartered in Detroit . . ."
"The union, headquartered in Detroit . . ."

That was management's constant refrain whenever it referred to our union. For a while we thought of changing the name "UAW" to "UHD"; it almost seemed more familiar to us. Management continually attempted to cast the union as an alien agent scheming to exploit a "family" disagreement. A union would "come between" the workers and management, disrupting the "pleasant" relations that existed. According to Cecil Murphy, you could no longer have a conversation with your boss, everything would become stressful, and your daily ups and downs would have to be run through the union *headquartered in Detroit*. Was there a race card being not so subtly played by Cornell with the majority Black, urban Detroit "controlling" the lives of the overwhelmingly rural, white Cornell staff?

Having a strong, visible, credible, and highly representative organizing committee that knew the union was us was a powerful antidote. We didn't just "know" it—we had lived it for over a year, making real decisions on strategy, timing, and message, and being the organizers workers saw every day on the job, on the bus, and at their front doors.

## Four: "The Union Will Force You Out on Strike"

This was a scarce tactic, again based on Cornell's ability to manipulate data. During the captive audience meetings, Cecil would put up a slide showing the duration of the average strike in New York State—quite long, maybe eighty or ninety days. Then he would confide that half of all university unions represented by the UAW struck in their first contract. The message: vote with the union and you will end up with a long strike. It was scary until we unraveled it and showed that Cecil must have been standing on his head or something. Sure, the university strike rate was high, but the average duration of those strikes was only about five days. Sure, strikes in New York were long, and getting longer, but only very few contracts—about 2 percent—ended up unresolved and in a strike situation.

The power of the captive audience meeting is that management can use whatever time and whatever methods it needs to convince the workers of its position, without fear of being contradicted. It took a great deal of courage for a worker to stand up at these meetings and in any way appear to be taking a pro-union stance. To do so could mean one foot out the door.

For a while there were question-and-answer sessions at the conclusion of the captive audience meetings. Then management realized that we were just using the question time to take away some of their leverage and power. It was an opportunity for us to speak. So they put the meetings on a tight schedule, leaving no time for questions. This made things a lot harder for us organizers. Hard, but not impossible.

The farmworkers at Cornell's cow farm in Harford, twenty miles from the main campus, showed a lot of us the way. Prior to one of Cecil's captive audience meetings there, a group of them placed a little bush on the floor in front of where he was talking. For a while he tried to ignore it, maybe thinking it was normal for these farm types, but it clearly was bothering him. About fifteen minutes into his presentation, it got to him, and he said, "What is this? Can I move it?"

This was the opening Quaker farmer Lyn Willwerth was waiting for. "Well, Cecil," he drawled, "this is our beat-around-the-bush bush, and when we heard you were coming, we thought we'd get it out for you." It just cracked everybody up, and totally undercut Cecil's whole talk. But it took guts.

Another time when Cecil came to visit the same bunch, I think it was again Lyn who put a tape recorder down right in front of him. "Do you mind, Cecil, if we tape your presentation?"

"Yes, I do. Please turn the thing off."

Lyn calmly continued, "But we want an accurate record of what you say. You know we're not as highly educated as you, so we need to listen more than once to your words. Why are you afraid? If you promise us something, we want to be sure to have it clear."

Cecil thought quickly: "I want you to turn it off. Having something like that on will make it too intimidating to your coworkers who may be uncomfortable speaking their mind" (as if Cecil really wanted this!).

Lyn was one step ahead of him: "Is anybody here afraid to speak if the recorder is on?" Nobody was, the tape recorder stayed on, and Cecil ended up pulling back from some of the less legal things he would normally say.

Each time we managed to embarrass or turn the tables on management we made sure the news traveled quickly around campus.

The UAW was fully behind us. They paid for buttons, food at meetings, a radio show that ran five days a week, shirts, hats, and a few full-time organizers. Barbara was the only out-of-towner. The others all had ties to Ithaca and

Cornell. The UAW International's president at the time was Doug Fraser. In the tradition of impressive, progressive thought leaders like Walter Reuther, Fraser was well-known nationally. As the UAW helped Chrysler out of bankruptcy by negotiating some tough concessions to save jobs, Fraser was given a seat on the Chrysler board, the first time a major labor leader took on such a role. Even the conservative *Reader's Digest* wrote a favorable piece about this left-wing union "boss." Thanks to Brendan's influence, Fraser agreed to come speak on campus during the drive. We decided that better than an ordinary address, Fraser would challenge Cornell's President Rhodes to a debate on the merits of unions. Our members loved this in-your-face idea. Who was afraid of a little truth? Not us. Two important leaders, icons in their respective spheres, duking it out. Of course, Rhodes declined, and that became a great story line. Fraser spoke in the jam-packed Statler Hotel auditorium. Workers, students, and faculty all cheered first the organizing committee, with Cathy introducing the UAW president. The media gave it tons of coverage, and scared service workers saw that the UAW was not just about autoworkers. They had our backs. When it came to organizing Cornell, they weren't messing around.

The UAW was also able to get moderately helpful public statements from both Governor Hugh Carey and then Lieutenant Governor Mario Cuomo asking President Rhodes to make sure the election was "free of intimidation, coercion and interference."

Cornell's antiunion campaign didn't miss a beat. The biggest and perhaps most important captive audience meetings occurred the week before the vote. There were about two hundred of us at the one I attended, not thirty or forty like at all the others.

This was going to be Cornell's last shot at us, and everyone knew the vote was going to be close. So they brought in the big guns. Cornell president Frank H. T. Rhodes had, for the most part, let Cecil carry management's ball. But things were too close. He had to enter the fray. But no way was he going to do his captive audience rap forty times over two weeks like Cecil. They decided on about five final meetings, with about two hundred of us at each.

Tall, aristocratic, charming, smooth, very British, Frank Rhodes was everything the average Cornell worker was not. He was almost a mythic figure for many workers—rarely seen by any worker or student, he kept himself well up in the Ivory tower. Employee relations were for others to do. His job was fundraising, public relations, and speaking at graduation every year. And flying in from a fund-raising junket in New York City to bust union organizing drives.

At our meeting, Frank stood at the entrance and shook everyone's hand as they went in. "Hello. So good to see you," he said in his British accent. "So glad you could make it" (as if we had a choice).

While ordinary workers got just one chance to shake Frank's hand, I got five or six chances. My record still stands: most handshakes with Frank Rhodes in an afternoon. I was frantically trying to prime my arriving coworkers for the meeting. We needed to make our points and didn't know if there would be a question time. I was running in and out of the room to talk to coworkers both inside and out as they straggled in or, in some cases, as they were herded in by supervisors. Each time I went back in I would have to pass Frank at the door, and each time it would be, "Hello. So glad you could make it." And he would shake my hand. But it was getting a little silly. About the fifth or sixth time, I finally summoned up my courage and said, "Look, President Rhodes, you've already shaken my hand four times. I'm a little busy right now getting ready for your meeting. You really don't have to shake my hand each time." It cracked everybody up.

They chose a large room in Noyes Student Center for the meeting and set up twenty or thirty rows of chairs. Two chairs were in the front facing everybody, one for Frank and one for their employee stooge George Peter. I remember how striking and symbolic the seating ended up being. Not one worker sat in the first six rows, establishing a huge gulf between Frank and "his people." President Rhodes was his typical smooth self, appreciating all our loyalty and hard work. The syrupy praise may have felt good to some, but it was a day late and at least a dollar short for most. Here was this guy from Britain—despite existing in the same small community, and working on the same campus, he was a stranger to us, talking with such a heavy aristocratic accent that many had a hard time understanding him. Here was this obviously upper-class, well-heeled guy, a guy who spent most of his time talking to the wealthiest people in the country, telling us—earning poverty-level wages, no pension to speak of—how wonderful Cornell was, and that any union would only be an "outside third party" disturbing our family relationship.

Poor Frank was not ready for what followed. Frankly, neither was I.

Frank finished and invited questions. There was quiet for a while. Then a hand went up. It was an elderly dining worker. I barely knew him; didn't even know if he was pro-union. Most of the union supporters brazenly were wearing our UAW buttons. This guy's uniform was bare. A sinking feeling engulfed me.

"President Rhodes, Josephine Brown retired last year after working twenty-seven years at Cornell. Her retirement check from you is fourteen dollars a week. How can you explain that? How can we be one big happy family when people give their lives working here and get an insult in return?"

I restrained myself from leaping up and kissing this guy. Rhodes seemed dumbfounded. He really was thrown off-balance for a moment. Maybe he really wasn't aware of the situation facing the other members of his "family." But at that moment it really didn't matter. This senior cook's challenge set the tone and opened things up to a lot of similar questions from many stepchildren of Frank H. T. Rhodes.

## You're Not Really Going to *Do* All Those Things, Are You?

"*Yes, No, Yes, No, No, No, Yes.*"

A sharp slap on my shoulder from my fellow organizing committee member Pam Mackesey jolted me back to the present. I had just been remembering, for some reason, how Rhodes had responded to my question at that last captive audience meeting: "President Rhodes, when we win, will you promise to follow the law to bargain in good faith with the union?" To his credit, he had said yes, they would.

Now, back in the present, I thought: But would we win?

"I think we're going to do it," Pam exulted. She was a little premature. Charlie Donner was still droning on, and it was close. After losing the first few clumps of fifty—not by much; we had gotten twenty-two or twenty-three in each—we began to win a few. It was getting close to our magic number of 480, the number of votes that we needed (or they needed) to achieve a majority. The tension was incredible. Charlie sounded the totals from the next batch, "Yes, twenty-eight; no, twenty-two."

Then from the side—someone was keeping track!—a shout: "We did it!" Others realized it at the same time. A palpable surge of deep unleashing emotion went through that room. It was incredible! Suddenly it was a giant roar of triumph echoing across the walls. But the formal count had not ended, and Charlie, in a matter of seconds, chastised us into a skin-crawling silence.

Then, in that eerie silence, with just the meaningless last few ballots being tallied, somebody started to hum "Solidarity Forever," an anthem most of us had learned together two years ago at the beginning of this fight. It started in a very quiet, ethereal way, as the count continued. It wasn't coming from one person. It just seemed to rise in the tense, thick air. I started to hum along, as the words went through my mind.

> When the union's inspiration through the workers' blood shall run,
> There can be no power greater anywhere beneath the sun.
> Yet what force on earth is weaker than the feeble strength of one?
> But the union makes us strong.

Soon everyone was humming defiantly. Even those who didn't know the words knew the tune, which was the same as "Battle Hymn of the Republic." This was who we had collectively become, a force of nature.

> Solidarity forever,
> Solidarity forever,
> Solidarity forever,
> For the union make us strong.
> They have taken untold millions, that they never toiled to earn,
> But without our brain and muscle not a single wheel could turn;
> We can break their haughty power, gain our freedom when we learn—
> That the union makes us strong.

A few moments—was it seconds?—and the humming turned to hugging, screaming, and general pandemonium, as the count ended and we were declared officially the winner. "Enthusiasm in the room was infectious," said of all the people, the Cornell personnel director, Cecil's boss, Gary Posner, quoted in the paper the next day. The vote was 483 to 375, with over 96 percent turnout. I didn't see Cecil Murphy hug anyone.

**FIGURE 7.** February 24, 1981: pandemonium breaks loose as two hundred workers observing the formal Labor Board vote count realize we have won. (Local 2300 newsletter)

**FIGURE 8.** Victory is ours. Custodian and OC member Al Davidoff, fist raised, celebrates the moment as greenhouse worker Bill Makepeace claps. (Local 2300 newsletter)

The pandemonium and celebration continued through the night at a victory party at the Party House, a local bar. Amazingly enough, I can still remember the "morning after." I remember it clearly, in fact. It was the only day I worked as a custodian for Cornell that I really wanted to get up and be there on time. The only day in almost two years.

Yes, I wanted to show off a little. I wanted people to congratulate me, and I wanted to congratulate them. But it was more than that. Even on the line to punch in, we felt a little different. We were no longer the animals in the zoo that the students in the adjoining laundry room could gawk at, as we waited in that line to stick that stupid card into that all-powerful machine to get "punched." We had changed a little overnight. We stood a little straighter and with more spirit, more pride, even a touch of "ownership." We weren't owners of anything concrete yet, not a contract, or even a functioning organization, but we did have more rights than before, and a little more ownership over our lives. And we felt a little more empowered, enough even to stare back. The front-page headline of the student newspaper declared our victory. The look on those students' faces reminded me of the scene in *Planet of the Apes*, when the humans suddenly realize that their enslaved apes could think, talk, and feel.

The election, of course, was only the first step. We had a union now, but what sort of union would it be? This was an issue that was not only of obvious interest to us, but also to Cornell.

This was brought home to me some months later as negotiations for our first contract with Cornell were getting under way. I remember a meeting between our bargaining team and Cecil Murphy. We told him that we were conducting surveys of the membership, as a way to reach out to all the workers to get their ideas so we could incorporate them into our negotiations. Cecil was dumbfounded. "You're not really going to do all that stuff, are you? I know you talked about it during the organizing drive all the time, but you're not really going to delay the negotiations because of that nonsense, are you?"

Murphy's questions reminded me of that critical issue. What kind of union would we be? Would we become the kind of union many of us were committed to—constantly reaching out to involve the rank and file in *their* union? Or would we go the way of many others—a bureaucracy largely divorced from the membership that does what it needs to do to service the contract, and little else?

As I thought about this in the aftermath of our wonderful victory, I was haunted by the memory of a little scene that occurred at our victory celebration at the Party House on State Street. Militant union man Doug DeHart was famous for two things: one was the odor of cows he perpetually carried with him; the other was his homemade frog puddle punch. I don't know where the "frog puddle" part came from, but it sure did pack a punch. UAW'S Tom Fricano found that out—the hard way.

Tom was then Western New York director of the UAW, in charge of all UAW activities in what was still a major industrial center. He and Tom Natchuras, the regional director for New York, New Jersey, and Pennsylvania, were the highest embodiment of the UAW for most of us, though we didn't see a lot of them during the drive.

A few hours into our victory party we found Tom Fricano in the bathroom, zonked by DeHart's brew. He was on the floor. He was a mess.

Was this a metaphor for the future of UAW Local 2300? Would this unruly, rural workforce, with little trade union experience, "zonk" the UAW bureaucracy in the process of knocking out our employer?

I remember that same night, John Earle, my first home visit partner, put the central dilemma differently. "We've been pregnant for two years," he said, "and now here we are a newborn babe."

"We're healthy now," he went on, "but what kind of person will we grow up to be?"

What kind of difference, if any, will we make in the world of the screwed-over service and maintenance workers at Cornell? How will we overcome the hostility, not only of our employer, but also of the 45 percent of the workforce that voted no?

Half a lifetime later, I still worry about these things. But not as much. But I'm jumping ahead of the story.

## Discussion Questions

- Why did workers begin to organize?
- What were the limitations of an informal organization like ACE?
- Why did management react so harshly against ACE, even though it wasn't a union drive and might have been easily co-opted?
- What were the risks and benefits of Barbara Rahke placing so much trust and authority in an inexperienced organizing committee?
- Was the decision to allow service and maintenance to move forward and vote ahead of clericals and techs the only possible move?
- In what ways did the organizing committee effectively counter the anti-union campaign?
- How is it easier or harder to organize in places like Cornell, where workers stay for many years? What advantages and disadvantages are there for organizing in more precarious and transient places of employment?

3

# CUSTODIANS—THAT'S ALL YOU'LL EVER BE

Two years of organizing didn't prepare us for what came next.

For two years it was worker to worker. It was Emily shooting the shit—talking union—with her friends and coworkers at the time clock or at the neighborhood IGA. It was John Earle schmoozing over beers with a worker in front of the TV set on one of our home visits. (I became a lifelong fan of *Charlie's Angels* that year.)

We were good at that. The final score proved it. We had our union. But now we needed a contract, and a good one at that. We needed to show the 483 that it was all worth it, and to convince the 375 that they had backed the wrong side, allowing fear to trump hope.

There was only one problem. For two years it was worker to worker. Even though management deluged us with antiunion literature and forced meetings, we were the only ones with our hands on the ballots. Now we had to go head to head with management. And we were playing on their turf.

We thought the hardest part was winning our election and establishing the union. And that really often *is* the hardest part. It's bare knuckles, winner takes all. But we won! We soon found out, however, that getting the "all" was anything but automatic or guaranteed.

We hoped, or maybe fantasized, that unionizing was all we needed to do, and that Cornell would follow the law, bargain in good faith, and respect the decision of its workforce. Good faith? Cornell would have none of it. We thought our vote meant we won the war, but quickly found out that the bargaining table was their second front. They were not through fighting, and they were on home turf now, relying on a contained, legalistic process *very* different from our grassroots organizing drive. We had won a union, but not the respect, livable wages, and stability we deserved and campaigned on. Cornell's intention was to show the newly unionized service workers, and the yet unorganized clericals and techs, that Cornell still had all the power.

We never expected Cornell to roll over and give us a great first contract, but we felt that with the UAW behind us we were well-matched for a fair contract struggle that would lead to a solid collective-bargaining agreement. In the 1980s the UAW was still a muscular international union, with 1.5 million members, a storied progressive history, a huge treasury, and national political clout. We realized we meant something to them, too, when we saw an article in the March 1981 issue of their national magazine, *Solidarity*. "Recently 900 workers at Cornell," the article read, "many of them badly underpaid, won UAW bargaining rights in a key representation victory for college employees." The UAW recognized us as part of a wave of campus organizing that included schools like Columbia and Boston University. Little did we know that the article's title, "The Union Goes to College," should have included a subtitle: "But Is the UAW International About to Get Schooled?"

Writing contract language, even the act of reducing our own big ideas to technical writing, was alien to folks like Emily Apgar, or Darlene, our bargaining team member from the dining services workers. It had been many years, decades in fact, since these two women had dropped out of high school. Emily had left to find work, to survive. Darlene left pregnant. Writing a contract, arguing with management bureaucrats in suits and ties, these were very different skills from cooking and cleaning. Also very different from organizing our brothers and sisters.

At first many of us didn't even know the significance of what we were doing. "Now it says here," I remember Darlene telling me one day, a dog-eared copy of *Webster's New American* clutched in her hands, "'a legal or business agreement.' That's what it says a contract is. What does that have to do with us?"

When we understood that a union meant that management had to sit down and negotiate a legally binding agreement with us, and that it would give rights and benefits we never had before, the thought invigorated us. But negotiate? With these bosses?

We knew how to clean management's offices, not how to convince them that merit pay had to go, much less draft complicated layoff language. We had spent years worrying that one wrong word would send us "down the hill," not how to sit across the table, eyeball to eyeball, equals in debate.

Intimidation was built into the system. And management knew it. They nurtured it. They were trained for it. Some, even born into it.

Dare I tell my coworkers what I learned in one of my ILR classes, that one-third of all new unions never even obtain a first contract? Management just disses them—stonewalls, stalls, punishes—till workers get tired, frustrated, worn out, even retire or go on to other jobs. Soon the union is forgotten, a joke, a shell. And they get away with it. The Labor Board mostly just looks the other way.

We did not dwell much on our fears, our low self-esteem, our lack of formal education. For six months, prior to the start of negotiations, we worked hard. The UAW reps began drafting language, running ideas by us, but mostly keeping the "technical" work to themselves. Our role was to survey the members, make sure we knew priorities. Two years of organizing left us feeling confident we knew what mattered. Thousands of conversations illuminated the big priorities.

Workers wanted to be treated with respect first and foremost. But how do you compel another human being with a lot of power over you to "respect" you? The organizing had kicked up all sorts of hard feelings. Some managers were vengeful, and some workers were too. Everyone was on pins and needles. Upper management blamed lower management for not "delivering" their no votes. There were high hopes and inspired expectations among our members and militant dreams of worker power and even control over the workplace from some of our dedicated, sacrificing activists who had risked so much. That profound idealism coexisted with deep fear and mistrust of a wounded Goliath. Our dread was fueled by the 45 percent no votes and nervous, blame-fearing bosses.

We knew our members hated the merit pay system. It was a constant source of abuse and favoritism, rarely linked to genuine performance standards. We knew we needed a fair grievance procedure with a neutral arbitrator making the final decision to hold management accountable. We also wanted a union shop, so that all members who benefited from the contract were part of the union, and that we all paid our fair share of union dues. Folks also wanted their years of service or seniority to count for something when it came to promotion opportunities, wages, and, in bad times, if there were layoffs.

Beyond those issues, of course, we needed to lift our members out of poverty. Only the top 10–15 percent made a livable wage, and even they were seriously underpaid for their skill levels.

The UAW reps listened hard to us and developed a set of contract proposals that had all the standard legal language but made clear what our members needed most.

## Over Our Heads at the Big Table

Our negotiations did not get off to a good start. Outside it was a beautiful Ithaca spring morning. Inside, winter still prevailed. Management was aggressive—no, hostile—right from the get-go. Cecil Murphy, the arrogant purveyor of the entire antiunion campaign, opened the first session with a speech about how terrific the university's track record of employee relations had been. He then went on to talk about how difficult it would be to take the "flexibility and friendliness" of the past and translate it into a restrictive binding agreement, that many aspects of our employment might be lost in the process. Translation: You'll be damn lucky to hang on to what you've got, and if you're the least bit weak we're gonna punish you for organizing.

Then Murphy introduced Ron Mathews. Here was the guy we'd heard all the rumors about, the one Emily kept referring to as Wyatt Earp: Cornell's new hired gun. We were all nervous about this guy before we ever met him. We figured Murphy was as bad as it could get, and we'd been fighting him for a solid year.

Emily stated her theory. "You see, it's like this. They fought us with Murphy and they lost, so the big, big bosses probably figure he wasn't mean enough. That's why they've hired the new guy."

Our apprehension was inflamed by the fact that we only knew a couple of things about Ron Mathews. He used to be a schoolteacher and active in their union. He then jumped ship and became a negotiator for school district management. The rumor was that his first negotiation ended in a bitter strike where a teacher was run over and killed on a picket line. Mathews was five foot six, wore glasses, had a bit of a gut. Maybe fifty years old, with greasy hair so black it obviously came out of a box. He was dressed in a very conservative, dark suit. Cecil was a flashy, hip collegiate dresser; this guy looked like an undertaker.

Mathews took charge, and Murphy never returned to another bargaining session. The rest of the management bargaining team were a hodgepodge of half a dozen heads of departments or representatives from specific colleges like the Vet School HR director Rita Harris. They never spoke, just sat there for months either scowling or looking bored out of their minds.

Mathews did his best to reinforce our inexperience and lack of confidence. At one session, he balked at our demand to establish a COLA—a cost of living adjustment, meaning that each year wages would automatically be adjusted to account for inflation. For us, this was basic justice. We were entitled to a living wage. Inflation—over 11 percent in 1979 and 13.5 percent in 1980—was a big deal for us and could cut a measly $5-an-hour wage to $4.50 in buying power in one year. That was unfair.

Not to Mathews. He never let us forget who we were and who he and his bosses were. And what he thought we were entitled to and not entitled to. He never stopped trying to undermine us in every way.

"Animal attendant, custodian, dishwasher, groundskeeper, waitress," he sneered. "These are all unskilled jobs. They require little education or training. Even the professors don't get a COLA. You just have to accept the reality of who you are." And then he smirked, "Custodians and the like."

I was enraged. We all were. Emily found her voice first. "To you, Ron Mathews, we may be a bunch of peons, dumb little children, but to us we're every bit as good as you. The girl at the checkout line at the grocery doesn't charge one price for bread if you're a custodian and another if you're a big boss, does she? We got to survive, and we ought to do it with a little bit of dignity."

"Listen," I coughed, and cleared my throat nervously, "you underestimated us during the organizing. Don't make the same mistake twice." I got the words out, but the nervousness was present in every syllable. I sounded like a petulant child angry at a parent. I was furious that Mathews could have so undermined me.

We were often terrified of saying the wrong thing at the table. This wasn't just shooting the shit with a coworker, or even a supervisor. This was *formal negotiations.* And we were carrying a thousand workers on our shoulders.

Fred Thomas, an amiable mechanic, confirmed our fears. Once, right in the middle of a statement on sick leave, he suddenly started talking about shift differential for night workers. "Hell, there aren't that many of them night-shift people anyway," he intoned, to our growing consternation. "You don't take those jobs for the extra money, you take 'em cuz you got a farm or another day job."

The famous labor ditty "Which Side Are You On?" immediately came to my mind, as I realized that Fred was, in effect, arguing against our own position and giving ammunition to management. Pam Mackesey, a gardener from Cornell Plantations and a key leader, tried to undo the damage, but Mathews swooped down on Fred like a vulture gobbling up newborn sea turtles.

"So, Fred, what you're saying is there are very few night-shift workers, and most of them actually prefer to work nights due to non-university commitments. Is that right?" Mathews stared at Fred, his masklike face now contorted into a sickly sweet smile. Pam tried to interrupt the flow, but Mathews would have none of it. "Now, Pam, Fred was saying something important, and I know how much your team values each individual's freedom to speak their mind."

Either Fred liked the attention, or he was entranced. "Sure, Ron, I mean, don't get me wrong, the night-shift folks want more money just like the rest of us, but I'd say better than half of 'em wouldn't take a day job if you offered it."

"Perhaps we should be offering those night-shift workers something *less* per hour, as they're just moonlighting from their main jobs. It seems the university is being taken advantage of." Mathews turned to all of us now, beaming. Slurp! Fred's little turtle tail was last to be sucked down Ron's throat.

A couple weeks later, after some more Fredisms, one of our fellow team members solved the problem. He made up a sign, to be seen only by our side: SHUT UP FRED. It helped control Fred, but the lesson was not lost on each of us. It didn't help our confidence.

Tom Parkin was harder to control.

Tom was the most hostile and aggressive member of our team. He was loud. He could be coarse. He was very much still the military drill sergeant he once was. Every other word out of his mouth was "shit" or "damn." And he said it as if he was mad and thought you were deaf.

Tom's vehemence wasn't the problem, though. It was a strength, making him an important leader. All the members knew management didn't scare him, that he would speak his mind. He was also a campus printer, often driving around campus making deliveries and seeing hundreds of members each day.

The problem with Tom was that his fusillades were shot out of a very loose cannon. One day at the table, Mathews had the gall to start pleading poverty. "Education is a sick industry," he said. He went on to roll through some dubious statistics about how this $2 billion corporation had to tighten its belt, and that our necks "just happen to be in the loop."

Tom exploded. "Well, it can't be too fucking sick an industry, cuz you're paying the president $500,000 and giving him a goddamn free house and car. What the hell are you pulling in, Ron? Sixty or seventy grand at least, I figure. Hell, the only way to get a raise at this place right now is to be a goddamn suck-hole kissing some dumb supervisor's sorry butt all day long instead of doing the job you hired me for."

It was thrilling. But it was out of nowhere. The team hadn't discussed coming on like gangbusters at this session. In fact, our main goal was to get a new wage offer out of them to show members that some progress was being made.

Mathews easily turned the tables. "I am shocked that you would disparage President Rhodes in that manner. You might want to reflect on the fact that this university's success is in large part due to his leadership. Many of you would have no job whatsoever if not for his important work."

He went on with the cool confidence of a spider seeing an errant fly twisting in the web. "Our team is not going to listen to such abuse and Cornell bashing. We had hoped your interest was in bargaining a contract, not in perpetuating the hateful atmosphere you cultivated during your organizing campaign. I guess we were wrong. Our next bargaining session is next week, Wednesday at 10 a.m. Hopefully you will rethink your approach to these negotiations."

Mathews pulled his chair back, shook his head, tsk-tsked us, and walked out with his team in tow like baby ducklings. Though we were momentarily energized by Tom's attack, we realized the membership might have a problem with bargaining breaking down because we had a temper tantrum. Mathews had one-upped us, put us on the defensive.

Tom was freewheeling, and our bargaining team was speeding downhill fast. I remember thinking, is this how first contracts are lost, and unions broken?

## Detroit Dave

One reason we selected the UAW as our union was that we understood that it, more than others, allowed its locals to exercise greater autonomy. That sounded good at the time. Now confronting Mathews and facing our own weakness and inexperience, we needed help. Where are you, Walter Reuther?

Our main rep at the table was one of the few UAW reps who was a woman. Sue was smart and could talk tough, but she had minimal experience bargaining first contracts. It was such a demoralizing process, and at times it felt like her heart wasn't in it. Most of all, we were lost, expecting some UAW savior to make Cornell behave. The UAW had unrealistic expectations too, and as we floundered, they decided to bring in a "bigger gun."

Enter Detroit Dave.

David Gordon. "International Representative, United Auto Workers," his card said. His presence said something more. Much more. Huge—maybe three hundred pounds—balding, white-rimmed pate, pink fleshy face, pink fleshy hands the size of a catcher's mitt. He could have been Hollywood's version of the tough union rep from Detroit. But this wasn't a movie. It wasn't Hollywood, or Detroit. It was Ithaca. And we needed help.

After our first meeting with Dave, it seemed that the Marines had indeed finally landed. He insisted we have a talk at a local bar. We chose the basement of one of our favorites, Rulloff's, and then ended up staying till closing. Rulloff's was named after the last man executed by public hanging in the state of New York. We were pinning a lot of hopes on Dave leading us to a better ending.

That first night, Dave told us his life story and even drew complex three-dimensional machine parts for us on napkins. He was born on the west side of Detroit. He had been a skilled design technician for Chrysler for twenty years, then a UAW rep for ten more. He obviously enjoyed his work, though second to the pleasure he got enjoying himself. He told us stories of management-bashing, stories of strikes, stories of the power of our union. He was intimidating and, apparently, unintimidatable. Detroit Dave was a pro, and just the right amount of radical nuts. He was the shot in the arm our bargaining team needed.

We fell in love that night. Or at least we were so drunk that it felt like the real thing. But would we respect him—or ourselves—in the morning, after his first bargaining session with Mathews?

As we trudged into that bargaining session, Emily whispered in my ear, "I hope he talks as good in here as he does at the bar when we're all drunk." He did. Dave changed the months-long dynamic at the table in five minutes.

He explained to Mathews how Doug Fraser, president of the 1.5-million-member-strong UAW, had personally assigned him to Cornell. Mathews acted unimpressed: after all, Frank Rhodes, president of Cornell, had personally assigned him to these negotiations as well. Those were the last words Dave let Mathews get in for a long while.

"Well, Ron," Dave started, "I know Frank Rhodes is an important man, running this important school here in . . ."

He paused for emphasis, looked around, suggesting how trivial this little town was, and then said, "Ithaca. He has to worry about how many students and how many classrooms, where should we put a library or a cafeteria or a new squash court. But you know, while *your* president is fretting about all those *urgent* matters, *my* president, Doug Fraser, is meeting with leaders of the Democratic Party deciding who the next president of the United States is going to be."

Yes, it was a new ballgame.

Dave Gordon had a great way of making threats clearly, but still so indirectly as to be virtually unassailable. When Mathews refused to move on merit pay as the sole basis for raises, Dave said, "Ron, let me tell you a story of a different negotiation where workers had become terribly bitter about merit pay. Workers there suffered from doing things like having to paint the supervisor's house or having to submit to sexual harassment to earn their merit raises. The money had nothing to do with how good a job you did. The whole system was corrupt.

"The workers were enraged that management refused to budge on this issue. One day, one of the workers had had enough. He was a big, strong, husky guy, almost as big as I am, but a few years younger. Not long before this, he had witnessed his daughter's sexual harassment at the hands of a supervisor. Well, he finally snapped, right at the bargaining table while management was, once again, defending this abusive policy. He took the huge two-hundred-pound table and just flipped it over right on top of the employer's entire bargaining team. Why, you could hear the bones snapping, you could see their ties flopping, as people tried to get out from under that weight."

As he spoke, Gordon pretended to reenact the murderous scene. Standing up, making full use of his ample girth, he suddenly lifted our side of the massive table slightly up in the air.

Mathews was dumbstruck, nervous enough to jerk his chair back away from the table. This was certainly not the Ivy League way.

"I'm telling you, Ron," Dave concluded after a long pause, "you just never know how upset some people can get over an issue like this."

We loved it.

Of course, management never budged an inch. Can you imagine Mathews going back to his superiors trying to justify compromising their position because he was afraid some three-hundred-pound, sixty-year-old labor goon from Detroit might flip the bargaining table on his lap?

Detroit Dave stories quickly made the rounds among the members. Most often it was a case of "You really had to be there." But the members wanted to see progress in negotiations, not improvements in bargaining team morale. The guy plowing the sidewalk and the woman cleaning the lab didn't want to hear about how their leaders felt. We were still stuck, getting nowhere slow. Some members started talking strike; others just lost hope. Those who had voted no in February snickered.

Lacking confidence in ourselves and seeing no progress, we started to experience internal divisions within our rank-and-file bargaining team. Pam Mackesey had been chosen chair of the bargaining team. This was in part because the original leader, the "Norma Rae" of our struggle, Cathy Valentino, had dropped back from full activity for a while. Pam had done a ton of work on the proposals that Cathy had missed, but Cathy was a natural leader, confident and clear-spoken. Pam, like most of us, was jittery, and tended to get tongue-tied, losing her train of thought. There were cultural differences, too. Pam was younger, more "alternative-y," and with broader progressive politics. She had earned the role with hard, steady work, but when the going got tough, folks on the team started to whisper about her weaknesses.

To make matters worse, our bargaining team member Darlene was starting to question the union entirely. It was as if management's bad behavior was eroding her loyalty to our cause. She had been less involved in the struggle to build the union, and less critical of Cornell. She also had a lot of friends in management, and her husband was a vulnerable low-level supervisor. It would have been

**FIGURE 9.** Cornell Plantations gardener Pam Mackesey was a key leader and the chair of our first bargaining committee. Pam went on to be a UAW organizer and was elected to the Ithaca Common Council. (Local 2300 newsletter)

devastating for a member of our bargaining team to quit, and we had to talk Darlene off the ledge several times.

## Are We Animals?

The International was frustrated too. Bargaining had gone on for six months with little progress. It looked like it could go on for six years. Maybe Frank Rhodes really was more powerful than Doug Fraser? It slowly began to dawn on some of us: Cornell had every reason to make a very bad example of our disloyalty. Thousands of other unorganized campus workers were watching this process, still debating whether to sign union cards and organize too. For our part, we had done nothing to pressure the university. We had gone into a cul de sac of preparation for professional negotiations. We had no serious campaign, and worse yet, no analysis to design one.

Frustration led to change. The UAW sent Tom Natchuras to replace Detroit Dave. The International's approach—they would have gotten an A in the MBA program—was to shake up the negotiating team. But their view of the team was limited. They assumed that they just needed to find the proper level of UAW authority, and then the university would act more reasonably. But Sue and Dave were smart and had made great arguments. What would make Cornell bargain fairly with another guy in a fancier suit? This was the same top-down approach that many criticized and ultimately contributed to a severe weakening of the labor movement. We didn't know enough or have enough confidence in the rank and file to question it.

The good news was that Natchuras was like a block of ice. Strong. Cool. But a control freak. He wasn't a storyteller, but a master bargainer, a technician extraordinaire. In an academic setting, Tom's intelligence and unflappability seemed to actually make an impression on the university.

The bad news was that his technical skills and controlling behavior left our rank-and-file committee in the bullpen. One of the first moves Tom made reinforced this. He insisted on moving the negotiations off campus, to a conference room at the Sheraton Hotel. We liked bargaining on campus because it made it easy for us to visit work areas during breaks and inform the membership. When things were slow at the table, say two out of every three hours, one or two of us could slip out and hold a clock meeting as workers punched out at the end of their day. Most of the time we weren't even face to face with management. We were in caucus, each side on its own, discussing and reworking proposals, or often twiddling our thumbs.

We told Tom this, but he insisted that if we were to make progress, our priority had to be concentrating on the bargaining. Tom did consult with us on his every move at the table, but we seemed more and more dispensable.

The move to the Sheraton also affected our diet radically. High-living labor aristocrats? Hell no. Bargaining all day there meant having to eat all our meals at the nearby McDonald's, sometimes two and even three meals a day. As our hopes at the table faded, we put more faith in Big Mac than Big Red. If we didn't get a big raise, at least we'd have a big belly. Or maybe win a million in the scratch-card game they were running at the time.

Tom's authority and negotiating skills slowly began to pay off. Cornell finally agreed to contractually guarantee us most of the rights and benefits we had prior to the union vote. They had played hardball for months, creating the impression that we might actually have to bargain away certain benefits in order to make any gains at all. Members with pensions or long vacation accruals, for example, feared losing them. Protecting our meager status quo was a big relief. But as victories go, it was pathetic. Cornell may have also feared our threats to file unfair labor practices for bargaining in bad faith. They had less to fear from weak labor laws but knew that any neutral government criticisms could lead to bad press and more outside scrutiny and interference.

We were down to half a dozen serious issues. A good wage increase, across the board with no merit system; layoffs by seniority; a grievance procedure with binding arbitration; health and safety protections that were grievable; an agency shop so that all who benefited by the union paid equal dues; and a better pension plan.

All these issues felt like musts for us. They were issues the members made clear were important to them too. Withdrawing proposals, compromising our ideals, made us feel sick. Sicker even than all those Big Macs we were consuming.

We knew what was fair. We knew what Cornell could afford. We also knew after six months, though, that we were not going to win a full measure of justice. Our organizing drive idealism had crashed head-on into the cold, hard realism of collective bargaining. We needed a level of strategic power neither we nor our UAW reps and leaders had figured out.

How low would we go? Should we recommend to our members a contract without some or any of their priorities accomplished? Which ones were undroppable? We felt we had a compact with the members that we were abandoning. What power did we have to stop this? Our power was us. It was many of the students. It was some of the faculty. It was to withdraw our labor, to strike, and to get the support of these others. What was our strategy? Ever since the glow of our February organizing victory, it felt like we were playing checkers with a powerful bully who was playing chess.

Tom clearly wanted to avoid a strike and the conflict that it would generate. And he doubted we could pull it off, given how divided our membership was and how complicated the campus would be to shut down. He also seemed confident that the university would move on these basic issues. He came out of the auto industry where multinational corporations filled with powerful, hard-nosed industrialists were routinely brought to their senses by the mighty UAW. How could an effete, Ivy League university truly brook a strike? How could they be so unreasonable?

Well, they could, and they would. Cornell made our decision, if not our job, easier by not budging on any of the remaining key issues. Our team found renewed unity and enthusiasm. We became organizers again. Even Tom began to encourage us to get our act together, because he too began to doubt the possibility of a good-faith settlement.

It was the first week in September. We set a strike deadline for October 1. That would give us enough time to make the necessary progress at the table to avoid a strike. Most important, it also gave us enough time to organize our members, to educate and prepare. By October 1, the campus would be in full swing, completely dependent on our services. And the Ithaca winter would not yet be upon us.

A week from the deadline, the UAW regional director Ed Gray suddenly announced he would enter the negotiations. Just like that. Nobody said boo to us. Worse, he offered to unilaterally lift the strike deadline if Cornell's vice president Bill Herbster agreed to join the talks.

We were livid. The strike scared us, but also invigorated us. It brought us back to the organizing drive. It gave us a new sense of power. And a new sense of control, like this really was *our* union. And we were finding more support from the troops than we expected. But now, our momentum, credibility, and confidence were upended. By the UAW.

We scheduled a mass meeting at Ithaca's Strand Theater to explain the situation to the members. Gray was flying in to address the crowd. Good, we felt; at least he can explain his big move. Gray's plane arrived. He called Herbster, who told him he would not join the talks. Gray just got back on the same plane and flew back to New York City.

"Fuck those naïve bastards," he told Natchuras as he boarded. Was he referring to Cornell, or to us?

The meeting was packed. The majestic Strand Theater, built in 1917 but now condemned and cluttered with pigeon shit and wine bottles, was still pretty grand. Eight hundred workers, hundreds of family members, kids, and dogs: it was pandemonium. The press huddled outside the hall snapping photos as film crews ran back and forth. We walked in like celebrities to a Hollywood movie opening, a little late, a little self-important, and very nervous.

As soon as we entered the theater the crowd began chanting: "*Union! Union! Union! Union! Union! Union!*" Hundreds of arms slapped our backs, hundreds of workers shouting encouragement. "We're with you!" "Don't back down!" "Tell it like it is!" We climbed up the stage and began chanting "*Union! Union! Union!*" back.

Each of us spoke about what bargaining had been like, what gains we felt we had made. Then we laid out what remained to be accomplished, and what we were stuck on. One mechanic yelled from the back, "Those are the reasons we organized." A fair grievance procedure, ending the merit system, an agency shop: these were fairness issues, these were respect and dignity issues. People said they could survive the low wages and the lousy pension till the next contract, but they would no longer tolerate favoritism and abuse.

Then Natchuras spoke. It was as if someone had flipped a switch. This icy labor bureaucrat delivered the most impassioned speech I had ever witnessed. He was a natural, weaving questions into his feverish pleas for strength and unity. He expanded the boundary of the discussion. "Are we animals?" he shouted. "Are we animals?" louder.

"*No!*" the crowd roared.

"Are we human beings?"

"*Yes!*"

"Are we human beings?"

"*Yes!*"

"Are you going to let Cornell treat you like an animal any longer?"

"*No!*"

"Are you sick of crawling? Are you ready to stand up with your brothers and sisters?"

"*Yes!*"

"Are you ready for justice?"

"*Yes!*"

"Then let me ask you one more question. Are you ready to strike?"

"*Yes!*"

"I can't hear you. *Are you ready to strike?*"

"*Yes!*"

"*Are you ready to shut these bastards down?*"

"*Yes!*"

People were screaming. People were smiling. People were crying. The roof had finally come off that old Strand Theater.

We stuck around for hours, talking to the members. And we needed to work out the details for one final meeting the morning of the strike, less than a week away. And a zillion more steps to take to get ready. To shore up the shaky few, and to speak with those who weren't at our revival meeting.

We needed to plan a strike.

Striking Cornell is exactly like trying to shut down a city. There are over forty entrance roads to the campus that need to be picketed twenty-four hours a day. And many hundreds of picketing members who need to be organized, directed, fed, informed, and supported continuously.

Luckily there are also leaders who emerge in precisely these types of crises. Folks who wouldn't touch a bargaining table with a ten-foot pole but who are brilliant at the logistics of coordinating hundreds of people's lives.

The strike was to be a war. As in war we had our generals and our captains. One of the strike generals was crusty old Larry Grey. He was an old army man, a "lieutenant," he whispered to me, so as not to sound elitist in front of our troops.

Larry treated me like a son, encouraging my leadership and having my back even when my ideas ran afoul of his more conservative thinking. Like many of the maintenance mechanics, Larry had worked with and around a lot of asbestos. Like many employers, the university kept using asbestos even as evidence was mounting about its severe health risks. A few years later, Larry got mesothelioma, shriveled and died from that exposure.

During that first strike, he was a leader among leaders. He wore a UAW baseball cap with five shiny UAW pins. Everybody called him "the General" or "Five Star." Larry and our other generals didn't want the bargaining team messing with their plans. Our job was to bargain, to write a daily news update, and to make the rounds of the picket lines to pass on news and boost morale.

We had such mixed feelings: buoyed by the Strand meeting, but very unsure of what we were getting into. The rumor mill was rampant: so and so was going to scab; Cornell would fire everyone who went on strike; the union would not provide strike benefits.

The truth was we just did not know how many would go out. We only won the election with a slim majority, and that was less than a year ago. We would've liked to kick Cornell in the teeth, but not if our toes ended up broken on Mathews's fangs.

Meanwhile we kept bargaining. A mediator was shuttling back and forth between Natchuras and Mathews. It was my first lesson in the relative powerlessness of mediation. Our differences were elemental; there was a kill-or-be-killed dynamic that the best mediator in the world couldn't have bridged. Tom kept us up to speed and asked our opinions before and after each of these private sessions, so being shut out of these sidebars didn't bother us too much. After Natchuras's speech we figured he knew what he was doing. We knew we didn't.

Some progress was made, but not on the big issues. Cornell still wanted some part of the raise to be what they called merit-based. But the amount of money they were splitting between merit and across the board was too small to tempt us. They seemed willing to respect seniority during layoffs, but we got bogged down in complicated details about exactly how it would all work. Would seniority be counted by department, by work unit, or university-wide? Nothing yet on a grievance procedure, a decent wage increase, a union shop, pension, or health and safety.

Tom assured us that "real" negotiations wouldn't end on a Friday with a Monday strike planned. He expected Mathews to agree to work through the weekend to avoid a confrontation that could leave thousands of students unfed, mail undelivered, buildings uncleaned, and hundreds of pickets clogging Cornell's arteries.

Tom was wrong. Cornell didn't know or care how General Motors did it. On Thursday, Mathews told Natchuras to make our best final offer, and he'd consider it. Friday, he rejected it. Tom just muttered, "Those stupid snobby bastards." He meant management, but despite his bravado and skill, we wondered who was schooling whom.

Natchuras now realized there really would be a strike. So did I. "What folly, Ron," I remember him saying. I don't know which was stranger, hearing Tom use the word "folly" or calling Mathews "Ron."

Mathews agreed with Tom, saying, "What a shame."

It was as if the two of them had forged some twisted bond of fatigue and familiarity in those sidebars, as if some larger forces had interfered with these two decent fellas' efforts to find justice. All I know is that to our relief Mathews stated that the university was prepared to continue bargaining during any "work stoppage." Everything else during that fleeting moment is a blur.

## Talked Out, Walked Out: The Strike Is On

Would the members really strike? It's one thing to cast a secret ballot for the union. To cease working, to cease getting paid, and to stand outside your work area while your boss and god knows how many of your coworkers walk past you, is something else. For union supporters in weak areas, this meant watching their bosses plus a majority of their coworkers walk past them.

To strike means standing outside in the cold October air wondering, *Will I ever regain friends I have lost over this strike? Will I ever be treated fairly by managers who feel I have betrayed them by striking? Will they always give me the worst assignments, the most dangerous tasks, the worst partners, all the little raw deals that function at a level below most written contracts? Will I lose my pension, my health care, or even my job? What is my spouse going to say? My family, my neighbors?*

For most of our members, those generic strike questions all came down to holding on to a whole lot of fear and insecurity. It takes a powerful idea to keep those questions answered or at bay. For us it was justice pure and simple. It was not about money, wages, or benefits, or any issue we were bargaining about. The strike was about the poorest, weakest, most exploited people at a vast omnipotent-seeming corporation, awakening to a sense of power, self-respect, sisterhood, and brotherhood. Maybe we *were* animals, but we had been pushed into a corner, and we were ready to fight with teeth bared.

For one of our key leaders, Ted Cunningham, a huge, softhearted cowhand at the Teaching and Research experimental cow farm, he had a very different priority. He took me aside and, quaking with emotion, told me he wasn't sure he could strike.

I said, "Ted, you are our leader there. If you don't go out, it will make our solid majority think twice, what's going on?" I was expecting the usual conversation we'd been having with all our members: What about money? What about our jobs? Will it really help? How long do you think it'll last?

Then Ted spoke. "It's the animals, Al. Who will take care of them?" At first, I thought he was messing with me, but I could see he was a wreck. This big old farmer was about to cry.

"If you don't feed 'em and milk 'em on a regular schedule, they get terribly sick, and that can happen in a few days."

I summoned my deepest sympathies and went at the heart of the issue. "What about your family, Ted? What about all your coworkers who end up in poor health or broke because of how Cornell treats them? It's Cornell that is putting your cows at risk. All they have to do is bargain fairly, and this strike will never happen."

He was nodding, but I could tell I wasn't hitting the bull's-eye yet. "I know that, Al," he said. "I know who's right and wrong here. I am just saying, I've worked my whole life with those animals, and I don't want them being hurt."

Finally, I switched tactics and said, "Cornell knows some of our jobs need immediate coverage. Between your scabs and bosses working OT, and a few temps they'll hire, they are not gonna let those cows suffer."

This seemed to help. Ted heaved a sigh on his way out, saying "OK, I'll strike, and let's see what happens."

The first day of the strike was revolutionary. Old women marching arm in arm, blocking traffic and screaming "Scab!" over and over at coworkers who dared cross their picket line. These custodians, so old they still called themselves "maids," were anything but passive and obedient that day. They turned away Teamster truckers, they turned away nonunion delivery trucks, they turned away nervous scabs, some of whom found a middle course. Don't work but also don't participate—just stay home.

There was real fervor, jubilation, but also the boiling over of a decades-long simmer of anger. Grown men, men with families, hunting rifles, and rusted pickup trucks, wept with joy, feeling their pride and power. Men who had shut up while bosses rode them, humiliated them, just to hang on to a small "merit" pay raise. Women who had survived by a sickening navigation of the sexual overtures of supervisors. Hundreds who lived in dire poverty amid Porsche-driving eighteen-year-olds and well-paid faculty. They all exploded onto picket lines.

People made up their own chants and songs. The Copy Center women doing a slow-motion, high-stepping chorus line of "Here's to you, Cecil Murphy, here's to you. . . . Here's to you, Cecil Murphy, here's to you. . . . Oh, you think you're upperclass, but you're just a horse's ass. . . . Here's to you, Cecil Murphy, here's to you."

Yes, there was some sabotage. Eggs were thrown, some roofing nails were twisted so that no matter how they were strewn they always landed point up under scabs' tires. Scattered acts perhaps, but still indicative of the powerful feelings we had unearthed.

Once when three of us from the leadership were making the rounds of picket sites sharing news and anecdotes, we saw construction work still going on in a remote section of campus. Workers had just finished pouring cement for a new sidewalk. They were thirty yards away. We thought all construction work had been shut down by the trades, so we were pissed to see this maverick operation alive and kicking.

"Screw that," hissed Doug DeHart. "Let's go do a dance on their virgin sidewalk." He told Pam to meet us at the other end in the car.

"C'mon, follow me," he barked, while yanking me out of the car with him. He started running toward the cement. But with a fifty-pound gut attached to the front of his waist he was huffing and puffing before he got to the first orange cordon. I sprinted past him, leaping over the plastic and digging my feet into the cement as I ran.

The scabs quickly discovered the intrusion and started yelling and running toward us. I glanced back over my shoulder to see Doug crawling under the orange plastic and stumbling in the cement. I jumped in the car, yelling at Pam to back up fast. We scooped up DeHart, still only halfway through the cement and a few seconds before some burly hod carrier could throttle him.

"We showed those scabs," he huffed. And we had a new story to tell.

The worst thing I heard that first day was that my good friend and fellow punk rebel West Campus custodian Leo LaMontain had scabbed. I could not believe it. Nobody was more militant than Leo. He had served as a union activist alongside me. I told the strike generals, "I'm going in," violating Cornell's requirement that strikers stay *out* of the buildings. I was on a mission.

I swept into his dorm shouting his name. Made my way into the basement still yelling, hoping no other scabs or supervisors would challenge me. I got to his break-room door, timing it for his usual break, and yelled, "Leo, you in there?"

"Yes, I am," he yelled back.

"I'm coming in," and I walked into the room.

Leo was crouched in a corner, holding a baseball bat. He had a goofy, stressed-out smile on his face. "Leo, what are you doing with that bat?"

"Just playing it safe," he said. "I didn't know if you were alone."

Given Leo's always vivid imagination, I guess he imagined we had a goon squad coming for him.

"What is going on, Leo? The strike is going great, and we need you outta here, man. This is what we've been talking about, and it is fucking fun out there."

Then I noticed that a side of Leo's face was swollen. "What happened to you there?" I said, pointing at his face.

"Oh that," he said. "I had to do a little dental work two nights ago."

I remembered that one time at his house he told me that he saved money by doing his own dentistry. It struck me as absolutely crazy at the time, but I knew it was just one more way he was trying to save a buck and take care of his family.

"So, what are you doing here, Leo?"

"Yeah, I know it's totally wrong, but Diane and I talked. She wanted me to strike, but she's out, so no paycheck for either of us if I walk too, plus the dental problem, I just freaked out, I guess. What are people saying?"

"They're saying come out and join us, Leo. It's sunny, and we're kicking Cornell's ass."

"People are pretty pissed at me, aren't they?"

"A little, but folks will be pumped up if you come out now. And we all understand about the pressures, man. Everyone will be happy as hell to see you. I know you, Leo; you can't live with this. You're a fighter. Everybody knows it. I damn well know it. Most of all, *you* damn well know it. Let's go."

Leo collected his stuff, walked out to his car with me, came to a picket line to great cheers, and never scabbed again. In typical crazy Leo fashion, he came up with some story explaining that he was a secret undercover spy for the UAW, gathering info on the scabs and management.

The strike itself seemed to work. People went to their assigned spots. Coffee trucks drove around regularly. Baloney sandwiches with mayo slapped on like mortar arrived at lunchtime. Some local restaurants even donated food. Moosewood, a cooperative-owned vegetarian yuppie heaven, was the most consistent. Their tofu burgers were too much for these blue-collar workers, but everybody loved those brownies.

We put out a daily newsletter as the strike wore on. In it, we recounted our little victories. Bill Floyd had scabbed the first day but gone out the next. Sage Dining was still 100 percent out. We forced Cornell to close the Print Shop. The building trades workers stayed out for us, at least three days, losing hundreds of dollars each. The strike was big news, and radio stations, TV, newspapers made instant celebrities out of our members.

We felt we had the upper hand. More workers went out than Cornell had expected. Just as they underestimated our support in the election, they leaned on the same unreliable supervisory structure for their strike projections. Our support from the students, long cultivated, was solid. And the press put us on page one every day.

Cornell, of course, mounted its own media blitz. Almost half the workforce came to work, they reported. We knew these numbers were inflated; we had signed lists of strikers proving we had 75 percent strike support. We invited the press to go on a tour of campus to see how much was shut down: no mail services, no printing, no meals in nine out of twelve dining units, some classes canceled. But the press had limited investigative energy. They'd quote our numbers, and they'd quote Cornell's, and leave it at that.

Despite heroic efforts by the members, the strike began to fade after a few days. A few dozen strikers defected. Bosses they were friendly with had called some at home. Others saw coworkers scabbing and felt isolated. Some confessed that spouses had pressured them to "stop messing around with the damn union and bring home a paycheck." We also knew the trades were going back to work. The thrill of the first day faded into a quiet, steely resolve for most and creeping fear for many. Students, faculty, community all helped out, donating food, showing up to picket lines, but none of that was organized, or on a scale that felt powerful.

At the first bargaining session during the strike, we didn't know if we'd get a lecture or a breakthrough. We got neither. What we did get were more sidebars and more small, steady progress.

We ironed out a seven-page layoff provision that we were very satisfied with. We also made some headway on a grievance procedure, and got protections written into the health and safety provision. Nothing on pension, nothing on the shop, and the money wasn't getting any better.

It was becoming hard to assess our progress. We had crossed many crucial hurdles. Negotiated some good language, but still so far from everything we felt we deserved and had campaigned on. But the strike had altered the equation in mysterious ways we had not expected. Some members were so fired up that nothing short of total victory would suffice. "I'll go back to work when they give us Cecil Murphy's head on a stick," shouted one worker from the picket line.

Other workers moved in the opposite direction. Just as the bargaining team's idealism had crashed headfirst into the realities of the bargaining table, now the membership's euphoria with going on strike was colliding with five straight days of cold, wet picket-line duty, baloney sandwiches, and debilitating fear of financial catastrophe.

Natchuras was frustrated, but he kept at it, spending more and more time away from us, writing language, sidebarring with management. At one point he reminded us that after the historic UAW sit-down strikes that won the first contract at GM, all they got was a one-page contract. He said, "That contract recognized the union, and set up a grievance procedure, that's it. But that contract was won with blood, and it was the foundation for the great wages and benefits we have now." We knew he was trying to lower our expectations, but taking a little bit longer view wasn't a bad idea, given we were sweating our future hour by hour.

Out on the line things were indeed getting tough. Over at the Collegetown gate I stopped to chat with the picketing workers and saw custodian Cindy Doolittle there. We'd spoken for a minute on the first day of the strike. She was incredibly wound up then. "You ever think you'd see me like this?" she joked, pointing to her sandwich sign, which read, "I love Cornell, it's being broke I can't stand." When I left her that day, I heard the chant she started that other pickets immediately picked up: "No contract, no work! No contract, no work!"

"My dad was an electrician," she had yelled at me as I waved goodbye. "He taught me that." Poor Cindy. At four feet and eleven inches, she probably had to take two steps for every one the other pickets were taking.

By this next visit a week later, things were different. She was standing around, shuffling, not really marching or even walking a picket line. The UAW's traditional method of striking "every entrance all day" kept people isolated, in small groups. Cindy had the old worried look I saw the first time we'd met. After I passed on the latest bargaining news to the whole group about one of the dining hall bosses trying to run the short-order grill and starting a fire, I chatted with Cindy for a few more minutes.

She looked tired, so I asked her to sit next to me on the curb. "No, I don't want to sit there, cuz some of the scabs will be going home now, and they're driving real crazy. Almost hit old Harold over there," she pointed.

We sat down on the damp grass with a picket sign underneath us. "So what do we do now?" she said.

"You know I came here to ask you the same question," I replied.

We both smiled tired smiles.

"How's your daughter holding up?" I asked.

"Are you kidding? She loves this. She's been out here almost every day. She loves making signs and chanting. Everybody's been really nice to her too. She won't love it too much when I don't get her anything for her eighth birthday in two weeks, or if Halloween comes around and she can't be something fancy. But she does understand a lot more than I thought she might. She knows what I'm doing is right. You should hear her yell at those scabs.

"People are mad. They feel stuck between their pumped-up selves and their scared selves. The support we feel for each other feels real strong when we're together on the line. We're stuck between all that good stuff that this strike has brought out of people and the doubts you have when you go home at night, or when you open the fridge. Thank God I'm not with my first husband, Joe. He crossed the line yesterday and today again. Last night he had the nerve to call me up and tell me to get my butt into work if I want to have a job. The nerve of him ordering me around. Those days are over. But it does make you scared. It does make you worry. People are tough when they're together, but we all know a few more sneak back in every day. People are afraid to be left hanging, but they're more afraid to lose their pride, their sense of right and wrong. It's hurting people how they're being squeezed."

I didn't know what to say. I told her to stay tough a little longer. That we were making headway and that we wouldn't leave anybody hanging. As I walked away, putting my best face and war whoop toward the line, and to Cindy, I knew I didn't know what "we won't leave anyone hanging" even meant.

"The troops can last another week but not much more," General Larry Grey told me. "Now, don't you take a bad contract, but don't keep us out a day longer than the day you get something we can live with. The most important thing is we got the union. Let's make damn sure we keep it."

**FIGURE 10.** The first days of our first strike were filled with rebellious energy. But long picket shifts in small groups like this were not the best strategy for keeping morale and confidence high. (Local 2300 newsletter)

**FIGURE 11.** Clericals and techs, as well as students and faculty, were key supporters in the first strike. Colette Walls was one of the most active members of the clerical workers' organizing committee. Many of the activists regularly included our sons and daughters. The fight was about families, and families were welcome. Colette's daughter stands holding a coffee can for strike donations. (Local 2300 newsletter)

Within the bargaining team, meanwhile, Darlene had begun to have a nervous breakdown, needing almost constant reassurance. She would go to each member of the bargaining team expressing her fear that we might all lose our jobs. The possibility that she might scab was terrifying. Cornell would have made a huge deal of it, and it would have given every shaky striker an excuse to give in to their fears. Her husband, a vulnerable, entry-level supervisor, was telling her that both of them would lose their jobs if she didn't get back to work. Darlene is white, and her husband is Black. Interracial marriages are not very common in our small and mostly conservative rural community; I imagined the two of them had weathered a whole lot together. Taking care of each other, keeping themselves safe and intact, were a lot more important to them than being a union leader or sacrificing for some good cause. Cathy and Emily were assigned to stay with Darlene all day and never let her out of their sight. Each morning they called to make sure she was coming to the table and not back to work. Natchuras used all his powers of persuasion. She hung in there but not by much.

While the absence of so many cooks, custodians, mechanics, and others caused a wide range of inconveniences for students and management, between the managers and 250 scabs working overtime, some of our work was getting done. We were a long way from shutting down the university. Building trades bravely honored our picket lines, shutting down construction. But their skilled-craft union reps were clear. They would do that for two or three days and then return to work. Beyond direct student services, most of campus was still nonunion, including faculty, clericals, techs, and grad student assistants, and their work continued regardless of our absence.

Whether we were winning or losing this strike felt like a subjective, minute-by-minute assessment. Our leadership's range of emotions from triumphant to desperate mirrored the members' volatile feelings.

We called a mass meeting after the first week. There was a huge turnout. Everybody wanted to hear news. Strikers also came to get their first $65 strike allowance from the International. Proving that our International was behind us by handing out these checks was a big boost, especially since scabs and bosses had spread the rumor that nobody would ever get a cent from the strike fund. The biggest boost, though, was simply having everybody together to hear and feel our collective might.

It was a raucous, rowdy meeting. Strike generals told many stories of bravery. We brought George Wegman up on stage. George was a shy, quiet custodian at the prestigious Johnson Art Museum, with over thirty years of service. His supervisor had personally threatened him that he could lose his pension if he went out. But George not only voted for the union; he was also an artist who would draw funny superhero cartoons for our leaflets. He got up to the microphone and thanked everybody for staying out. "I'll stay on strike for as long as it takes, cuz that's where my friends are." All seven hundred of us sang happy birthday to George, who had turned sixty-five on the picket line. Every face in that crowd showed tears or a smile, or both.

Then Tom pulled out his ace in the hole. It wasn't a fiery speech. At this point I believe he was more worried about getting the genie back in the bottle than whipping up the militants. He told us that Governor Hugh Carey had contacted both Cornell and the UAW, telling them to get this strike settled. Cornell was now under more pressure to bargain. Tom said not to expect a miracle, that every first contract had its disappointments, but that if the strikers could hang in there a little longer, we would bring back a proposal to vote on. Later he let the bargaining team know that he had called the governor's chief of labor relations and "arranged" for the intervention.

However it happened, it worked. At bargaining on Monday Tom played dumb when Mathews mentioned that the governor was going to send his head labor relations honcho in to help the negotiations. Good. Tom had finessed some more uncertainty into management's equation. With the state providing hundreds of millions to Cornell every year, management worried about this meddling. They were not going to offend the governor. The pace of bargaining picked up. The strike was a huge embarrassment to Cornell. The strike was having some impact on both services and reputation.

In a few days of nonstop bargaining, we established an excellent grievance procedure with binding arbitration, and we ended the merit raise system. These were huge, emotionally powerful issues for us. It meant the end of abuse and favoritism in pay, and a process to challenge management misconduct that didn't end in Cecil Murphy's or Ron Mathews's lap. We also won a raise of fifty cents in year one and fifty-eight cents the following year. That averaged over 10 percent. These were the biggest raises any of us had ever received, and we all would get them.

On the downside, there was no progress on pensions, and no additional cost of living raises. Decent raises still left a majority of our members under the poverty line. We only made tiny progress on ending the open shop. Once people signed up, they could only withdraw and thereby stop paying dues during a once-a-year contract window period. Mathews was adamant about protecting the scabs' right to enjoy the fruits of the union and the strike without sharing the cost. The open shop gave the scabs a financial incentive to remain outside our union, and that meant less unity to win the changes we all deserved.

We decided to take it to the membership. We had been on strike for twelve days, and while we greatly appreciated the sixty-five-dollar check from the UAW strike fund, we were hanging on by the skin of our teeth. Natchuras gave a spellbinding speech about the bravery of the strikers. To his credit, he wanted people to feel proud of what had been accomplished, even though the bargaining team knew he believed that it was the UAW's influence with the governor that turned the tide.

Oze Richardson, a Black man in his sixties whose job involved carrying giant electric typewriters to and from offices, up and down stairs, said it best. It was a good contract, and he'd be voting yes. Then, tears streaming from his eyes, he spoke of brotherhood, the family of the union. "Like any family, we've become close during our crisis, we've grown together during this strike. You've treated this old Black man with more respect, more true equality than management at Cornell ever did for twenty years. This union is what we've really won. That contract is great, but it's a distant second to winning respect from management, and from the friendship, and dare I say it, love from each other."

The bargaining team all spoke. Cathy got choked up, and it was powerful. She talked about how this all started out so small, a few flyers posted, just the desire to be heard. "And now we have a legal document, a binding contract. It's not perfect. I wish we could have got more, but it's a damn good start."

The vote was 554 for and 98 against.

Oze was right. There wasn't one person on that campus whose life would ever be quite the same. Whole reputations grew or shriveled based on the bravery or cowardice exhibited during that strike.

At the huge victory party, we sang and drank and, as Emily called it, "speechified" all night. DeHart once again brought some of his homemade 150-proof frog puddle punch. This time he got the usually stoic Natchuras to drink an entire glassful. Later we found DeHart dragging our semiconscious regional director out of the bathroom, laughing, "I guess old Tommy boy could use the governor right now, eh?"

A young custodian named Becky who had become a feisty picket captain came to the party, and I gave her a big hug. She laughed, "You guys really did it, but boy I had my doubts about you." She added, laughing, "You know something? I just figured it out tonight. With the new raise I'll lose my public assistance for day care, so I just about break even."

I must have looked ready to cry. She put her arm around my shoulder and said, in her quiet voice, "You did a damn good job, and we got it all in writing. They can't take anything away, and they can't do to me or anyone else what they did years ago. I know that, and that feels real good. Maybe next time I'll get in there with you and see if those suckers will listen to me."

"You know what else?" she whispered. "I'm not so afraid anymore."

Lost in the night of celebration were the many questions we still faced. Could we approach and sign up scabs, the very people we now loathed? Could we implement our new rights effectively? Who would handle grievances and arbitrations?

Who would be our elected leaders? Would Pam and Cathy continue the internal sparring and division that emerged between them during bargaining? Was management going to accept the union now or try to somehow punish us for the strike? If we'd stayed out one more day, what else might we have won . . . or lost? With a contract, and dues coming in, we would really be on our own as a local union. Were we ready? Would that autonomy we wanted leave us better off? The UAW circus was about to leave town. Or was it? Would the thousands of techs and clericals be motivated to organize, or turned off by twelve days of striking?

It was clear to me that whatever the answers, we needed to start doing a better job of figuring things out ourselves. After all, if we could shut down a city, wage war against the most powerful local institution we knew of, feed, care for, inform, and mobilize seven hundred workers, we could run our own union in peacetime, couldn't we? And, perhaps most important, come back stronger the next time. As p.m. changed to a.m. and the party ebbed, there were more questions than answers, and they would be coming at us fast.

## Discussion Questions

- How well did the union handle the transition from organizing to bargaining?
- Did the union get a good contract?
- As an organizer or workplace leader, how do you deal with feelings of disappointment, impotence, rage, or fear that can come from a struggle with mixed results?
- Was the strike necessary?
- What strategies and tactics seem missing from this first contract fight?
- How did the UAW's approach help, and how was it ineffective or harmful?

# 4

# WE MEET THE ENEMY AND IT IS US

After our two-year-long struggle to organize, and our harrowing bargaining and strike, I was ready to move on. I was tired of cleaning a filthy freshman dorm every day. I wanted to be full time in this movement I had come to respect and love. I felt I had been blessed to be part of an amazing journey with a courageous group of sisters and brothers. I had learned a ton about organizing from Barbara Rahke. I had handled grievances, been at the bargaining table, and on strike. I had learned more about labor relations in this fight than in the best classrooms. Most of all, my respect for what workers could really become, individually and collectively, was sky high. I wanted to learn and grow and continue to be in exciting fights for the rest of my life's work.

While we had elected a negotiating team to hash out a contract, which ended up also including leading a strike, we had no officers or administration. No president, no vice president, no treasurer, no executive board, no trustees. But the UAW and our constitution insisted on all of this. All our titles, while earned through rank-and-file geographic campus zone elections, had basically been interim, until we had a contract, collected dues, and became our own local. This would be the first time we chose all our top positions local-wide, through elections involving the entire membership.

As the process of sorting out who might run for what leadership positions was slowly starting, I literally began to pack up my stuff. I even went to one interview for a job with FAST, (Food and Allied Service Trades), a strategic campaigns group based in Washington, DC, connected to the AFL-CIO and led by a tough and brilliant organizer named Bob Harbrant.

There were two obvious options for the top leadership posts at the local. The two credible top leaders had been part of the struggle since the days of ACE, before the word "union" was even spoken out loud. Cathy Valentino launched this fight; she really was our Norma Rae. Pam Mackesey had chaired our bargaining team, and while not as charismatic or seen as salt of the Ithaca working-class earth as Cathy, Pam had been steadier in her union activism and represented a younger, more socially progressive option.

It was clear to our leadership group that Cathy and Pam did not like each other. Cathy saw Pam as shaky and not capable of standing up forcefully to management. Pam saw Cathy as a bit of a prima donna, a good talker but less of an organizer. Tensions had emerged during the pressures of bargaining, and a good strike and decent settlement had not regenerated any love between our two most prominent leaders.

Unfortunately, after years of our all working together for the greater good, with minimal internal tensions, we were about to have a full-blown political war.

Personally, I thought either Pam or Cathy would be good leaders. Our strength all along was that we had forty to fifty solid leader activists. We would never have won our drive without a big organizing committee. We were used to making decisions collectively, and there was a ton of earned respect, love, and loyalty built up over years of home visits, clock meetings, OC meetings, bargaining, the strike, socializing, and struggle. What we could not afford was to work this hard to build our union, still be facing a very hostile and powerful employer, deal with an open-shop "window" while at least a quarter of our coworkers were still antiunion, and do all this with the 75 percent that went on strike split into two political camps.

The larger group of top leaders went back and forth with Cathy and Pam, trying to feel out a solution. How about one of you be president and the other VP, and we give the VP major responsibilities? How about if we create a powerful position, chair of grievances, which would oversee the whole zone rep and steward structure?

We tried every configuration we could come up with, but neither Pam nor Cathy would back down from being president if that meant her rival got the job. Part of the problem was that we had never had a local-wide election; and from what we could tell from among the top activist group, support was pretty evenly split. Democracy is great, having a choice is important, but a fifty-fifty divisive, personal fight, with few if any apparent differences in goals or vision, would squander our hard-won unity over egos and personality differences.

Finally, after every effort to get Pam or Cathy to take a half step back for the sake of unity failed, the larger leadership group decided to seek a compromise choice. Jack Evans, a bushy-bearded, redheaded materials handler from General

Stores had also been active since the beginning. Jack was calm and soft-spoken. He was smart and articulate, steady and sweet. We all liked and respected Jack. But Jack was way too mellow for the intensity of being local president. He turned us down, saying he was honored to be asked to run, but just didn't think he could give the job what it demanded. Jack served as a trustee and key leader for many years.

As one of the founding activists and an elected bargaining committee member, I had been involved in the efforts to get Pam or Cathy to compromise and then to ask Jack Evans when we failed. Still, I was surprised when a few of the top leaders came to me, starting with Emily Apgar. I guess you could say I was the fourth option. I was only twenty-three years old, and at times felt more like a son than a peer to many of the leaders. Truth is that my best qualification was probably the only one that mattered. I got along with both Cathy and Pam and had worked diligently and steadily with all our leaders for a long time. My biggest advocate was Emily Apgar.

Emily didn't want the job. She was the most credible, beloved, and effective organizer, but the stress of the fight had worn on her. No matter how much we reassured her, she felt insecure about her own abilities to debate upper management or interpret the legal nuances of the contract. Emily was a diehard Cathy supporter and felt Pam "couldn't get a damn sentence out of her mouth." She had a traditional sense of what mattered in a leader, and toughness and charisma were important to her. But she was also determined not to divide the local. Emily and I were close. I loved her and learned from her every week for years. I'd spent hundreds of hours with soup and a sandwich in her trailer, in our cars, in other workers' homes, and in hundreds of meetings with her. Her support gave me confidence and also helped forge a consensus among the broader group of leaders. I gave up my notions of moving to a big city, making some "real" money, and agreed to run for president as long as the leadership group was united in the decision.

We created a structure where Cathy was VP and Pam was second VP and chair of the grievance committee. Our slate got elected easily; there really wasn't any opposition or division once the Pam-Cathy conflict disappeared. Cathy and Pam continued to wrangle, and Cathy criticized Pam's handling of issues in a way that undermined support for Pam among some zone reps. But Pam had become good friends with Barbara Rahke, and as Pam struggled, Barbara offered her a job as an organizer on the ongoing clerical campaign.

I unpacked my bags and tried taking a deep breath, which turned into a hyperventilating freak-out. Whatever hubris and elitist confidence a kid gets from going to an Ivy League college had long ago faded, thanks in part to my growing politics that knew that attitude was privileged bullshit. More importantly, the experience of being one of a few dozen rank-and-file activists had humbled me. I had the diploma, but I wasn't the best strategist. I wasn't the best organizer. I wasn't the best bargainer. Emily worked harder than I did.

The day after the officer election, I realized that I was now expected to have the answers, to inspire confidence, to lead in a way no one had before in our less-hierarchical organizing days. I was in a fog thinking, "These are grownups, with kids, and trailer payments, and they now think I have the answers." I was a compromise candidate, and I was twenty-three.

I had become friends with the new UAW regional director, Tom Fricano, a wise and kind leader. Like me, he came from Buffalo. He respected my efforts and was influenced by Brendan Sexton's love and support for me. More importantly, he was genuinely moved by the courage of our members and the righteousness of our fight. I called up this powerful leader of three states and asked for advice about leading the local.

What he told me only deepened my fears. He said, "Al, you know I just took over as regional director a little while ago. I have a lot of big ideas, things I've been wanting to do. But every day it's like getting on a wild, bucking bronco. You start out thinking you're going to take it someplace important, toward a vision for the union. At the end of the day, you're not sure where you are, and you're happy just to have stayed on the damn beast."

Tom was honest, and it was a good message about the challenges of leading with purpose. If highly experienced Tom couldn't "steer the beast," what the hell was I going to do? I made the only decision I could come up with. I started to grow out my facial hair and hoped I'd at least *look* older.

The UAW did have a strong commitment to rank-and-file education, and an amazing Education Center at Black Lake in northern Michigan. The family-inclusive programs there were designed by my mentor Brendan Sexton. Tom Fricano appointed me their regional fellow, and I spent six weeks in the woods learning more about leadership and eating wild boar and frog legs on "game night."

We had so many decisions to make: about our steward structure, when we would hold meetings, whether to share offices with Barbara Rahke and the UAW organizers still working on the clerical and tech campaigns. We also had to decide what I, as our only full-time staffer, would get paid as local president. We made a decision few organizations make. We felt being on staff was a privilege in and of itself. My pay was set at exactly what I had been making as a worker. As a low-skill, low-seniority custodian, I was at the bottom of the poverty wage barrel. I was young, single, and agreed with the principle. That principle meant I continued to make $4.29 an hour. Anyway, it meant I was done cleaning freshman toilets!

With all these decisions upon us, my guiding light was that I knew we didn't want to lose the egalitarian activist energy that had defined us through the organizing and the strikes. We did our best to shift our activists into elected roles as stewards, zone reps, and exec board members.

With the next round of negotiations only a year away we quickly found we had much bigger and more complicated problems than we had imagined.

That first contract was a pretty good one. There was only one problem. It was almost our last.

## Hey, Close That Window!

The first thing that almost killed us was an open window. Neither car fumes nor a cold draft threatened us; it was our members who we feared would flee the union through that window. Call it collective suicide.

Let me explain.

Once a union is established, usually by majority vote, it is authorized, in fact obligated, to fairly represent and bargain for all the workers. It's called "the duty of fair representation." All the workers, however, are not obligated to pay their dues. It's called freeloading.

The same worker who voted "union, yes" two months ago may say "union, kiss my ass!" today. "I'll be damned if I'm going to hand over any of my hard-earned money for dues so you can vacation on the Riviera." Now, in our union, full-time officers get paid their regular working salary. So there have been no vacations on the Riviera for us. And dues equaled about two hours' wages per month. No matter. Some folks just didn't want to pay. That meant we had to spend a lot of energy just convincing people to join up. Why didn't they have a course on marketing in the ILR School when I was there?

Cornell fought hard to get us to accept just such an "open shop." They wanted to keep the union weak by building in a crude economic incentive for financially strapped workers to freeload, get all the benefits of the union without paying any dues. Once we won our election, the National Labor Relations Act certified the UAW as "the exclusive bargaining representative" for all service and maintenance workers. We resisted Cornell's effort to weaken us, managing to get a clause called "Maintenance of Membership." It was an open shop with this difference: once you signed on you were in it for the duration of the contract. Your membership was maintained, with the exception of an open window a couple of months prior to the expiration of the contract.

Despite Cornell's entreaties and our coworkers' empty pockets, over 75 percent chose voluntarily to pay dues. That seemed remarkable to us, considering we won our organizing vote with only 55 percent support. Even better, some areas of campus got strong enough to keep mini union shops. You simply didn't work as a material handler at General Stores, or on the Grounds crew, and not join. Folks worked closely together and shared a culture of mutual support that predated the union and was deepened by their new labor activism. In the weakest areas, the reverse was true. The union was getting more and more polarized by area, with the half-organized areas the major battleground.

Our members hated this open shop. It meant that almost all of us worked alongside "freeloaders." These people didn't join our organization even though they benefited from it. We had to bargain for them, represent them in grievances, even pay the cost of taking their grievances all the way to arbitration if need be. Not only had these folks voted no, and not taken the risk of going on strike for a better life; they didn't have to pay dues yet got all the same rights.

When a poor person believes in something strongly enough to risk his income by striking and then pays out $150 a year in dues, it's hard to work next to somebody who ends up with the same rights, same benefits, with none of the sacrifice. "Harry," Emily gently explained once to a scab she worked with, "how'd you like it if you had to work alongside some asshole who stole ten bucks out of your wallet every month?"

It kept us divided. It meant that every new hire was a target for some anti-union boss. It was almost like the merit system all over again. "Hey, Joe, I got you this job," the boss might say, "and I sure as hell hope you're not stupid enough to throw your money away paying dues to that goddamn union."

The freeloaders fell into two categories. There were the principled ones—the ones who just didn't want the union in the first place. They stayed clear of the union entirely. They were consistent. They never signed a card. They voted no in the union election. They scabbed during our strikes. They almost never came to the union, even when they were having problems at work. When they did come to us, it had to be serious, because it meant swallowing a lot of pride. When they did come to us for help, we were usually able to organize them, show them we were just workers like them, and that their notion that the bosses would treat them fine had been a mistake.

The other kind of nonunion workers were the cheap opportunists. They openly flaunted the power an open shop gave them. "I'm not against the union, but why should I pay if I don't have to? I'll wait and see what the union does for me and then I'll decide." Of course, their staying on the outside meant we would never get strong enough to accomplish half of what we wanted to. It drove us crazy. We tended to see this simple selfishness among some newer hires and younger workers, less steeped in the history of abuses and with less attachment to coworkers.

Management played up this advantage. They screened new hires in subtle ways, and sometimes in some not so subtle ways. Once we overheard management lecturing an innocent job candidate about the evils of the union and then asking him, "How do *you* feel about unions, Larry?" We filed charges, but under the Reagan Labor Board, Cornell slipped away with a slap on the wrist. It didn't matter, because they were rarely that blatant; they didn't have to ask a lot of questions when they hired whole scab families.

Now, spending time organizing and educating new hires is important no matter what kind of shop you have, but the union itself ought to decide how many scarce resources ought to be diverted from other pressing needs. We didn't have that choice. The deck was stacked against us.

The shop wasn't our only problem. There was that "open window." As our contract neared expiration, and a new one was negotiated, dues-paying members could escape. They could renounce their membership and stop paying dues—just when we most needed maximum solidarity. It gave Cornell another powerful wedge to wield against us. We wondered, as the window approached in 1985, would our members engage in a giant, debilitating free fall on the eve of contract expiration? "Once that window opens, watch all the little birdies fly away," our Syracuse-based International rep John Geer cynically warned.

Our wonder turned to fear. And our fear became panic, as we realized a "decert campaign" was also in the works. Decertification is how a union can get voted out. It requires 30 percent to sign cards asking the Labor Board for a vote to dump the union. Suddenly a new organization appeared. WAU—Workers Against UAW. Either the organizer had dyslexia, was quite clever, or maybe both.

We saw their literature. It was everywhere. It wasn't particularly well written or designed, though. And more importantly, their antiunion meetings were poorly attended. But the decert petition was making the rounds. If they got three hundred signatures—only 30 percent of the bargaining unit and fewer than voted against the union initially—we would face a new and dangerous vote, a vote that would be a no-win situation for us. Even in victory, our energy would be dissipated, our divisions heightened. Exactly why management everywhere loves decerts. We feared the worst.

We organized furiously. Each area had stewards, and we worked hard to get leadership people visiting every area we thought might present problems in terms of window jumpers or a decert. Worker leaders explained that to be antiunion right now was to weaken our chances of a good raise and a good contract. We talked about going backward to favoritism-based raises, promotions, and even firings. And we appealed to every openly pro-union member and striker to recognize the possibility of a purge of activists if the union was voted out.

I went with Emily to one clock meeting where two of the antiunion leaders showed up to take us on. A dozen custodians sat around a basement break area beneath the grand stage at Bailey Hall. The dumpster was right outside our door, and the room was buzzing with flies. The three custodians who had invited us to the meeting sat at their break room table, each with a different-color flyswatter. Written in black magic marker across each swatter was the custodian's name. "Bob," "Chuck," and "Amy" had asked us to come. Bob was antiunion, Amy was on the fence, and Chuck was pro-union.

Chuck started the conversation. "Well, Emily, we asked you guys to talk with us because the three of us all get along about everything—everything except the union, that is."

Amy butted in, "That's what he thinks."

People chuckled. Chuck continued, "As I said before I was so *rudely* interrupted, we don't see eye to eye on the union. Then we got to thinking, other folks must be in the same boat, so we invited the rest of the clock."

Emily began to clear her throat, but then one of the big-time antis jumped in, "We've heard plenty from Emily Apgar about the union. I'd like to hear who here can tell us what the union has done." There was total silence. A couple of the younger, long-haired male custodians looked at each other and shrugged their shoulders.

"Not much, I guess," one muttered sarcastically, loud enough for everybody to hear. The antis chuckled.

Then old Jim Wooden, a longtime custodian who struggled with poor health, began to talk. "I was your steward once, some of you who have worked here more than a few months may recall. Damn it, I know I did not do a very good job. I had problems with my damn heart, and I suppose I couldn't take the stress—at least the doctor and my wife convinced me I couldn't. Nobody picked it up after I dropped out. You want to know what the union's done? I'll tell you; it's given us a chance to get something decent for ourselves. The way I see it, if we don't take that opportunity, we got nobody to blame."

"Why do we even need the union? I can take care of myself," one of the long-hairs mouthed off.

Emily jumped in, and nobody was going to interrupt her this time. "Look, young man, you're healthy and beautiful with that ponytail of yours flapping around, and you think you can kick the world's ass and keep on smiling. But it don't work that way at Cornell. You can be minding your own business and find yourself out the door at this place. And if you kick the wrong ass, I guarantee you, you won't be smiling."

Amy swatted a fly with the force of a gavel hammering down. "I was raised antiunion, but I think we'd all be crazy to trust management, to just give up on the union. It's here; we'd better give it a chance."

The antis were shaking their heads, a few starting to leave. The pro-union employees had held their ground and swung at least one fence-sitter. Emily got in a final shove. "Listen, everybody, we're at the bargaining table right now. We're fighting every week for better wages. Let me ask you, do you think we're gonna get more if Cornell sees us fighting among ourselves? More or less if we're really united? Let's get off our butts and stop cutting off our nose to spite our face."

Chuck ended, "Well, that makes sense, Emily, more or less!" The remaining gang laughed. Emily smiled and flopped down hard on Chuck's lap. "I'll give you *more*, Chuckie boy."

Our efforts to define antiunion behavior as antithetical to a good contract and a good raise made the decert signers perceived as traitors in many areas of campus. Nonetheless they were plucking up signatures from the antiunion diehards. We held our breath and kept talking, break rooms, clock meetings, on the bus. The tactics were similar to our organizing drive, but this felt defensive. We had just won the union, and already we were fighting among ourselves just to keep it. We also had a contract and a strike record to defend, not just hopes and dreams. But most of those who went on strike felt real ownership of the contract, ongoing pride in having stood up. Finally, it became clear that the antiunion decert committee was falling apart; they couldn't get anywhere near the three hundred signatures they needed. They got about one hundred and then imploded.

Lesson number one: the type of folks drawn to an antiunion committee tend to have little faith in their fellow man and are not likely to work well in groups.

But there was still the window.

A lot of folks didn't like paying dues and weren't so sure they'd gotten their money's worth. The union hadn't made poor people middle-class and hadn't won many new benefits. They weren't ready to dump the union either, though. They liked knowing they had a written contract, a grievance procedure, and trained coworker stewards to assist them if a problem arose. They just wanted somebody else to pay for it. We had great momentum from crushing the decert. But the window was scarier because it appealed to people's private selfishness.

If this wasn't bad enough, we also had UAW area director John Geer breathing doom and gloom down our necks. This wasn't just a prediction on his part; it felt more and more like it was becoming a struggle between his way of looking at people and our way, our local union's way. A campaign like this requires a sense of urgency but also buoyancy, spirit, a sense that this fight to organize and reorganize our members was part and parcel of building for our best contract ever. Geer's fatalism suggested this was just some losing, defensive, uphill war against human nature's selfishness. John was demoralizing.

John Geer was the UAW area director for all of central New York. It was his responsibility to oversee the locals in his geographic jurisdiction including

Syracuse, Elmira, Massena, Plattsburgh, and Cortland. He came out of the Syracuse Chrysler plant, after serving one term as local president. He was never part of the original historic struggles to build the UAW that had shaped early leaders into creative fighters.

From what I could tell, his main attribute was his joke-telling ability. As much as I grew to detest him, I had to admit he knew a thousand jokes, and told them all better than I could tell my best one. He imitated any ethnic accent but specialized in stutterers and "hair lip" accents. Sometimes it wasn't funny at all.

Geer was the worst kind of business unionist, more likely to trust management than the rank and file. He saw every strike as automatic suicide. His approach with us was to schmooze with the bosses and try to cut a deal. He would then convince workers it was the "best we could ever do." Geer never for an instant led with ways workers could organize creatively in the workplace to fight concessions.

Like most business unionists, Geer religiously avoided taking any responsibility for labor's sorry state. For him, and others like him, the two main reasons labor is in trouble are the "apathetic and uneducated" rank and file, and politicians selling workers out. In the 1980s, Geer was at his best as a militant critic of Reagan and Bush. Rather than talk about what we could do to organize more workers, or build alliances with other progressive groups, Geer just acted like we were stuck until we voted in a Democrat.

Worse for us, Geer had opposed the UAW's decision to help us organize Cornell. "Why do we want to mess around with universities?" he said. He couldn't cope with Barbara Rahke, a strong, brilliant, undeferential organizer who was a woman. Worse, he couldn't stomach that she was calling the shots on his home turf. Barbara routinely rubbed salt in his wounded ego by constantly "forgetting" UAW protocol and ignoring John.

In addition to their different union philosophies, their styles clashed as well. Barbara was a fit thirty-two years old, and the whole time she lived in Ithaca she continued to dress like she was in Boston. Geer, in his fifties, appeared to be carrying twins, and had enough grease in his pompadour to keep a Mack truck lubed. Geer's usual attire consisted of green suits he couldn't have buttoned if his life depended on it.

John met with us a few months before the window opened and argued strongly that we would lose the unit entirely unless we cut a deal with Cornell. Somehow, despite five years of our getting kicked in the teeth by Big Red, after our strike, and after UAW leaders more powerful than he had tried, Geer thought deals could be simply "cut."

Geer preferred we not even ask my fellow local leaders, but I went to the exec board, and they authorized the two of us to meet with top management to "feel out" the possibility of closing the window before the contract talks began. We met in some awful little restaurant in Cortland, halfway between Ithaca and Geer's HQ in Syracuse. Cornell sent two bigwigs. Geer led us in male bonding small talk for two-thirds of the lunch and eventually got down to business. He definitely had the gift of gab. Sports, vacations, all the little things that might make us four white men feel like we had something in common.

But Geer was too crude for these Ivy League administrators; they did not vacation in Atlantic City or joke with working-class strangers about their slothful wives. When the conversation drifted into national politics, with management praising Reagan's stewardship, Geer changed the subject by telling a joke about geriatric sex. John's idea of a tactful segue.

The bottom line was that Cornell was well aware the decert was stumbling along, dividing our attention, and there was no way in hell they were going to close that union-weakening window for us. The suited sharks smelled our blood, and they were very happy to let the bleeding continue. Management was not going to bandage up our union for us. All the schmoozing and all the bluffing were no substitute for a clear-eyed analysis of the power dynamics. Geer and I spoke in the parking lot after. He had lost face, but instead of channeling that into helping us fight, he fatalistically said, "Oh well, you guys are really screwed."

Management's thirst for our blood, and its high hopes of weakening us through the window, also became clear at the bargaining table. For sixty days we got nowhere negotiating a new contract. Management wasn't about to remind people that the union could accomplish anything. On the other hand, their stonewalling did remind workers of how unreasonable and callous they could be.

About a week before the window opened, every member of the bargaining unit received a letter from the failed decert antiunion committee encouraging them to withdraw membership and explaining how to do it. We wondered how they got a complete set of mailing labels and assumed Day Hall had spit out a set for them. Illegal, but how could we prove it?

Then before you could say "Don't jump," Cornell itself put out instructions on withdrawing, claiming correctly this was a contractual right and incorrectly that they had been deluged with requests for information.

That first day we got about eight certified letters asking to withdraw. We had a team of rank-and-file organizers primed to talk to every worker who wanted to withdraw, as well as going into their immediate work areas to do damage control and limit the spread of the disease. By the end of the first week, we had only received eighteen withdrawals. The membership was holding solid. In addition, we had signed up nine new members during that week. We whipped out a bulletin announcing that the union was "turning lemon into lemonade." When it was all said and done, only forty-three members out of 670 withdrew, and we signed up forty-five during the same time period.

Once we realized we were going to survive the thirty days, it became a campaign hell-bent on signing up more new members than the number of old ones lost. We even ran a newsletter interviewing a member who withdrew and then decided it was more important to help win a fair contract and then rejoined.

Our victory felt good. We had concretely proved to the antis, to management, and most of all to ourselves that our members still wanted the union. We were a little shell-shocked from the stress of fighting just to keep our union, but all of the organizing work had left us stronger than we were before the failed decert and window.

I knew, however, that a different kind of crisis was brewing. Our growing strength and confidence exacerbated our tensions with Geer. Weak unions are easily manipulated and controlled by conservative business unionists. But the more creative, animated, and involved our membership was and the more assertive our leadership, the stronger we became, and that threatened Geer's whole way of "doing business." He was getting annoyed.

Events the following week brought the conflict more out into the open. We had scheduled another bargaining session for Wednesday, the first in a month. Bargaining had been going nowhere, a sideshow while both sides fought over the allegiance of the rank and file, over power. To keep the momentum of the window victory going, and in the spirit of finding new forms of leverage, we decided to try something new. We invited a couple of professors and three students to sit behind us at the table. We knew management was being unreasonable and thought that other segments of the Cornell "community" would agree. They just needed to be there in person.

It worked. Management clearly was rattled. There they were defending the most atrocious takeaways in front of an audience that included key stakeholders from the Cornell community. I had visions of twenty thousand faculty and students honoring picket lines. Management must have had the same vision. Mathews grabbed me and Geer and told us to cut the shenanigans.

I did have to admit that one of the student reps was a bit too funky for our team. Lorisa was an anthropology major with hair down to her knees and an intimidating tattoo of an angry unicorn on her shoulder. During a union caucus, halfway through the bargaining meeting, she whipped out her guitar and sang "they paved paradise and put up a parking lot." We gently discouraged her offer to play mood music during bargaining.

Not surprisingly, John Geer saw things the same way management did. He collared me after the meeting.

"Do you think management is really going to buy into this grandstanding? Are you going to start charging admission? This is not a show. This is serious bargaining, not a three-ring circus."

"John, to make progress at the table, we have to make progress *outside* this room. We need to mobilize our members and get the support of the community. We need to expose Cornell's behavior."

"Bullshit. We need to sit down and negotiate a damn contract. And you better give up your fantasies about what you might get. They just don't have a lot to give. The longer we prolong this the harder it will be."

"They're the ones prolonging this. We got a thousand people out there who want a decent contract, and they're willing to work hard, maybe even strike, to get it."

"*Strike?*" He spat the word out. "You'll get killed. Don't you read the papers? Maybe you should get that cute tattoo to read them for you. Remember PATCO? This union won't survive a strike. Al, you're educated. You're not even twenty-five—you don't need this. Do you think these farmers would go on a long strike? They can't even spell the word! This is too personal for you."

"That's bullshit, John." But he had hit a sore spot. Only a few dozen of our members had a college degree, let alone one from an Ivy League school. Yet during my four years of helping organize this union, cleaning up shit as a forty-hour-a-week custodian, nobody ever cited my formal education as a dividing line. I recalled fellow custodian Jeff Clark asking me during a break, "Hey, don't you have a degree from this place or something?"

"Yeah, why?" I replied. "Does that seem strange?"

"Nope. Everybody around here has some messed-up story," he concluded.

Geer ignored my retort. He wanted control, to be in charge. "I'm not going to let you do this. To strike you need authorization from the International. Fuck your voting. Your precious members can vote to strike till hell freezes over. That doesn't mean I'll let it happen."

I suddenly realized this struggle was not only over a contract, but over the soul of our union. We were not only fighting management, but Geer too. Could we let him determine our interests and how to achieve them? Could we let him undermine and disarm our local and its autonomy? Could we let him stop us from involving, mobilizing, and energizing our membership for the best contract we could get? We were fighting business unionism. And we could lose.

## Cow Shit by Any Other Name

It was our instincts against Geer's experience. But the proof of the pudding is in the tasting. So far, we hadn't had a nibble; management hadn't backed down once. The next week at bargaining, however, an incident occurred that confirmed more creative agitation might put us on the right track.

Most of the members of management's bargaining team were nondescript. Mathews, the chief negotiator, never permitted any of them to speak at the table, so we couldn't take any measure from the negotiations themselves. Nor did we know them from work. Who were these people? We'd never seen any of them in our buildings, eating on campus, driving through campus, parking. Who were they, where did they work, eat, live, park?

During the long hours of bargaining, I developed various theories. Maybe they were rented! Maybe this was one of those fast-emerging "management services" that you could subcontract out for. All they had to do was wear suits, ties, dresses, stockings, and be able to sit expressionless for hours at a time. These folks probably were being paid five dollars an hour, plus a clothing allowance, to sit there. I couldn't stand what they represented, but I confess to fleeting bouts of pity. They couldn't speak, they couldn't nod or smile or frown.

There was one exception to the cardboard stick figures facing us week in and week out. Rita Harris. She was the personnel director at the Vet School. This seemed strange to us. Other much larger Cornell colleges didn't have their own personnel director. Why the Vet School? Did she boss around the sick dogs and cats? "Give Skippy a second written warning for peeing on the floor again," I could hear Rita barking out the discipline.

Rita never spoke, but her dress and carriage were worth a thousand snide remarks. While I honestly believed that the others on management's team were dying to jump into the fray, to debate the issues with us, to defend their management prerogatives from our infringements, Rita radiated such repulsion for the very idea of bargaining with such louts that I believe she strongly preferred contemptuous silence.

Rita was perhaps fifty years old. She seemed conflicted between severe, steely gray intimidating business suits and, alternatively, fuzzy yellow and pink sweaters. Unlike her clothes, her facial expression and posture didn't change much. If Wikipedia needed a graphic for "turning one's nose up," all they had to do was snap a photo of Rita Harris. She maintained her head at a forty-five degree upward tilt at all times. This not only jutted her nose high in the air but enabled her to be perpetually looking down past her nose to examine us. Of course, she never actually made eye contact. Typically, she sat at the end of the table and stared unblinking off to the side, away from the entire bargaining table, as if to say, "Oh, why must I be here among these barbarians one more minute? Why can't we just fire them all and start over with some employees that understand their place."

Doug DeHart was a slob. He was a brilliant mind trapped inside a mess of a body and a mess of a life. He tended to cows at Cornell's experimental dairy. He was a constant wiseass, always in trouble at work for mouthing off. He was a runner-up in the election for bargaining team members, but the guy that won ended up getting promoted to management, in a nice coincidence.

Brilliant? Toward the end of the negotiations, when we were holed up in our regional director Tom Natchuras's hotel room night after night, I recall Doug challenging our erudite, well-dressed labor leader to a game of chess. Doug sat there, with his belly half on the chessboard and an unlit cigar stub drooling out of his mouth, whipping the cuff links off one of the brightest labor leaders in the state.

Doug used to sit at the end of the table by Rita. They made for a lovely couple. Doug often smelled bad from working in cow shit all day. This may have affected Ms. Harris's attitude. Maybe she wasn't turning her nose up at us at all; maybe she was just gasping for oxygen. Management was harassing Doug because he was a night-shift worker. While we were all permitted unpaid time off from work to attend bargaining, for which the union compensated us, Mathews refused to release Doug from his night work, reasoning that the bargaining wasn't going on at night, so why let him off.

This meant that Doug could be in bargaining from nine to five and then be expected to work from eleven that evening to seven the next morning. Doug was basically working sixteen-hour days. We complained over and over but got nowhere until Doug took things into his own hands.

It seems that there is a scent much stronger than cow manure, and that is fermenting corn silage. Doug came straight from work one morning after intentionally rolling in this nauseating brew, soaking it into his overalls. Our whole team was gagging the second he came into our caucus room. When he sat down four feet from Rita, her eyes just bugged out, and I thought she would flip backward in her chair. To ice the cake, Doug was chewing a giant wad of tobacco, which he proceeded to dribble out of his mouth into a Styrofoam coffee cup in front of him, not two feet from Rita's Maybelline mask of horror.

Mathews called a caucus, and the nebbishy mediator assigned by the Federal Mediation and Conciliation Service to help the negotiations came into our room to air management's complaint against Doug. We told him there was no way this could be avoided if Doug was being refused time off for bargaining. We held our ground, and lo and behold, management agreed to give Doug the time off, on the condition that he leave immediately and get cleaned up. Our hearts said, "Play hardball," but our snouts said, "See ya later, DeHart."

It was one of those small examples of how we were beginning to learn that the way to beat these bosses was to rewrite the rules. We sure weren't getting too far playing by Hoyle. And Geer was getting more and more pissed off.

## Geer-illa Warfare

I found out Geer was willing to go beyond an occasional speech to our bargaining team, after my conversation with Walt Smithers. Walt was our new local union vice president. He was tall and skinny, with a pimply face that made him look younger. His voice—deep, powerful, mature—was almost a shock, a sharp contrast to his features.

I noticed him during the first strike. We needed a skeleton crew to maintain the picket lines—thus preventing deliveries while we held our mass meeting at the Strand Theater. Nobody wanted to miss the excitement of the meeting. But Walt stood up and not only volunteered to stay behind, but he also offered to take responsibility for convincing twenty others to stay with him.

When the strike was over, he and I became friends. I learned he was Jessie Smithers's son. Tall, with a bony, jutting jaw, she had been a custodian for over twenty years and a head custodian for five more. She had voted yes and gone on strike even though the bosses put a lot of pressure on the head custodians to be loyal. They were dangled promotions into bossdom, but Jessie had backbone. Walt came from good stock.

Walt moved up our short union ladder. He handled grievances as well as any of us. He had that rare ability to be strong and confident with management staring you down without descending into pettiness or name calling. And he had great respect for the International, Natchuras in particular.

Walt unfortunately transferred some of that respect to Geer. He liked John's jokes and was always egging him on to tell one more. Geer milked Walt's admiration for all it was worth. He'd take him out for a drink after a meeting, and he'd sit next to him at meals. I imagined that Geer did not hesitate to criticize my leadership or to suggest that perhaps Walt ought to be president. I knew that we couldn't afford to have Walt more loyal to Geer than to our local union. Or to me.

During our debates at the table, Walt rarely weighed in. When we'd challenge Geer's recommendations to cave in on an issue, you could see Walt's uncertainty. I realized Geer wasn't going to let a few punks like me push him away without a fight. When Geer shook his head, tsk-tsking us, he always made eye contact with Walt. I kept close to Walt during the rest of the contract struggle. Only once did I directly confront him about Geer.

It happened at Ides Lanes, when Walt and I went bowling with his oldest boy. Walt had three sons who lived with their mom, and Walt usually had one or two of them on the weekends. He was a great dad but had never gotten over his wife's running out on him. It was especially tough for Walt because she worked at the Pyramid Mall where he fixed vending machines part time. The "other man" worked selling shoes at the same mall. Walt had the whole situation rubbed in his face every Thursday and Saturday on that second job.

While we were bowling, I asked Walt what he thought of Geer. Walt said he thought he was the funniest person he'd ever met.

"But what about the disagreements we've all had with him? What do you think of those?" I pursued it.

"Well, Al, I don't know. He's no dummy, but neither are you. I do think he wants what's best for us, and he's got a hell of a lot more experience than any of us."

"Yeah, but not experience at a place like this. He was against the UAW helping us organize in the first place. Remember, he was sure we could get Cornell to cozy up with us and agree to eliminate the window," I added.

"Well, none of us had much faith in that, but it still was worth a try. You gave it a try too, Al."

"I guess if there's one thing I learned from the first contract and strike it was that the International is great, but we've got to rely on ourselves and our own judgment a lot more. We are this union, Walt."

"I know, I know. But I think you ought to show John some respect though. He's been through a lot of shit, and you just ignore him. You know you're cutting your own throat, Al."

"How am I cutting my own throat?"

Walt answered, "You got a future to think about. You'll have kids someday. You'll want to drive a new car, own a home. You can't get there from here, you know; not the way you're acting. The International's got opportunities. Don't forget that. You fuck with Geer, and he may just fuck with you."

I was a little dumbfounded by Walt's last comments. Was he really worried about my future? We were friends and had been through a lot together. Was he figuring that with me moving on up, he could be president, and then *he* could move up? I just pushed aside the whole can of worms.

"Look, Walt, I just want a contract with decent money for our people and with no more windows and no more open shop. You and I both know that the members will never swallow less without a fight. Sometimes it's healthier to fight the good fight even when you don't win everything than it is to eat shit and walk away with our tails between our legs. I think we got Cornell a little scared with the professors and students supporting us."

"Yeah, that's great, but it'll be our asses on that picket line while they go on with their cushy lives. We'll see," Walt concluded. "Hey, seeing as those pins aren't falling down from all our hot air, maybe I ought to throw a ball at 'em." He grabbed his black ball with his name on it, stuck his fingers in, and rolled it at an impossible seven-ten split.

"Pick that up and I'll kiss Geer's fat ass," I shouted. He missed the split but hit a chord in my psyche. Geer's way had support. We really were in a battle for the soul of this union.

I soon found out that Geer had some more aces to play.

## Shutting Up John

As we continued bargaining through the summer of '85, working without a contract, John Geer concocted a new obstacle for us.

Our contract with Cornell had a dues checkoff provision, meaning that members could authorize Cornell to just deduct the dues from each paycheck, sending it to the union. This made life easier for us and was pretty standard stuff.

But now we had no contract. The old one had expired, and we were still bargaining for a new one. Geer's revenge was to tell us that we would have to pay dues in order to be eligible for strike fund benefits. To pay dues without the checkoff meant we would have to collect it ourselves! Each week . . . from seven hundred far-flung employees! That night I dreamed that federal withholding had been outlawed, and I was the IRS commissioner faced with the task of collecting taxes monthly from each taxpayer.

About half the union dues members pay goes to the International, not the local, for various services. One of the services we get, a key one, is access to the strike fund. If we strike, we still get a portion of our pay, thanks to the strike fund. Without it, we couldn't even consider a strike.

I argued strenuously that there was no reason to deny us strike fund eligibility over monies we couldn't collect now but clearly could reimburse a few weeks later! We had even settled on continued contract language regarding dues checkoff with Cornell, so there was no question that we could make up the lost money. But Geer wouldn't budge. Nor did I get anywhere trying to go over his head.

It was clear to me that this was Geer's way of forcing us to eat shit and settle a mediocre contract with Cornell. It was his way of getting back at us for being creative insubordinates and for proving him wrong about the birdies flying out the window. Now, without the strike threat, we had no leverage with Cornell. It was a sellout.

I met with our executive board and explained the situation. After the decert, after the window, I was exhausted and assumed everyone else was too. I honestly did not believe that we could jump this hurdle. But the leadership decided we could. We would collect dues by hand, the old-fashioned way. We agreed we would not tell the membership that the reason we were doing this was Geer's ultimatum to strip our strike benefits if we didn't pay dues. They would have felt horribly betrayed by the UAW. We loved the UAW enough to cover for Geer.

It was a slippery step. We had gone from representing our brothers and sisters to deciding we knew what was best for them. Geer had boxed us in. It was as if we had to act like him by withholding info from our members, to fend off his poisonous defeatism. While some of us wrung our hands about this choice, Emily blurted out, "This being a leader isn't so much fun after all. But listen, we're just a bunch of peons elected to make hoity-toity choices. Any other ten members in our shoes would do the same thing." We couldn't put doubt about the UAW into the workers' minds.

The recordkeeping was a nightmare. So was the organizing and outreach effort. Once again, however, our members rose to the occasion. More than 85 percent paid dues "by hand" over the summer, after the contract expired. Geer was flabbergasted. For once we had something in common.

Poor John Geer's ego. He was supposed to be in charge, but the fundamentally democratic nature of the UAW and the relatively high degree of local autonomy were two major reasons we chose the UAW. We wanted our fate to be in our own hands. It felt great. No Detroit Dave gimmickry, no sidebars without clearance from the rank-and-file team and one of us present. But we were pissing off management and pissing off our link to the International. Once again, it seemed like our idealism was colliding with some powerful forces.

By now we were all exhausted, but triumphant, and pretty pissed at Geer. We felt like we had spent the last four months fighting the dregs, our most antiunion coworkers and our UAW rep, more than we had fought our employer. The key issue was getting rid of the old shop: no more windows, no more card-pullers or window jumpers. We wanted union security. Cornell would not give it, though. The wage offer was still too low as well. It looked like a strike was inevitable. But what game was Geer playing now?

The bargaining team, unanimous but shaky, scheduled the strike for Friday. We had hashed it over two or three times. Geer tried hard to pour cold water over our militancy, pointing out other area unions that had been crushed on strikes. He even brought in newspaper articles about defeated strikes where everyone lost their jobs. But Cornell had never hired permanent replacements during any previous strike, only temps.

We had taken a strike authorization vote earlier and been given overwhelming authority to do this. Thursday night we called a mass meeting. This would be critical. Waiting at the auditorium for five to six hundred members to arrive, I overheard Geer verbally working over Walt, trying to sow disunity.

"Listen, Walter, it's one thing to play Barnum and Bailey at the bargaining table, that's what's got you into this mess. But it's another thing completely to take these people out on the street. Look at them—they can't afford a strike. It's easy to whip 'em up, to get 'em mad, to take 'em *out*, but how long will they be out for? How long will they *stay* out for? How fuckin' easy will it be to get 'em back? Do you really think Cornell is going to cave in in a few days or even a few weeks? Let's get real here. Your responsibility is to those people, not to fuckin' Al Davidoff."

Walt stood there listening, sometimes nodding, looking worried and conflicted.

I came fully around the corner. "Gee, did I hear my name? Hey, Walt, could you lend a hand passing out the contract summary sheets up front? Thanks." With Walt out of earshot, I lit into Geer. "I'm sick and tired of you trying to undermine us. This union has an elected leadership, and your job is to support it. You've had your say; now you better get on board with our recommendation to strike or just leave."

"You guys don't know what in hell you're doing. A strike is suicide. I've got thirty years in this business. What the hell do you have?" he sneered. He was beet red and angry.

"What I have out there are one thousand people and their families. Hardworking people. Good people. People who are being fucked over on a daily basis and on a grand scale. We're gonna win this strike and build this union. *Our* union. *We* are the union, and I'm the elected president. And I'm running this meeting. You might as well head back to Syracuse now."

The meeting went very well. Our members had been through a lot and were in no mood to settle for the crap Cornell was offering. Every member of the team spoke in favor of the strike, including Walt.

Geer stayed, but I never let him get within ten feet of the microphone.

## A Day Hall Invasion

We decided to run this strike differently from our first one. Maximum publicity, maximum rank-and-file morale, and maximum intensity right from the beginning. We knew our members would not stay out for very long, so we promoted militancy and creativity. We urged members to make it a tough, inventive strike from the very first minute.

Cornell seized on this as if the union leadership was calling for violence. The press went along, spitting it out as the university's press office wanted it.

Our weekend strike began with "Fighting Friday." I had reached out around Geer to UAW friends with a new strategy. Let's shock Cornell by going beyond Ithaca, a town where people proudly attached bumper stickers saying, "Ithaca: Centrally Isolated." There are elite "Cornell Clubs" in many major cities, fancy places where alums and faculty meet and socialize. Why don't we leaflet them the day we go out? In Boston, New York City, DC, and Albany we were able to line up students and UAW activists from other universities to hand out flyers exposing the poverty fight at Cornell. We got press coverage of the strike in the *New York Times*!

Closer to home we hoped that students were our ace in the hole. Radical students had grown in strength and now represented a small army, ready, willing, and able to fight beside or even in front of us when called upon. Diarmuid, a grad student from Northern Ireland with IRA sympathies and, even better, some IRA training, was one of the best. Diarmuid sometimes forgot that he was in Ithaca, New York, and not Belfast. Like when he had some of us almost convinced that ringing the campus with roadblocks of burning tires was a winning strategy.

At least it was a better idea than Byung-hoon's. That veteran of labor-management strife back home in South Korea (he was a young union leader there before coming to Cornell's grad school) wanted the leadership to go on a hunger strike till our demands were met. Most of us didn't even have to think about that one. Especially our 350-pound zone rep Harry Evans. Cradling his massive gut, he gave one of his signature guffaws (sort of like a high-pitched wheeze). "Hunger strike?" he laughed at Byung-hoon. "Now I know why you guys are so thin!"

The students helped us keep tabs on any important campus events. We brought dozens of service workers and radical students and infiltrated President Rhodes's speech to the arriving freshmen and their parents. We entered the massive Willard Straight Hall—"the Straight"—and immediately campus cops set upon us. Unwilling to shackle and arrest us in front of a thousand wide-eyed parents and freshmen, the cops just eyeballed us and kept close. They left us free to distribute our literature and to solicit donations in our plastic buckets. Here at a speech welcoming freshmen and proclaiming the greatness of Cornell were Cornell employees begging for strike donations. Our finale was unrolling a two-hundred-foot banner with the first and last name of every employee making wages below the poverty line. Led by our most artistic members, we'd been up all night crafting this shameful statement, toxic marker fumes filling the office and our nostrils.

The banner was the last straw. With the banner turning everyone's head around to the back of the hall, Rhodes digressed in mid-speech. "Some of you may have noticed," he said, "we have some special visitors with us." Yeah, special as in a cancerous wart.

"These are our employees, and we value them greatly." There was a collective boff from our side. "They are on strike because they believe they are underpaid, and they are probably right about that. We are working on resolving these issues, and bargaining is continuing."

We stopped eye rolling long enough to realize we had won this round. Rhodes's off-the-cuff remarks made it into the local newspaper. We got a tape recording of what Rhodes said, acknowledging we were underpaid, from a friendly local radio station reporter.

I brought it to bargaining the next morning. I said, "Who is speaking for Cornell, you or President Rhodes?" Management spokesperson Pete Tufford got royally ticked off and lectured us about our disruptive and disrespectful "stunt."

I said, "We unfurled a banner with two hundred names of your staff who make less than poverty wages. What is disrespectful is paying your community too little to live on, and we appreciated that President Rhodes agreed we are underpaid."

"He never said that," Tufford deadpanned.

I leaned under the bargaining table and pulled up the tape recorder. "Should we play the tape of what President Rhodes actually said?" I asked.

Tufford grimaced. "No, let's move on and see if we can actually make some progress today, Al."

"OK with me," I said—but progress was not going to happen without more pressure.

On campus, instead of spreading ourselves thin across forty picket sites twenty-four hours a day, we assembled en masse in a few key strategic areas, like the major dining halls. The biggest crowd of workers, strike leaders, bargaining team leaders, students, and faculty all spoke to the wildly enthusiastic crowd in front of the Straight. We then led a march across the quad to the main administration building, Day Hall, the true seat of power. The cops started to freak out. They were union brothers and sisters who often had done the absolute minimum to police our activities. I told their man in charge that we planned on briefly marching through the building and not taking any hostages or doing anything illegal. I assigned one executive board member to watch Diarmuid, just to make sure we didn't end up with Rhodes's severed head bobbing up and down on a stick.

We found ourselves entering an inner courtyard I didn't realize existed within Day Hall. With four stone walls encasing us, the chants grew deafening. We chanted so loudly that all work in that building ground to a halt. Some administrators fled; a few clericals clapped and smiled. We felt great.

"What do we want?"

"*A contract!*"

"When do we want it?"

"*Now!*"

"Hey, hey, what do you say? UAW is here to stay!"

Given the failed decert and window, this last chant was belted with gusto. True to our word, we returned to the Straight to finish our rally.

## Hitting 'Em Where It Hurts

We also lavished attention on Cornell's rich alumni during the campaign leading up to the strike.

Image is everything to Cornell, because the university's major constituent is not the students, it's not the staff, it's not even the esteemed faculty. Nobody has as much clout as rich alumni. These folks are wined and dined and then whined at for a "major gift." These corporate moguls are presented with an idyllic image of harmony and purity at the university. This image industry, known as development at most colleges, creates a facade that is quite different from the undoubtedly more mixed real-life experience these alums had as students. But reality is readily forgotten in the Image Factory.

Now the rich are popular folk. They are in demand. So, if Cornell alum Richie Rich is also being wooed by Stanford, the Cancer Foundation, and the local opera house, the last thing Cornell Development wants is for Richie to get any static, any negative vibes whatsoever about Big Red.

Cornell's fund-raising goal was $1.25 billion over several years. To raise that much, you really have to hit up the biggies. Big as in individual contributions of twenty-five mil. That got an entire college renamed after Samuel Johnson, the guy with the "real wax shine."

Cornell Development spares no expense in landing the really big fish. In order to yank another five mil out of one group of artsy alums they gave them a tour of the half-completed new Performing Arts Center. They made all the construction workers stop building the center and clean the entire construction site from top to bottom for this tour. Then they ordered the workers to leave the premises for two hours so the grand tour wouldn't be disturbed by their flannel shirts, hard hats, and missing-digit waves. They got the five mil.

Another time, the university took the largest gymnasium on campus, Barton Hall, spent $10,000 on black tarpaulins and another $10,000 on dirt and re-created the renowned Arnot forest, Cornell-owned but fifteen miles from campus. A neat $100,000 for the trees. Gives new meaning to "a lot of green." The trustees, the cream of the rich and powerful, were then treated to a gourmet meal at their tables in the "forest." It makes you wonder what people who have their fantasies handed to them on a silver platter have left to fantasize about.

Our local union decided to go after these alums, too, especially the trustees. During negotiations they met on campus once, and we greeted them in a variety of eye-catching ways. First, we had our members who cleaned their hotel rooms all wear UAW pins. They made sure that each trustee had a leaflet describing the miserably low wages the Cinderellas of the Cornell "family" lived on.

We then got hold of the menu that our talented chefs were preparing for the big trustee banquet. Duck from France, stuffed with lobster from Maine, in a medley of fresh artichoke hearts flown in from California . . . and that was just one of the appetizers.

We hit on the idea of reprinting the menu on the back of a blown-up food stamp that one of the workers preparing the meal used to feed her family. We leafleted the banquet with our menus. The press just happened to show up too.

If you've never leafleted rich people, it's a memorable experience. Most were what we called the cowardly rich. Looking down, they rushed through our line trying to behave as nonconfrontationally as possible. No eye contact, hands in pockets, never a glance back over their shoulders until they were a safe distance from our line of leafleters.

Other trustees either had more guts or were more ideological. They would want to crush us intellectually. "Look, it's a free market," they'd stop and say. "I'm sure the university is paying you what the market rate is. If they weren't, you could just go elsewhere." Yeah, elsewhere, as in McDonald's.

The smallest group of trustees were the handful with liberal leanings. They seemed sincerely bothered by our plight. These people actually took the leaflets *and* spoke with us.

One fashionably formal but friendly elder stateswoman of the silver spoon set once gushed to a young, single mom custodian, "The campus is so beautiful! You get to work here every day. Money isn't everything." I was standing near our activist member, close enough to hear her yell back, "Money isn't everything? Yeah, well, I'd like a chance to find out."

How many trustees, I wondered, realized that every meal they ate for their lovely four student years here was prepared by us, that every toilet they threw up in after too much expensive imported beer was wiped clean by us, and that everything they broke we fixed so that the next chicks entering this corporate hatchery would find their world shiny and new.

We hadn't yet truly figured out how best to activate the alums as a lever to change Cornell's behavior, but we were experimenting, starting to develop our own theories of power and some pretty fun ways of expressing ourselves.

## Nailing the Window Shut

Back at the table we now had many members in the audience, as well as our coalition of supporters. The university continued to move toward us on the remaining issues. Geer stood on the sidelines shaking his head. Once again, we didn't know how far to push. Did we have the university where we wanted them? Should we play it out further, squeeze a little harder, and to what contractual end? Is it worth the risk of our strike losing momentum to get another ten cents an hour? It was Saturday, and we had bargained from 10 a.m. till midnight.

When they came around with an offer we could live with on the shop issue, we knew we were about to wrap up a very short strike. Management agreed that they would give us a modified agency shop. Everybody hired from then on would be a dues payer, every current member would remain a dues payer, every current freeloader would have the option of joining or remaining a freeloader.

This meant that the university had capitulated, accepting the long-run existence of the union. Each new hire would not be a life-or-death battle; the union was going to get stronger over time. We would never face another open window. If we did our job and organized our brothers and sisters, if we never got lazy, we would never face another decert either. We had a long way to go to get the middle-class wages we deserved, but we had overcome the efforts to divide and destroy us.

We called a mass meeting for that Sunday afternoon. First, though, we had one more action to pull off. Cornell had invited the parents of the freshmen to a special university brunch at Noyes Dining. Instead of blockading it or ruining it, with our tentative contract in hand we decided to join them. Every striker was given a five-dollar bill and joined this massive brunch. Strikers ate and ate and ate. Meanwhile, we brought our portable sound system with us and spoke to the parents, thanking those who had understood us and supported us. We let them

**FIGURE 12.** Traditional labor allies stood with us in the first strike. Teamsters and trades workers refused to cross our picket lines. Here, UAW leaders from Rochester hand Cathy Valentino a donation. New York State AFL-CIO president Ed Cleary, *far right*, came to show his support. (Local 2300 newsletter)

know we had a proposal to vote on that very afternoon, thanks to their pressure and the solidarity of our members. We finished with students and workers and even a few parents clapping and singing union songs.

The contract was ratified, but not until we had squeezed exactly one more nickel out of Cornell. Geer had been wrong every step of the way. By the next negotiations, after I begged our regional director and Geer's boss, Tom Fricano, Geer was replaced as our UAW rep. Our new guy, Bill Kane, was terrific. He told me, "Don't worry about John Geer, brother. You're the future, he's the past."

## White-Collar Wipeout

History showed that while we built an incredibly loyal and hardworking nucleus of support among the clericals, it would never really get close to a majority. The techs organized a bit faster and made it over the minimum 30 percent needed to hold an NLRB vote in 1983. But any organizer knows that you need more than a majority expressing support for the union on cards to win an election. In nine out of ten campaigns, the employer, using high-paid union busters, will whittle away your majority. That happened with service and maintenance, even without a lengthy delay. We petitioned with about two-thirds and hung on by our fingernails to win an election with about 55 percent.

The techs petitioned "light," with around 38 percent, but felt like they needed to bring their very long campaign to a vote. Over the couple of years since the service/maintenance union vote, two things happened that made it even less likely for the techs to win. First, our Local 2300 had two strikes, and important but modest gains to show for it. Our loud, rowdy blue-collar strikes may have generated sympathy among clericals and techs, but that kind of militancy was culturally uncomfortable for many white-collar workers. Second, Cornell had given out the best raises to clericals and techs in decades. We could show that this was happening because of the threat of a union. We could argue that the union would allow the techs to lock in and guarantee those kinds of raises in a contract. But the truth is, Cornell had sent a message that they had learned their lesson and would do better by their white-collar folks. Cornell also learned a lesson and did not rely on an easily despised bureaucrat like Cecil Murphy to be their main antiunion spokesperson. They effectively activated many faculty who feared that their labs would be disrupted and their techs less fully loyal if a union "came in." The techs lost their election by a wide margin.

The other negative effect of the failure to build a powerful single union of all workers on campus was that our fledgling service and maintenance union was under a permanent magnifying glass. Cornell knew that any concession they gave to us would be proof that unionizing helped employees. We were doubly disadvantaged. We didn't have two thousand sisters and brothers alongside us in the fight, and Cornell was determined to make a negative example of us.

Many tech and clerical leaders worked closely with Local 2300 UAW for years. They were key strike supporters, helping with everything from providing food to speaking at events. The full power of a 100 percent "wall to wall" organized campus remained elusive and drove our service and maintenance local leadership to search far and wide for every ounce of power we could find.

## Discussion Questions

- What are the benefits and disadvantages of the local becoming more formalized, less an organizing committee and more a traditional organizational hierarchy? How was the UAW structure and approach both a burden and a blessing for Local 2300?
- Imagine that a union like this gets pretty good contracts over the course of ten to twelve years, so there's less need to strike or engage in a militant confrontation. Does the union necessarily become demobilized, bureaucratic, weak? Do unions need to have a big fight every few years to stay strong?
- Were there other options that may have been missed in sorting out the rivalry between Cathy and Pam? Are some "internal politics" inevitable and a healthy part of democratic organizations?
- Was the larger activist leadership group wrong in finding a compromise as opposed to letting the two leaders fight it out?
- How might gender dynamics and sexism have played a role in the leadership conflict and the local's resolution?
- What are the pros and cons of a union paying its officers no more than what their regular job paid? What about paying staff that it hires no more than the average worker?
- Why do you think John Geer had an analysis and approach so different from that of most of the local's leadership?
- At this stage of the relationship Cornell capitulated enough to give the union a more secure future but didn't bend significantly on benefits and wages. Why did they go that far and not any further?
- The local began to experiment with new tactics that included students, faculty, alums, creative disruption, and publicity. How does a union know what is working and what might backfire in a fight like this?

- What was the impact on Local 2300 of having thousands of unorganized clerical and technical workers on campus?
- How might the UAW's slowly emerging militancy and creativity have helped clericals and techs organize, and how might those approaches have turned off some white-collar staff?
- What do you think were the major factors in techs and clericals failing to unionize? How much were gender, class differences, or the structure of the workplace key factors?
- Most unions in the US focus exclusively on winning a majority in order to be certified for collective bargaining. How might a union of clericals and techs have continued functioning with less than a majority?

5

# FRANKIE MCCOY

Frankie McCoy. Our first arbitration. Even after our first strike, even after winning a decent first contract that included a legitimate grievance procedure with binding arbitration, workers didn't believe Cornell could ever be overruled. Not only the rank-and-file believed this. Even our own leadership. Even those who had fought Cornell for two straight years and won. Even they were pessimistic.

"Cornell's too damn powerful," Emily Apgar told me after the local union executive board first discussed Frankie McCoy's firing and the possibility of going all the way to arbitration. "Once the muckety-mucks make a decision, they are not gonna let us just turn it around."

"But, Emily, you know the arbitrator is independent. And we have equal say with Cornell in picking the arbitrator." I said it but wasn't sure I really believed it. Emily was sure she didn't.

"Yeah, sure, maybe we help pick the arbitrator, but how many of them are working folks? Aren't they all lawyers and professors? We aren't on strike; we can't win this with muscle or by tearin' them a new asshole in the newspaper. This is legal, Al. How are we going to compete with all their lawyers at this hearing? And how do we know they haven't bought off the arbitrator to begin with? Probably he'll be some big kiss-ass Cornell graduate."

Making matters worse, some members believed Frankie may have deserved his termination, that he was lazy, or stupid, or at least irresponsible. And if he didn't deserve it for these reasons, some felt he deserved it for another: Frankie was Black.

During our organizing drive our coworkers' deep-seated racism rarely surfaced. Some typical racist tropes didn't resonate in ways that management could use as a divide-and-conquer union-busting narrative. The service and maintenance group was around 90 percent white, so while there were always visible Black leaders in the campaign, there was no talk of this being a "Black run" union. Another racist antiunion tactic is to suggest the union would protect "bad" workers, and to some that can be code for Black workers. But that too didn't ring true with our daily reality on multiple levels. First, everybody worked pretty hard, most working second jobs, and second, everybody was subject to a lot of favoritism and low pay. The overwhelming majority of white staff saw the Cornell pay and promotion system as unjust or even rigged. Few worried about our being so powerful that we would stop Cornell from legitimate oversight of "bad" staff. Most of all, we believed deeply that this union was ours, and that we would not misuse it to defend truly inexcusable behavior by one of our own.

The fact that Cornell had not been able to use racism as an antiunion wedge issue the way many employers do did not mean there wasn't significant racism just below the surface of our membership solidarity, however. Frankie's firing brought out a wave of ugliness that showed we had a long way to go. At first it manifested itself subtly as doubts about taking his case to arbitration.

Custodial zone rep Cindy Doolittle told me one night on the phone, "Jesus is the only person I know of who came back from being terminated. I don't think Frankie is any kind of Jesus."

"You never know," I told her. "The powers that be did a number on both of 'em, if you ask me."

Cindy wasn't dissuaded by my joking around. "But, Al, don't you think it's important that our very first arbitration be a real winner? Y'know, to show the people, to show Cornell?" Cindy had a Socratic way of gently leading me along logic's path.

"Yeah, I know what you mean, but the union can't just walk away from a fight because we might lose. Should we tell Frankie and his family we're waiting for a real winner?"

"Now, don't get me wrong," Cindy was prepping me for something she knew I did not want to hear, and started to almost whisper, "but Frankie is not too popular out there. Doesn't this arbitration thing cost a lot of dues money? Doesn't it have to come up for a membership vote?"

"Yes, it does, but those decisions shouldn't be popularity contests. Besides, this is what our dues are for. Hell, I don't want to end up like one of those unions with a fat bank account and no fight."

Finally, I figured I should just ask her. "Cindy how much of what's being said has to do with Frankie being Black?"

Cindy sighed. "Well, there is some of that kind of talk. Fred, you know him, he's a diehard anti, he's saying at the clock, 'See, I told you the union's just gonna fight for the lazy ones.' The people in the field sure don't see Frankie as deserving of a big fight, not with their dues money. They know he missed an awful lot of work. And people say he's nice but hasn't got any sense, having all those kids and not showing up for work over and over."

I was getting ticked. "Cindy, if Jesus Christ was a custodian at Cornell and turned water into wine, they'd fire him for drinking on the job. Frankie McCoy was sick. He has doctor's notes for almost every absence. Everybody, even management's own evaluations, say he was a hard worker when he was there. What do you yourself think, Cindy? Really, the truth."

Cindy sighed in a way I had come to know was her reckoning with her old and newer self. "I don't want our own people to lose faith in the union. I don't really know how much of people's bad feelings have to do with him being Black. Most of the whites live out in the country; they don't even associate with the Blacks. Personally, I don't care if he's purple. I just don't want to take a case we can't win. But if you think we got a good case . . ."

"Hey, I never said this was a good case in the sense that it was a sure win. I just think we've got to go to bat for the guy. If we lose, Frankie's no worse off; but if we win, it'll be great for Frankie and great for the union."

## "Not Fired for Just Cause"

Frankie McCoy was a forty-two-year-old African American man from very rural Alabama. We eventually learned he had to go to work before finishing junior high and had a hard time reading. He was full of a southern, rural working-class black deference to authority, especially white authority. He had survived many hardships in our very white world of upstate New York and immersed himself in family and church.

He and his wife, Mary, had arrived in Ithaca in the late 1970s, bringing their family—ten kids—north during a religious migration. Other members of their church had relocated in Ithaca, and they helped bring the McCoys. Frankie was no stranger to hard work; he started at fifteen in the woodcutting industry in Alabama. Hard worker or not, Frankie had begun to rub Cornell the wrong way in the past year. They said he was chronically absent from work. And they fired him after nine years of service.

At first, we didn't realize how strong a case Cornell really had. We also hadn't realized the controversy Frankie's firing and our grievance had stirred up among our members. I remember talking with the union steward in Frankie's area, shortly after Frankie got notice of his termination.

"Sure, he's missed some work," Tom told me. "But so have a lot of other guys. I know you don't want to hear this, but a lot of our own fucking people at the clock are asking me why we're fighting so hard for some goddamn colored. I tell them Frankie gets his work done. White or Black, you can get sick. His supervisor, Charlotte, just doesn't like him. Doesn't like that he's Black. Doesn't like the way he talks. God knows what else. She's had it in for him for a while." I was getting concerned that this case might never make it to arbitration and instead go down in flames at a membership meeting.

I visited Emily on a break so we could talk about Frankie's case. She was a coworker of his. She liked Frankie. "He's a sweetie," she told me but then added, "I don't know, Al, he's irresponsible enough to have ten kids, and then to miss so much work—he was practically asking them to can him." Was this plain racism or Emily's prickliness about "irresponsible workers," folks who missed a lot of work or didn't work hard, people Emily constantly told us all "make us peons and our union look bad." Nobody had a higher work ethic than Emily. I asked her point blank, "What about the fact that he's Black?"

Emily had that furtive look she always got when about to share some dirt. "Well, I heard two of them talking on the bus. They didn't want me to hear, but I told Robin to shut up so I could catch most of their words. One of them said, 'So what do you think of the union spending all our money on that colored?' Then the other said, 'You mean the one that's got a dozen kids? Why, they ought to put a clothespin on the end of his thing, that's what I think.' They laughed and laughed. That's all I heard. I know that's racist, Al, and a pretty disgusting thing to say, but that's the kind of talk out there."

I knew we had two battles to fight. The membership's attitudes and management's case. The membership vote was in three weeks. The grievance steps were well under way. We appealed the firing within the mandated ten-day period. This was the first step of the formal grievance process. The termination, we said on the grievance form, violated our contract. Specifically, he was "not fired for just cause."

At the first-step meeting, Charlotte, Frankie's immediate supervisor, explained to Tom and Frankie how she had warned him over and over, how he had missed more work than anyone in the whole department. She would not rescind the termination. We persisted.

At the second-step meeting, the head of the department rolled out the statistics. Single spaced, it took two pages to list the days Frankie had missed in the course of a year. Management was not budging. We played it to one more level.

At the third step of the grievance process the appeal goes beyond the department involved, to Day Hall. Ron Mathews scoffed at us for even going that far.

"This is a real waste of time, gentlemen. We walked this man through the entire disciplinary process, from oral warnings to written warnings to a suspension without pay. Then we backed off and gave him time to straighten out, and a year later we started over and gave Frankie a clean slate. We could have just fired him a year ago, but instead we gave him more written warnings, and another suspension. If the department had asked me, I would have fired him a year ago."

We made a valiant defense of Frankie. He had been sick for virtually every absence, and he had documented it. There was absolutely no evidence suggesting that Frankie had invented illnesses to get off work. That didn't matter to Mathews. "This was not abuse of sick time, it was 'gross overuse,'" he stated. We countered that he'd worked at Cornell for nine years without any other problems. His evaluations showed he was a conscientious worker. "You can't be a good worker when you're never at work," Mathews deadpanned.

My high rhetoric to people like Cindy and Emily about fighting the good fight was reverberating in my mind and sounding pretty tinny. Was I just trying to make a hero out of somebody I felt bad for? Our members had no experience with evaluating a case like this. Strangely, my four-year degree in labor relations never covered "how to defend a worker." It did provide me with a relationship to a great and wise professor, Jim Gross. He taught arbitration, and from that point on became my go-to, off-the-record ally in case analysis and strategies. This time he told me, "Dig into every detail. You don't have a strong case . . . yet . . ."

Matching our legal challenges, we were also struggling with an internal political reckoning. Many Cornell service staff had an old-fashioned puritanical sense of work ethic and could be as hard on a coworker as the boss. It was true, Frankie had one of the worst attendance records in a big department. I was beginning to think there might be no way we could win this case. To drop the case now would give the appearance that our most narrow-minded and prejudiced membership had won. It would look like the union had capitulated to racism if we dropped the case before the membership meeting.

It was another one of those definitional struggles where the choices we made, made us.

I felt the added pressure of knowing that Cornell was not going to work out a compromise on this grievance. Firing is the labor relations equivalent of capital punishment. There was not much room to work something out, to find some middle ground. Either Frankie McCoy was fired or he was employed.

There was a lot at stake. The union wanted to prove that our grievance procedure really meant something. We had elevated its significance during bargaining and during our strike. "This will be your system of justice," UAW regional director Natchuras had proclaimed. "The contract is the law, but the law is nothing more than paper without the means to enforce the law. You are the law's police, and the grievance procedure is your court."

In the first year we had resolved some grievances. We had won some partial victories. But we hadn't had any knockout success stories, and no case had gone all the way to arbitration. We wanted the first case to be a strong one, a winner. Frankie's case did not fit the bill. Cornell wanted to prove that the union hadn't won anything special, that the grievance procedure was a lot of hype. They had cracked down on arbitrary firings, making sure that Mathews reviewed those decisions prior to their implementation. This meant the union, and the grievance procedure, were having a valuable preventive effect, but it denied us the chance to loudly and publicly confirm the power of our contract. Mathews was not going to hand us our first arbitration on a silver platter.

It was clear from his taunting arrogance at step three that Mathews would like nothing more than to have us take Frankie's case to arbitration. We would lose, and arbitration, the contract, and the union would be discredited.

The union doesn't have to take any case to arbitration; we call the shots as to how far each case goes. We do have a legal duty to make a fair assessment of the case, but a union has a lot of latitude as long as it is not arbitrary or discriminatory. Our local membership votes on whether to take any case to arbitration, to spend the couple thousand dollars that represents our 50 percent share of the cost of paying an arbitrator six hundred bucks for each day he or she hears the case, thinks about the case, and writes the decision.

The few firings we had that first year were so blatantly justifiable that the union never had to think about going to arbitration. One printing assistant got caught stealing expensive ink. A food service worker didn't show up or call in for five straight days without a decent explanation. These workers didn't even ask the union to fight for them. But Frankie came to the union right away. "I was sick a lot. I came in whenever I could," he pleaded. "I got papers from the doctor."

We voted on Frankie's case at our January membership meeting. I had been warned by Emily and Cindy that a few coworkers hostile to Frankie might show up to vote it down, to in effect let management send him packing.

Straight shootin' Tom Parkin opened the discussion with the crucial numbers: "Yeah, Frankie misses a lot of goddamn time, but he's got nine years' service, ten kids, and about two dozen notes from his doctor."

Frankie smiled. Nobody said anything for a minute. Then Millie Lovett spoke. "Well, when he's there, Frankie is a hell of a good worker. He went out of his way to help me with my carpets. Then that fool supervisor, Charlotte, chewed him out for leaving his work area." People shook their heads knowingly.

One burly member I didn't recognize had never even taken off his coat. "I want to hear what Frankie there has to say for himself," he tensely blurted out. "He's asking us to spend a whole lot of dues money to get him back to a job he don't really seem to want." A couple of heads nodded, and everybody turned toward Frankie. The room went dead silent. Frankie paused so long I wasn't sure he understood how hard he had been challenged, that his whole chance at arbitration, at employment, might be hanging in the balance. He just smiled, then finally spoke.

"Well," he began, then paused. His voice was soft, and I was worried. "I do want that job. I been there nine years straight. I can't see how a man can lose his job for being sick. That just ain't right." Frankie was not going down without a fight.

But the doubters were just getting warmed up. "I've been sick as a dog with pneumonia, and I made it into work. I think old Frankie spends a little too much time making more McCoys and not enough time at work." People giggled nervously, glancing at Frankie, who just kept the same neutral smile. The high-seniority, high-skilled mechanic continued: "I say Frankie made his own bed, now he can lie in it. When I voted for this union, you guys said we weren't gonna spend all our time protecting the lazy ones. I'm against this." It was the first time in over two years of fighting he'd ever come to a membership meeting. Interesting what launches different folks into action.

I saw a hand near the back of the crowded room. I knew who it was before I saw his face: one of only three Black workers present, Oze Richardson. Oze was almost sixty. He'd worked hauling coal for Cornell's heating plant, a filthy, poisonous job. He was part of a small union of operating engineers on campus, but he would still come to our meetings sometimes to show his support, and he eventually ended up in our unit, the only person to get to vote to organize two different unions at Cornell. Oze used to come to organizing meetings still covered with the black dust. He'd say, "This dust doesn't bother me. I was Black before I took this job, and I'll be Black the day they plant me."

Oze was an elder Black statesman on campus. He was a leader in his church and had formed the Black Elks when the regular Elks decided they wouldn't admit anyone who wasn't white. Younger African Americans on campus sometimes criticized Oze for "getting along" a little too well with white folks. Oze once told me, "I got nothing against white folks in general, just the stupid ones."

Oze cleared his voice and began, "May I speak to the issue before us?"

"Of course, Oze," I replied.

"Thank you, Mr. President. Brothers and sisters, most of you know me, the rest of you don't. It is plain to see, I am a Black man. If you look a little closer, you will see I am an old Black man, and if you look real close, you'll see I've worn the same union button for two solid years. I supported this union from day one. I did not support it because I thought it would fight for the lazy. But I did support it because I thought it would fight for the sick, for the abused, for a man terminated for missing work due to documented illness." His voice was rising.

"I too have had my share of illness. Sick as a dog. Think of those words. Sometimes I've come to work anyway, sometimes not. But I am not a dog. None of us are dogs. We are men and women, human beings. We have minds, we are able, unlike a dog, to decide whether we are sick or not. The only person, sick as a dog, who always comes to work is someone who, like a dog, fears his master. Brothers and sisters, I fear no master. Frankie McCoy is not a dog. Cornell is not Frankie's master. The doctor declared him unfit to work—that is all the evidence I need. Thank you for your patience. Now when are we going to get some cushions on these chairs so my Black ass can get some relief?"

"What the hell did we organize a union for anyway?" Bernie Lamphere, a huge, taciturn farm tractor driver of few words was not looking for a response. "If we don't fight this, we lose. Fight it, and win or lose, we make Cornell take us seriously."

There was not much more said. The motion to take Frankie's case all the way to arbitration passed handily. I was relieved that the better side of our union had shown itself. But I also felt a little uncomfortable with all those "we got 'em now" and "how can we lose" comments. Expressions of solidarity and fifty cents will get you a cup of coffee at arbitration.

I wondered whether the silent majority who had not bothered to show up at the meeting were typified by the racist banter Emily overheard on the bus. I wondered if more racist staff were afraid to speak their mind at our union meetings. I wondered if that was a good or a bad thing.

## "Semen Lab?"

If we weren't going to look like fools at the arbitration, as ILR professor Gross had challenged us, we needed more to go on than we had gotten so far. The harder I scraped for information, the more complicated our case was becoming.

We started with the fact that Frankie had indeed been sick and was able to document most of his absences. He had severe headaches and what he called "breathing trouble." Frankie gave us permission to talk to his doctor, who told me that Frankie had a condition that resulted in wrenching, debilitating, chronic sinusitis, and headaches.

Cornell knew this. It was written in the doctor's notes they had been given, but they pointed out that no matter how legitimate the cause for many of his absences, he did miss work at other times, and that sick or not, they simply could not keep someone who was not available for work a couple days each month.

Probing further, we found more bits and pieces that gave us hope. Frankie's absences that were not related to illness centered on his need to leave work on two different occasions because his family was about to be evicted. Frankie described his wife Mary's desperate call. He said that he told his supervisor Charlotte that he had to leave immediately to help keep his family sheltered. He missed the next day as well, according to Frankie, because he had to watch the kids while Mary went to see a lawyer and Neighborhood Housing.

Weeks later Frankie explained that the reason they were having such house problems was "the other house burned to the ground."

"And did you miss work when that happened, Frankie?" I asked.

"Oh, yes, sir, I missed two or three days then," he replied.

"When did this happen?"

"Well, it was about four months ago. It was in the paper—didn't you see it?" he added.

"So some of the days they fired you for missing work were due to your house, where your family lives, burning down?" I was excited at the newfound, albeit tragic, information. "And there was a story in the paper?"

"That's right."

"Family of Twelve Lose Everything in Blaze," read the headline that it took me about half a day to track down. If we were going for a sympathy plea with this arbitrator, Frankie had just casually mentioned a real tearjerker that accounted for some more of those missed days.

It was time to discuss this with Bill Kane, our new UAW rep. Bill was young for a UAW International rep, only in his mid-thirties. He was out of an industrial shop in Philadelphia. He was tough as nails, a former paratrooper with a long scar down the side of his face. After we became friends, I asked how he got it. "From growing up where I grew up" was his growling answer. Bill the rep used his toughness to intimidate management, not to confuse and coerce members into selling out their own union.

Bill came out of the struggle to make his workplace safe. He hadn't risen by way of the usual ladder of steward to local president to rep. He came out of the ranks as a health and safety activist who had impressed Natchuras. Bill even achieved national recognition when he testified in front of the Philadelphia City Council about a proposed right-to-know law. The law would have required employers to tell their workers the hazards of the toxic chemicals they worked with. The Chamber of Commerce decried it as another step toward socialism. Bill brought a tall gas cylinder into the high-ceilinged council chambers. He began his presentation without uttering a word. He turned the nozzle on the tank, and an ear-piercing screech of escaping vapors filled the room. Some council members dove under their chairs; others gasped and covered their noses and mouths.

"The way you feel right this instant," Bill's gravelly voice boomed, "that's the way the workers of Philadelphia feel every day. We never know what we're being exposed to or what it could do to us or our families. The only difference is, we're being exposed to a lot worse than compressed air."

Bill had brought the press in tow, and it made the next day's front page. The law passed. Bill was our kind of rep.

At first even militant Bill was skeptical of Frankie's case. "Look, Al, I'm a fighter, but do you really want to take on such a loser of a case as your first arbitration?"

My heart sank. "We were in a damned-if-we-do, damned-if-we-don't position, but the membership voted," I replied. "Maybe this is naïve, but I'm hoping an arbitrator might give Frankie a second chance."

"Try about a hundred and second chance. I'll do my best, but I'm no F. Lee fuckin' Bailey." Bill was flipping through the stack of written warnings. "All right, let's get to work."

I spoke with Bill about the problem we faced regarding how careful management had been to walk Frankie through each of the incremental steps of progressive discipline. When I pointed out they had literally done the whole series of warnings and suspensions *twice*, Bill's eyes lit up.

"You mean they took poor Frankie to the brink of termination and then started over again with rinky-dink warnings?"

"Yep. Mathews claims they gave him an extra series of chances."

"Maybe they did," said Bill, "but they also negated the corrective value of progressive discipline. You see, by letting him off the hook, they sent Frankie the message that he would not be terminated for missing work. They did not enforce their own rules, and therefore they undermined those rules. They should have given him a longer suspension or fired him the first time around. By starting over at square one they made a mockery of the discipline procedure."

"Interesting," I said, unconvinced. But I appreciated working with someone who could be this creative.

Bill was on a roll. "This argument makes even more sense given how, shall we say, uneducated Frankie is. I bet he didn't know what the hell was happening to him with all these warnings. Hey, can Frankie read?"

"Shit, if he can't, how the hell could he have fully understood what those warnings meant? I bet Charlotte never explained the warnings to him."

We were right. Frankie told us, "I can read a little, but not too good." We gave him one of his warning letters and asked him to read it to us. It was sad, it was embarrassing, but the fact that Frankie couldn't comfortably read one sentence of that letter was the best news we'd had in weeks.

"Frankie, did Charlotte know you couldn't read too well?" Bill pursued.

"Well, once I asked her what this was all about with these letters. And when I got my red book, my union book—she saw the steward hand it to me—she said, 'What are you doing with that, Frankie?' I said, 'I'm sure I ain't making heads or tails of it.' Oh, wait a minute. She gave me my evaluation one time, and I asked her what it meant."

"What did she say when you asked her what it meant?" Bill asked.

"Well, she said she would read it to me."

"And did she? Did she read it to you?" Bill was gobbling up every word, every step in the progression.

"Oh, yes, sir, she read the whole thing to me."

"And Frankie, did Charlotte ever read any of the warning letters?"

"No sir, she'd just hand 'em over to me, paper, paper, paper. I could tell she didn't want to talk about it."

"Frankie, did you ever take the letters home and have Mary read them?" I asked.

"I left 'em in my locker. No, I didn't want to trouble her. I really didn't think anything of it, I guess. Should I have?" Frankie shook his head.

After Frankie left, Bill and I walked through our line of thinking. Frankie was functionally illiterate. His supervisor knew he had trouble reading. They relied almost exclusively on handing him written documents, full of technical jargon to confront his absenteeism problem. The contract stated that discipline should be for the purpose of "correcting" a problem, not just to punish the employee. How could Frankie correct a problem when management made no effort to communicate with him in a way he could understand? Maybe it wasn't a huge point in our favor, but it could help.

"You know what this means?" Bill asked me, cocking his head and raising his devilish, Jack Nicholson eyebrows.

"What?"

"This means we have to make Frankie out to be one dumb son of a bitch." Bill was shaking his head. "But you know, Frankie isn't stupid. He can't read much, but he knows enough to take care of a family and survive on $5.85 an hour. He knows how to find housing and food. He knew to come to us. And you know what else he knew? He knew enough to get the fuck out of Alabama."

Bill continued: "But for the arbitrator, we need to show how wealthy Cornell is, and we need to contrast that with this poor, southern Black man with a dozen mouths to feed and a burned-out house. Here he is at an Ivy League university for nine years, and nobody ever offered him a chance to learn to read." Bill was disgusted, drawing righteous energy from the contradictions and hypocrisies so many Cornell employees experienced.

"What about his health? Can we get his doctor to testify that Frankie couldn't help it, that he really was too sick to work?" I wondered.

"What's wrong with Frankie's nose?" Bill asked. "I know you told me once before."

"He's got some nose disease. Sinusitis that leads to migraines."

"And the poor son of a bitch had to spend all day sweeping floors and dusting. I bet that job causes half his problems." Bill, the former health and safety rep, was talking. "Hey, what building was he in? Does it matter? Are some buildings worse than others? Dirtier? Dustier?"

"I don't know. All I know is he worked on the Engineering quad. I don't think those buildings are especially dusty." The next time we met with Frankie, Bill had not forgotten this line of questioning.

"I work in the basement, in the semen lab," Frankie told us—or at least that's what it sounded like.

"Frankie, what the hell is a semen lab? You mean sperm? In the Engineering School? What exactly are they engineering down there?" Bill chuckled.

"No, *cement*, like sidewalks and roads and stuff. It's a terrible mess down there, they always bustin' it up all day long. They got this big machine, and they break the cement, then I clean it up." Frankie lit up talking about work. He clearly missed it.

"Does it get dusty, real dusty?" I asked.

"Oh, Lord yes, it's a mess from all that concrete they break. I'll show you if you want."

So Bill, Frankie, and I took a field trip to the Cement Lab in the basement of Thurston Hall. Officially known as the Bovay Civil Infrastructure Lab, its 12,500 square feet houses the largest biaxial direct shear apparatus in the world, which applies 3,597 tons of pressure, simulating small earthquakes. The outside of the lab was surrounded by piles of crushed concrete and granite. Inside it was a disaster area. One of the techs took us aside and said, "Hey, Frankie, where you been, buddy? Hey, you can't stay in here much longer, we're about to smash some stuff."

"Why do you smash it?" Bill asked.

"We test the tensity of different materials in this lab and check out seismic waves. You heard of 'between a rock and a hard place?' that's all we do here," the technician said.

"Put your goggles on," Bill shouted to the tech as we walked out.

"Is it always this dusty?" I asked. Frankie nodded his head. Bill was smiling. I was smiling. We came back with a Polaroid and took a roll of pictures. Dust, dirt, and a pile of rubble from every angle.

In a department where over two hundred custodians were transferred from building to building at a supervisor's whim, Management had never put two and two together and offered Frankie a transfer to a normal building. Instead, knowing from doctor's notes that severe sinusitis caused his absenteeism, they left Frankie McCoy in the dustiest building on campus. We were starting to feel like we had a case.

As we walked back to Bill's car, Frankie looked back at Thurston Hall and said, "I sure do miss that place."

Bill grabbed Frankie by the shoulders and said, "Friend, you will never work there again." Frankie's eyes dropped sadly. Bill continued, "We're gonna get you back to work in a nice, normal building where students track snow into coffee lounges and miss the urinal."

"That'd be OK too, I guess." Frankie grinned.

The day before the hearing Frankie called us from the pay phone near his house to say their car wasn't running and he couldn't come in to prepare. Frankie's testimony was the lion's share of our case, so we asked if we could go to his house and work there. Frankie said, "Well, let me check with Mary." He called us back ten minutes later. "It's OK with her, but she said to make sure and warn you things are a little messy right now."

"Frankie, you tell Mary I got two kids, and I bet my house is messier than yours." Bill had met Mary McCoy and loved her toughness, her strength. "Tell Mary to make some coffee, cuz I'm bringing something she's gonna like."

We sat on the tattered green couch, Bill and I slumping toward the indentation surrounding big Frankie. We ate Bill's coffee cake and talked about the case. As we spoke, waves of little McCoys would drift past. It seemed like we met the whole family. Two older girls watching the baby. They were all polite, well clothed, respectful to us and to each other. Maybe that kind of restraint was due to our presence. Maybe it was the socialized necessity of having twelve people trying to live together in a four-bedroom house.

Right before we left, I watched as Frankie sat his eight-year-old boy on his lap and carefully rebuttoned the white shirt that Tommy was still growing into. On our ride back to the office in Bill's big white Buick, probably more space than most of the McCoy children had in their bedroom, Bill shook his head. "Shit, we gotta win this. Not just for the money or for the job, but because Cornell took away some of Frankie's dignity. And that is a family working overtime to hang on to every inch of dignity they can. I hope to hell we beat those bastards. There's a lot more at stake here than meets the eye."

## Judgment Day

I was only assisting Bill, but as we walked into the hearing room I was as nervous as the day of our union vote. We'd heard that Mathews was so certain of their case that he had lobbied to handle it himself instead of using one of Cornell's many attorneys. Mathews was there ahead of us, chatting with the arbitrator. Their banter about a recent Labor Relations Association luncheon held at Cornell put me even more on edge. I recalled Emily's crackly voice, "Cornell will buy 'em off, or he'll be some big alumni type."

Bill Kane walked up to Mathews, interrupting his chitchat with the arbitrator, and boomed out, "Ron, how the hell are you?"—the effect of which was to end the schmoozing. Without waiting for Mathews to reply, he extended his hand to arbitrator Joseph Gentile. "Bill Kane, and you must be Joseph Gentile?" Bill had pronounced his name *gentilee.*

"That's Gentile, like Jew and Gentile," the arbitrator responded. "Let's get started."

Bill came back to our chairs and rolled his eyes at me. He handed me a bunch of our photos of the Cement Lab and said, "Make sure they're in the order we want." I flipped through them while the arbitrator gave a few solemn instructions. In the middle of the photos of rubble and dust was one Bill had snapped of me wearing his Christmas gift to me. An authentic "John Geer UAW International Rep suit," the caption said. It was a polyester green plaid number with bright orange pants. It even included a cigar stub stapled to the pocket.

I snorted, Bill choked back a laugh, and we both began to loosen up.

An arbitration hearing is like a mini trial, only less formal. Each side makes an opening statement, then each side presents witnesses who can be cross-examined. Finally, each side either makes closing statements or, a few weeks later, submits a written brief.

The burden of proof is on the employer to demonstrate the discharge was warranted, for "just cause." This meant Mathews went first. The advantage for us was we got to hear their whole case before making any last-minute adjustments to our own. The disadvantage was the arbitrator gets inundated with management's perspective. By the time we presented our case it felt like we were at the bottom of a deep, dark well.

The good news that day was that Mathews's presentation held no surprises. Charlotte testified about Frankie's extensive absenteeism, and Mathews submitted the warnings, demonstrating that Frankie had been properly marched up the ladder of progressive discipline. Charlotte laid it on thick about the hardship his absence caused his coworkers who had to cover his floors.

On cross-examination Bill asked her how many buildings she was supervisor over. "Eight," she answered.

"Did you ever consider transferring Frankie to one of your other buildings?"

"What good would that do?" she replied.

"Then your answer, I take it, is no, you did not consider transferring Frankie?" Bill concluded.

"No, I had no problem with his work, just with him showing up to do it," Charlotte responded.

"And is it possible to transfer custodians from one floor to another or from one building to another?"

"Yes, it happens now and then." Charlotte clearly was being waltzed out into territory Mathews hadn't contemplated or prepared her for. She kept looking over to him.

Finally, Mathews objected. "What is the relevance here?"

"I'll establish the relevance during Frankie McCoy's testimony," Bill shot back. "Five years ago, I was working in a factory. I'm not very educated in this process, Mr. Arbitrator, but my simple understanding is that legal rules of evidence are not what we are bound by. Besides, I only have one more question along these lines."

Arbitrator Gentile said, "You're right, we don't adhere to formal rules of evidence, and you're doing fine. Please make your point and move on."

"Charlotte, I understand that you were a custodian for fifteen years before becoming a supervisor. During those fifteen years, how many different buildings did you work in?"

"Oh, Lord, maybe ten or twelve."

"Thank you, Charlotte. No further questions."

The bad news that day was that our health and safety expert had canceled on us. We needed her testimony that twenty years of Alabama woodcutting caused Frankie's medical condition, and that his exposure to cement dust in the basement of Thurston had exacerbated it. So at eight that morning, Bill had told me I was going to have to testify as a health and safety expert.

"How can I be an expert? What are you talking about?" I knew Bill was a cowboy, but this was freaking me out.

"Look, Frankie needs this. You can say you've taken courses through the ILR School, right?"

"Uh, Bill, I never heard the word 'adenocarcinoma' until a month ago. They don't even offer a health and safety course, and Mathews probably knows that."

Bill was not budging; he had bullshitted his way past bigger pricks than Mathews, and he expected me to do the same. "Well, you could have taken classes through the union, that's true, right?"

"Could have? Sure. Did I? Just a little basic stuff, not really."

This was not about "if" for Bill, it was about "how" I was going to do this, so I saddled up.

"Read these two articles we're submitting on adenocarcinoma. That's some kind of nose cancer or something. They link the problem directly to exposure to wood dust. Frankie's got an occupational disease, and management's lack of proper attention to the cause of his absences was negligent. I'll bet dollars to doughnuts Charlotte didn't even think of transferring him to a normal building. Now you have to shed light on all the notes from the doctor. The doctor doesn't make the connection with the dust in any of his notes. You've got to do that." Bill was talking, and I was hyperventilating.

Frankie's doctor had refused to testify against Cornell. Even though we had asked him more than a month in advance, he was mysteriously unavailable. Once again, Emily's warning had been sounded. "They've got this town in their pocket. Nobody wants to help us take on Big Red. They're covering their own butts."

"Bill, this is crazy. Mathews will blow me away," I pleaded.

"Read the articles, then I'll run you through the questions. You'll see, it'll go fine." Bill had jumped out of airplanes when he was seventeen; he was not going to let my nervousness get in the way of our game plan.

On the stand I took the oath. I wondered to myself, am I going to lie? My answers weren't exactly lies, but I definitely was creating a false impression of my expertise. I made my peace knowing three things. Frankie deserved a job. Mathews would lie in a heartbeat. I was already going to hell, and at least I'd run into Bill Kane there.

"Adenocarcinoma, yes, that would appear to be what Frankie has developed." Christ, twenty-four hours ago I couldn't even pronounce the fucking word! What next? Tomorrow maybe I'd write a few prescriptions.

"As these two articles indicate, Frankie's prolonged exposure to wood dust is likely to have caused his nasal condition. As they both also indicate, exposure to abnormal amounts of dust post adenocarcinoma will typically cause severe headaches and other symptoms." So sayeth I, with a heavy emphasis on the words "abnormal amounts of dust."

Bill handed me the photos of the cement lab debris. He had me testify that I was familiar with every building on campus and that out of two hundred buildings, this floor on this building was the dustiest I had ever encountered. I seconded Charlotte's testimony that custodians were frequently transferred to different buildings, and that Frankie easily could have been.

Mathews was pissed. He questioned my credentials, then he examined the two articles. I said I had been trained by the UAW and was a UAW health and safety specialist.

"So, as a custodian and health and safety expert," he paused, letting his sarcastic tone reverberate, have you read the other studies footnoted by this article?"

"I believe so," I cautiously replied. "Perhaps I should check the titles." Mathews handed me the article with a sneer.

"Perhaps you should," Mathews scoffed.

As I flipped through the citations on the back two pages, I knew we had a problem. Every citation but one was in a foreign language. It appeared that the Dutch and the Finns had done quite a bit of research into nasal cancer. Thank God there was one article from the *Woodworker's Journal.*

I winged it. "Yes, I am familiar with the study published in *Woodworker's Journal*," I stated.

"Oh, you are?" Mathews grumbled. "And what does it say?"

"It establishes the link between inhaling wood dust and the particular condition Frankie appears to have."

Matthews rolled his eyes, looked at the arbitrator and said derisively, "No more questions for our young expert."

It was my first lesson in the Alice in Wonderland quality of arbitration. An arbitrator comes in with no knowledge of the case and often no knowledge of the employer or the union. Reality is concocted for the moment. Both sides stretch that reality to fit their needs.

I got off that witness seat as fast as I could.

Frankie was great. He knew our strategy. He knew we had to establish that he couldn't read. He knew we had to get into the miseries of his life, his house fire, his eviction. Frankie testified clearly and with dignity. He even got Mathews's goat by making him repeat a question now and then when Mathews talked fast.

Bill whispered to me during Frankie's cross-examination, "I've never seen Frankie do this, no matter how fast you or I talk. He's driving Mathews crazy, breaking his rhythm and showing the arbitrator that management never broke things down in a way he could understand. This is brilliant."

The more elusive Frankie was, the nastier Mathews became. The more abusive old Ron got, the more revictimized Frankie became.

"Mr. McCoy, isn't it true that you were fully aware that your repetitive absences from work had brought you to the brink of termination in 1981?"

"I'm sorry, what was that you said, what kind of absences? I was sick, but I came to work even with the headaches quite a bit, sir."

"Repetitive absences, Frankie, repetitive. Like when you miss a day every two weeks, that's repetitive," Mathews explained testily.

"Oh, OK," Frankie said.

"Could you answer my question?" Mathews pushed on.

"I'm sorry sir, could you ask it again?"

As Mathews became annoyed with Frankie, he stopped calling him Mr. McCoy. Now it was only a patronizing "Frankie." He berated Frankie, who seemed to be trying his hardest to understand and answer, even though Bill and I knew Frankie was dumb like a fox. Mathews's frustration led him to treat Frankie with the same insensitivity and disrespect that characterized the very firing Mathews was trying to justify.

In the end Mathews may have been our best witness.

The arbitrator rarely intervened during the hearing. Once Bill objected to Mathews's badgering Frankie, and Gentile agreed, saying, "There's no reason for an angry tone, Mr. Mathews."

After the hearing, as Frankie got out of the car in front of his dilapidated home, Bill and I got out too. Mary came out. Bill held Mary's hand and told her, "Today your husband did a great job. He told the truth. He may even have outsmarted that s.o.b. Ron Mathews today. I hope we win. But you should know that Frankie McCoy did you proud today. If we win, it's because of Frankie's testimony."

Mary just nodded her head and thanked us.

As we walked back to the car, Bill turned to Frankie and yelled, "Hey, Frankie, you know what the word 'repetitive' means?"

Frankie grinned a huge, ear-to-ear smile and waved goodbye.

## Turning the Eleventh Cheek

We wrote our briefs after the hearing. It took about a week. We felt we'd done our best. Frankie had come through with flying colors. We pulled off the medical argument, the illiteracy argument, and the transfer argument. For management's side, Mathews had done a good job shooting down Bill's theory regarding taking Frankie through the process twice as being unfair. And there were a lot of absences.

We certainly had painted a picture of a hardworking man who desperately needed this job, a man Cornell knew had health problems they never cared enough to comprehend, much less accommodate, and a reading limitation they ignored as they papered him up with discipline.

The question was whether the arbitrator had a heart. The question was whether management's litany of warning after warning convinced Joseph Gentile. The question still was, could Cornell be beaten, overruled.

A month later the answer came. It was yes. Frankie McCoy had been unjustly fired and would be reinstated with full back pay. Gentile found great fault in management's lack of diligence in comprehending the nature of Frankie's problem.

"Corrective discipline is more than simply marching an errant employee through a series of documents. The employer has an obligation to attempt to understand the causes of the problem. The employer provided no evidence of that effort."

First, I called Bill in his Philadelphia office. Then I drove to Frankie's home and told him the good news. He had no phone at that point, a function of months without income. He smiled and kept saying, "That's wonderful, just wonderful. Wait till I tell Mary." Later that night we cranked out a leaflet. At five the next morning we stood at the giant B parking lot handing them out to all the custodians. "McCoy Wins Job, Full Back Pay."

I called Emily. She was thrilled but ended our talk by saying, "I'll believe it when I see him at the time clock."

I assured her there was no appeal. But I was wrong. Cornell did try to appeal the decision. It delayed Frankie's return for another two months, but it could not stop it. Cornell had taken the trouble to contest Frankie's claim for unemployment insurance after his termination, leaving him with no income whatsoever. The back paycheck grew thanks to Cornell's callousness—and Frankie's photo with a $6,000 check made the local newspaper.

Everybody loves a winner, and Frankie was the first working-class winner in Cornell history. I never heard another bigoted comment related to Frankie or the case.

The next time I spoke with Frankie he asked what he could do for me and Bill now. I told him the next time Bill Kane was in town he could have us over

**FIGURE 13.** *Bottom row*, custodians and union leaders Cindy Doolittle, *left*, and Emily Apgar; *top row, from left*, strike general and mechanic Larry Grey, Al Davidoff, and Frankie McCoy. We were celebrating Frankie's arbitration victory, which reinstated him with full back pay. (Local 2300 newsletter)

for family dinner. I told him the most important thing was to show up at every monthly union meeting for the rest of his life.

Frankie did show up at the next meeting and every meeting for years. He wore a suit, probably his churchgoing suit. He sat with a straight, prideful posture. There was a glow of resurrection about him. Cornell had terminated him, and he had returned from the dead. No one had done that before.

"Jesus Christ and Frankie McCoy," I muttered to Cindy during the local's financial report.

"Yeah, I guess they both suffered enough," she whispered back, smiling.

Frankie's suffering left him with no bitterness toward Cornell. His religion taught him forgiveness. The McCoys named their eleventh child Charlotte.

## Discussion Questions

- Does arbitration seem like a fair process? Would you feel that way if Frankie had lost?
- If Local 2300 were stuck with a less combative and creative rep than Bill Kane, what might have happened differently?
- What creative strategies were important to the union building a winnable case?
- Does an employer have an obligation to continue to employ someone who misses a lot of work because of illness? What could management have done given Frankie's illness and job location?
- What else could the union leadership have done about the members' racism surfacing around Frankie's case?
- Was pointing out Frankie's illiteracy, large family, and challenging circumstances to the arbitrator a good strategy? Did it reinforce racist stereotypes?
- Is it reasonable that members get to vote on whether to take a case to arbitration?
- Was it unethical and unfair for the local president to stretch the truth about his credentials in the arbitration?
- This confrontation happened in the 1980s. What, if anything, might be different about the employer, the union, or the members' reaction to these issues today?

6

# BLACKNESS ON THE CORNELL PLANTATION

Frankie McCoy's victory was a breakthrough that proved we could beat Cornell, forcing a public reversal of a serious decision. But Frankie's treatment was far from unique. Cornell had exercised its prerogative to "send workers down the hill" hundreds of times before. Sometimes there were good reasons, many times not, but that power had never been effectively contested. But Frankie's experience was not unique for other reasons. Unchecked by union action, Cornell departments, typically functioning with great autonomy, had long engaged in discriminatory practices within the workforce. Our efforts to fight and change these patterns won us praise and allies in the Ithaca community and from faculty and staff. We built relationships with families of developmentally disabled workers, supported a small but diverse caucus of Asian staff intent on fending off racist stereotypes and comments from management and coworkers, and we prioritized promotion opportunities to lift women and members of color out of the lowest labor grades. We were aggressive at confronting sexual harassment, and cosponsored training for all members where the union made clear we had zero tolerance of abuse from managers, students, or coworkers.

Ending anti-Black discrimination at Cornell was a deep and daunting challenge. It had strong historic roots and was widespread on campus, with some departments worse than others. The Cornell Bus Garage was one of the bad ones. Just how far Cornell had to go to remedy this history, and how hard we would have to push, became clear when we put a spotlight on aspiring bus driver Roy Lee Clements.

The tinderbox of 1960s radical social protest came home to roost in 1968 when festering tensions and racist attacks pushed Black Cornell students into a militant, armed takeover of the largest student union building on campus. This became national news, deeply divided the faculty, and cast one of the longest shadows across Cornell's history in the twentieth century. Within ten years, race at Cornell was again front and center as students, faculty, and community members carried out an intense, decade-long struggle to persuade the university to divest from South Africa and thereby help end apartheid. This included a protracted, excruciatingly embarrassing presence of a student-occupied "shantytown" directly behind Day Hall, the university president's office and starting point for all campus tours. The divestment struggle was linked at times with a number of labor struggles and was where my student self cut a few activist teeth.

Racism affected the lives of many faculty and students, and efforts by a large and diverse group of activists to force Cornell to confront these issues frequently made headlines in the campus newspaper. The average service and maintenance worker, however, lived in a separate universe from student political struggle. Out of one thousand service and maintenance workers, about fifty were African American. That's not out of whack with the 5 to 6 percent African American slice of the general population in the forty-mile commuting radius of Cornell employees. That benign framing changed, however, once you looked at the population of Ithaca, which directly surrounded Cornell and was closer to 10 percent Black, or a hiring pool double the percentage of actual employees. But aggregate numbers are only one-third of the story.

The second third is all about *which* jobs those fifty Black workers held. The gleaming campus on the hill had not only a severe class hierarchy, but a separate and distinct race and gender history of occupational segregation. It wasn't just that Blacks were not evenly distributed across the fourteen labor grades that spanned unskilled, semiskilled, to highly skilled. It's not only that this meant that Black workers' poverty levels were twice as high as whites'. It's that the one skilled job that Blacks could rise into on a consistent basis was cook. The university that had named its vast, forty-three hundred acres of gardens and green space the "Cornell Plantations" imagined Blacks as best suited for the most traditional, racialized role of cooking for a mostly privileged, white population.

So while Black workers were generally last, there were also some carefully curated firsts. There was one Black general mechanic, one Black printer, one Black material handler, and one Black high labor grade animal attendant. There were also zeros. Not one Black gardener, or dairy plant operator, or heavy equipment operator or bus driver.

The third leg of the three-legged stool of what to me was managerial racism and white supremacy in our bargaining unit was how individual Black workers were treated. The overwhelming whiteness of the power structures on campus projected a nonstop sense of otherness and "less than" racist thinking that was at times subtle and quiet and at other times brazen and loud.

As to Black workers' attitude toward organizing, while we won our union election with about 55 percent of the vote, we had support of forty-five of fifty Black workers. We had Black worker organizing leaders, including most of those "firsts." Having come the closest to "making it" in terms of livable wages and respect for their skills, they were subject to daily racism from bosses and some coworkers. There were a few Black workers who didn't sign union cards or who made a point of keeping their distance from the union. But our Black leaders told us every one of them voted yes in the privacy of the ballot box.

Hoping that the union might be a counterforce to Big Red's racism, Black workers played key roles in our leadership and tested the union with some of our most formative grievance struggles. Our first set of thirty-six elected stewards included six Black leaders. Two Black organizing committee activists took visible, formal roles in the Local 2300 leadership. Oze Richardson served a term as our secretary treasurer, and Al Butler as our community service chair.

The organizing drive gave written voice to the experience of Black workers. As a Vet School tech, Peaches Bell wrote, "Sure as water is wet, there is racial discrimination at our great Ivy Tower of Cornell University. My husband and I have four generations of roots in this area and we don't want to move to find equality."

Less than six months after our organizing victory, Oze Richardson was given space in the *Bear Facts* to comment on the burning issue of racism in and university divestment from South Africa. "As Reverend Jesse Jackson has said, 'You can't be against prostitution and invest in a brothel, and you sure as hell can't be against apartheid and invest in South Africa.'"

The union struggled at first with trying to win respect and dignity for all with a decent grievance procedure and training shop stewards at every work site to enforce the contract. We knew those struggles specifically meant defending Black workers who were more likely to be punished or just taken advantage of with onerous assignments. We struggled to win livable wages for the most impoverished, the majority of the thousand-person unit, and that meant lifting Black workers out of the deepest poverty of any group of workers.

What we hadn't at first directly tackled was how to confront the segregation of women and people of color in those lower labor grades. One hard reality was that there were maybe 750 lower-grade jobs like food service worker and custodian, and only 250 middle- and higher-skill jobs. Even in a fair system, it was not easy to move up. But that reality only made it more painful for long-term, lower-grade staff to see opportunity after opportunity go to nonemployees, too often family of white bosses. So those rare internal promotions were not distributed evenly, and people of color's chances were closer to none than slim.

When we confronted him, Human Resources' Pete Tufford acknowledged the facts of where Blacks and women worked in the labor grade system but denied that anybody in management was racist or sexist. He would say that people needed to apply for those higher-grade jobs, and they needed to be the best qualified. Nobody was trying to hold anybody back, we were told. We had many frustrating cases where long-term, lower-skill-job-holding union members, folks who had been custodians for ten or twenty years, desperately applied for the middle-skill or higher-skill jobs, only to see those jobs go to outsiders. In a small community, this often meant friends, or family of bosses, getting the plum jobs. Even if nothing that nefarious was happening, there were so few good jobs for working-class folks that every high-skill job opening had a dozen perfectly qualified external applicants, just trying to get a foot in the university door. As bad as the wage scales were, and as infamously arrogant as Cornell management could be, for a local, construction or factory worker, there were decent benefits and greater job security at the university. But our low-wage members were stuck. This was true for most white workers and almost all our Black members.

We had grievance after grievance where we would defend a longtime, loyal, positively evaluated custodian trying to win a material handler job or printer or machine operator post. Time and time again we couldn't make the case contractually that the qualifications were relatively equal, and the outsider won the job. As we won contracts that began to strengthen worker rights and slowly lift the lowest-paid workers out of poverty, we began to focus more on this issue of upward mobility and the critical race and gender discrimination subset of this reality.

One "rising tide lifts all boats" approach we took was to fight for training and development opportunities that could give longtime staff a leg up to winning better jobs. We established a program that helped advance literacy and math skills. School-smart Cornell students from the College of Human Ecology were paired with service workers to tutor them in math or English. In return, the workers were expected to teach the students about their work and their history. It wasn't perfect, but it happened on paid time, and those who participated often built close friendships. Students got a window into the hard lives of our members and the dignity with which they carried themselves.

We also worked with New York State to see if we could establish that certain of our highest-grade jobs like maintenance mechanic, cook, and printer could be recognized as apprenticeable positions. This would provide a clearer set of skills needed to become qualified, and we could work from there to provide more training opportunities. Our existing high-skilled folks loved the idea of their positions being recognized that way, and it helped us argue for boosting their pay too.

Those overall systemic efforts were slow to change the culture, and as constructive as they were, they didn't directly confront the racism that doubled the barriers for longtime workers of color. And then along came Roy Lee.

## Front of the Bus

Roy Lee's story is really a story of a rock meeting a hard place and not giving up. The hard place was the Cornell Bus Garage, an area about two miles from central campus where a massive fleet of buses was housed, repaired, and dispatched. Cornell had a full-service bus system that ran 24/7 and moved thousands of students, faculty, and especially staff. It even provided long, overnight trips for sports teams. There were maybe ten mechanics and forty drivers. The drivers were four grades above a custodian, and the mechanics a few grades higher than that. In the blue-collar service and maintenance world at Cornell, these were respected, middle-working-class jobs. While the wages were still below most measures of poverty, they were still 20 percent higher than those of a custodian or food service worker, and there were opportunities for overtime.

Every single Bus Garage position was held by someone who was white. In fact, there had never been—not once since Henry Ford invented the automobile, not once since a bus transported its first rider—even a single African American employed as a bus driver or bus mechanic. For the past thirty years, all the generic reasons mentioned above were only part of that story. The main reason was Bill Crissey.

Bill Crissey ran the Bus Garage with an iron fist. He was known as one of the toughest bosses on campus. He scared the crap out of most drivers during the union campaign. He was short, still muscular even in his fifties, with a military haircut and a drill-sergeant personality. During the organizing fight, we only had about five drivers willing to wear union buttons and speak up, and not a single mechanic. We maybe got eighteen votes out of fifty possible. Bill hired every driver personally, and he set the driving schedules, which meant he could not only screw you by not hiring you but could screw you every week by giving you awkward split shifts, too few hours, or too many hours. Even five years into the establishment of our union, the Bus Garage still felt like a nonunion workplace. Favoritism and fear ruled.

We knew Bill was a racist. Our shop steward, a courageous, equally tough driver named Jim Royce, told us Bill had once muttered in front of drivers, during a particularly loud anti-apartheid demonstration, "I wouldn't let those n-----s with signs on *my* bus." It was a sick environment where one's good job and daily existence were all wrapped up in keeping Boss Bill happy.

Bill had a seemingly impenetrable system for hiring. You can't be a bus driver without a special CDL license. It was very difficult to get that license without practicing on a bus. Bill controlled every bus. His friends were given ample opportunities to learn. Nobody got promoted from within the larger bargaining unit, with the exception of one or two of Bill's clan.

The reality that was openly understood was "No coloreds need apply." Cornell HR would admit Bill was old-fashioned, or a throwback, but would just shrug their shoulders and say, "We need qualified drivers." We also could get no pressure to change the system from within the staff at the Bus Garage. Even those who occasionally suffered from being out of favor with Bill were reluctant to grieve anything, much less challenge the system of privilege that got them in the door or could always send them "back down the hill."

As we escalated our arguments that Blacks and women were stuck on the lowest rungs, the Bus Garage was becoming one of a couple of "poster children" for the campaign. We met with women's groups and Black faith leaders. At one point we even had a Black city bus driver considering applying. But he ultimately decided that working for a guy known to be a racist control freak wasn't a good career move.

Roy Lee Clements had been working as a custodian at the Statler, the campus hotel. He had a few years seniority and had always been a solid union supporter if not an activist. He was known as a bit of a tough, no-nonsense guy. When it came time to strike, Roy Lee was not only one of the first out the door, but he said he'd help make sure shaky coworkers knew not to scab. One day he called the union office and told me he had applied to be a bus driver. As the words "That's great" came out of my mouth I could feel my heart already sinking under our previous failures.

I said, "Roy, you know we've been trying to change things at the Bus Garage for a while. Great that you applied—"

Before I could finish, Roy interrupted and said, "I didn't just apply. I'm planning on getting that job, because why wouldn't I?" I knew he was testing me, testing the union.

I said, "Well, you know you'll need a CDL, right?"

He said, "I've had a CDL for ten years. I drive our church bus every week."

That was it. I called HR and told them. I wanted them to know we were watching this closely and that here was an opportunity for the right thing to finally happen. Tufford did not share my enthusiasm. He was not willing to do anything, saying instead that each department makes its own hiring decisions. I reminded him our paychecks say "Cornell University."

"Cornell is our employer," I said. "We are on this, and we aren't letting go."

Roy Lee went through the process. He was interviewed, he even demonstrated his driving skills on a Cornell bus. We waited. Then I got the call from Roy. "They turned me down."

Crissey had said, "Sorry, Roy, I guess it just wasn't your time."

That pissed Roy off. He said, "I don't need some buzz-cut cracker telling me what time it is. What are you going to do about this, Al?"

I said, "Roy Lee, we are going to grieve it, and we are going to fight it. I'm ready. Are you ready?"

Roy just chuckled and said, "Hell, yes, I'm ready."

We could have relied only on the grievance, but this was way bigger than that. This was the spotlight we needed on a system that was blatant at the Bus Garage but pervasive throughout many Cornell departments. After years of fighting, we had learned a thing or two about power at the university. As Andre Agassi used to say, "Image is everything." We engaged local political leaders, Black faculty, and local clergy. We said there was apartheid at Cornell, where people of color could only access the bottom of the economic ladder.

Crissey claimed the driver he hired was more qualified, that management met the standard in the contract where he proved the two weren't equal. The contract language was not in fact good for us. It left a great deal of subjective interpretation of qualifications up to the boss. Roy was clearly qualified, but he didn't have as much full-time driving experience as the driver Crissey hired. We didn't want to go to arbitration and lose the case and have this boss and this system vindicated. Our contractual case was weaker than our commonsense moral case. This fight was all about public, moral pressure.

After months of fruitless effort, we put Roy's case in the context of a set of statistics that proved the overall campus segregation. We reached out to two of the leading Black ministers in town and to the prestigious director of the Africana Studies Center on campus to see if they would ask the question: Why are there no Black bus drivers? Finally, after months of agitation, with bargaining approaching, Tufford called me. He got right to the point, saying, "I have one word to tell you about the Roy Clements situation: "uncle."

They refused to strip the new guy of his job, but they guaranteed Roy a driver position that had just come open. The "no need to apply" racism that had kept people of color out of that garage for fifty years was now "no need to apply," the job is yours, Roy.

I asked Roy if he could stop by the union office after work. When he came by, I told him the news. A man whose face I'd only seen express toughness, determination, and bitterness broke into the widest, happiest smile I'd ever seen. "I told you that job was mine." He laughed and grabbed me hard.

Roy's first day driving the bus was a big deal. We put out a flyer announcing it to all. I made sure to be around his route. He wore the uniform, he looked crisp, and he seemed to have that victory smile permanently etched.

One of the great things about the position of bus driver is its visibility. Jim Royce used to show every rider that he was wearing his union button and UAW hat during the heat of our organizing fight. He used to shout back and forth to pro-union friends while driving with dozens of workers in the early mornings, running a veritable pro-union captive audience meeting.

Roy Lee Clements was an eight-hour-a-day, every day for years to come, visible, campus-wide reminder that the union could change some of the hardest things. That the most prejudiced and dictatorial boss could be beaten, that the union stood for more than just an end to poverty. The fight had educated our members, most of whom shared frustrations with a general lack of upward mobility but hadn't thought much about the added barriers facing Black coworkers. It showed that weak contract language didn't have to be the end of a good fight. We had created pressure that contributed to new cracks in that plantation mentality.

## Discussion Questions

- What do you think about the limits of the contract that allowed supervisors to choose the best-qualified candidate regardless of years of service or the need for affirmative action? How could this be misused?
- These events happened in the 1980s, after the civil rights movement and before the Black Lives Matter movement. How do you assess Cornell's imperviousness to racism and occupational segregation?
- Were there other approaches the union could have taken to fight racism?
- Students and faculty were focused on divestment from apartheid South Africa. What are some strategic reasons for or against the union becoming more involved in that struggle?
- If you were a union leader today and most of the workers were white, would you seek to counteract underlying feelings of racism within the membership? Why or why not? What might you do?

# 7

# NOAH'S AMALGAMATED ARK

One unanticipated result of taking on the largest employer within fifty miles was that other workers took notice and started to consider their options. It wasn't just that workers were inspired that we were taking on the big dog; it was the *way* we took them on that whetted the aspirations of other working people. We were in the news and in the community. We were feisty with the big shots and having fun with each other. News articles, radio, TV, T-shirts, teams in the bowling league, a food bank, the Singing Bears all provided a steady stream of mostly positive impressions. Other workers were aware that we had political clout, that community leaders often stood by our side. On the other hand, our strikes created a mixed message. For risk-averse, fearful workers, going on strike seemed dangerous. While none of our striking members ever lost their job, it still seemed to some upstate New Yorkers as awfully radical.

During the initial organizing drive a few other workplaces approached the UAW for help. Most of us were excited by the prospect of workers around us unionizing, but Barbara Rahke and the UAW had a firm and well-reasoned view otherwise. Barbara told us we simply couldn't risk the distraction, or the possibility that all would not go well. What if we lost the vote? What if the workers went on strike or had a hard time getting a contract? We were on a mission to organize thousands of workers; we couldn't risk damage to that effort by getting tied up with a few dozen folks somewhere else.

We found a good approach during the organizing drive. We would turn over any non-Cornell organizing leads to other unions in town. Those workers would get their chance, just not with us. This approach also helped us build relations with other local unions, some of whom felt all our flash and swagger had left them in the dust. We were happy to help out by seeing if any of our Cornell activists knew workers at those workplaces. This led to the largest union in town, the Machinists Union, which represented most factories, to organize a local nursing facility, the Reconstruction Home. Those workers won, and urged on the Cornell staff with a message: "How wonderful it is to win! The suspense of counting the ballots, the screams and hugs of victory, a moment none of us employees will ever forget. We will finally all be equal."

Once we organized and had a first contract, we took a different approach. We persuaded the UAW to give Local 2300 an amalgamated charter. This meant we could have multiple shops, organized as separate legal bargaining units, all under the Local 2300 UAW umbrella. For about a decade we helped several other workplaces join us. This proved challenging and exhilarating. It also tied us to an interesting theory of power, one based in community support.

Our Cornell members were broadly supportive of these efforts. The spirit of our union was that *every* worker deserved the fairness that only a strong union could provide. We never refused help to any group that came to us. We became the "Noah's Ark" of local organized labor, with one or two of everything on board the UAW 2300 boat.

We organized the maintenance staff at the Ithaca Housing Authority; the workers at our weekly newspaper, the *Ithaca Times*; two different bargaining units at the Tompkins County Library, including the professional librarians; staff at the local homeless shelter network; a major bakery and eatery; and a center for developmentally disabled adults. Two fights that went very public were at the largest downtown hotel, at that time a Ramada Inn, and at a very popular chain of video rental stores.

The Ramada was our kind of fight: low-wage workers, very rich boss. In fact, the owner was the richest man in Ithaca, an attorney and longtime liberal benefactor, Wally Wiggins. It was yet another lesson in how even the most liberal employers would do everything in their power to thwart their workers sharing in that wealth. In fact, I found that the more liberal owners were the worst employers, partly because they had delusions of benevolence. They took it very personally that, god forbid, *their* workers would be less than thrilled to be part of *their* family. And for all that liberalness, the idea of sitting down across a bargaining table as equals was just one liberal bridge too far.

But the good thing about liberal employers was that they cared about their reputation, and we knew their friends. We won the Ramada vote and a first contract, but not before a public campaign that included picketing with one of my all-time favorite slogans, "Wally Wiggins Welches Workers' Wages!" We also learned that very low-wage employers also meant very high turnover. It was hard to organize and maintain leadership. Cornell, for all its faults, did have a basic pension and health insurance package and stability that engendered long years of service. Places like the Ramada would have 50 percent turnover every eight to ten months.

A few years later, Wiggins sold the Ramada, and it went through several corporate hands. One of those faceless corporations was called Interstate Hotels Corporation. They produced my all-time favorite artifact of any campaign. A custodian who cleaned the hotel manager's office came by our union office to pass along a tiny, laminated card she "had found" there. The card opened with "The following events should require an immediate call to the Corporate office." It then listed seven such catastrophic events. To show they meant business, they then listed six corporate execs and their personal cell phone numbers. The list of catastrophes was the impressive part of the card. I'll just share four:

"Fire in the Hotel"
"Floods, hurricanes, tornadoes"
"Loss of life in Hotel"

All of the above would certainly be cause for some emergency calls, with 24/7 access to the top national brass. But these were numbers three, four, and five on the list. What was numero uno?

"Union activity"

The hotel custodian looked at me through exhausted eyes and deadpanned, "They really hate us, don't they?"

I said, "that's one way to look at it. The other way is that they really *fear* us. That our union, if we stick together, can be more powerful than a hurricane or a tornado."

I've kept that card in my wallet for thirty years.

## Win a Union, Lose a Friend

The other highly public fight destroyed one of my closest personal friendships and put at risk our broad progressive coalition. Richie Berg was one of two co-owners of a highly successful chain of three video rental stores, Video Ithaca. They had cornered the local market with a lot of smart strategies that jibed with their college-town customer base. Richie himself was a bit of a hippie. He was friendly, charming, and a major activist in the local slow-growth, environmental world. Before the rise of labor in town, this was the most powerful wing of local liberal activism.

Richie and I bonded during the Nichols mayoral campaign. We became great friends, socializing and schmoozing over politics. Politically, we were an unlikely couple. I was the hard-core union agitator, and Richie the liberal green hippie entrepreneur. In some ways our friendship symbolized our at-times tenuous political coalition. And in some ways, our personal closeness helped provide some added glue in that partnership when trust might have been tested.

This all held together until the day the workers at Video Ithaca walked into the Local 2300 office. Part of how Richie and his partner Alex built their brand was by hiring a lot of cool, film-smart, and even well-known hip local folks. You could go in to rent a video and end up in a great conversation about the actors or the director. It also meant that these workers had more than an average amount of spunk and sense of self-worth. The small workforce also included a few activists from the gay and feminist community.

The Video Ithaca workers in their view were what made the stores cool. They knew they were the brand. They also knew Richie and Alex had a near monopoly of the market and were making money hand over fist. The workers were expected to be knowledgeable about film and cool with customers but were still paid like very low-wage service workers. Richie once told me that the workers loved being there because it was such a fun environment. The workers told me they felt ripped off.

There were only around fifteen regular staff, but within days fourteen of them signed union cards. They knew I was close with Richie, and they hoped I could talk to him. I asked Richie to come over to our house, a place he had been many times before. We sat face to face on our couch, and I told him I had some difficult news. I told him that if he stayed with me, we could navigate this and it could all go smoothly and ultimately end in a good place. I told him I knew this, and that we could figure this out together.

And then I told him his workers were organizing. I told him there was a way he could respond to this that would allow us to build a positive, progressive model, something that would enhance his reputation and the stores' image. But Richie was devastated. He barely spoke. He was in shock, and he seemed not the least bit interested in exploring a high-road approach. He walked out on shaky legs, with me saying, "Richie, we can work through this together. We need to keep talking when you're ready."

Richie fought the union every step of the way, and that fight not only ended our friendship, but it in many ways also destroyed him.

He did all the usual antiunion things. He tried to talk workers out of it and tried to figure out who the ringleaders were and get to them. But the staff was too united and too unflappable. He was awkward, and his efforts to defeat the union included being oblivious of legal boundaries at times. Every negative step he took was met with a response from us. The clever, politically sophisticated staff made a mockery of his efforts to defeat them. It got increasingly personal.

I meant what I said to Richie on that couch. He could have taken a deep breath and said, "Tell me how we work this out where I don't go broke or look like an idiot."

And I could have told him. "We have fourteen of fifteen signed-on cards, so you have a legal right to recognize the union. You don't need to force a long, drawn-out election." I could have told him, "We can do something called interest-based bargaining, where we approach this respectfully and in a win-win mind-set. And yes, you will have to pay the workers more, and yes, you may have to make some other improvements, but you will have even higher morale, lower turnover, and we can publicly hold your business up as a model of positive worker relations." Not for nothing, this would also be a great message about our larger political coalition and help us organize other employers. Not for nothing, our labor coalition represented close to twenty thousand workers, who were potential added customers to a local business with great union relations.

But Richie chose the opposite path, and it got ugly. I've organized more than a few liberal bosses, and they are always worse than traditional employers. They live in a bubble, clinging to a delusion that they are the benevolent patriarch of a loving set of adult children. In smaller businesses, this is all extremely personal. In another hippie-owned business we organized they used to give each staffer a free cookie every shift. The owners thought that was cool; the workers thought it was insulting when they didn't have affordable health insurance. That same employer had purchased a painting from an artist who worked in his bakery and store. The artist-employee later signed a public petition saying he was voting yes for the union, and the next day the painting appeared, destroyed, on his front lawn.

There are always some workers who out of true friendship or out of currying favor enable those liberal employers to feel like all is right with their staff. But underneath, it never is. Because there are class differences and power relationships and basic economic needs that speak to different interests. Straight-up, traditional, middle-of-the-road employers have fewer of these delusions. They want to make a profit; they don't want to share power, and they are not too worried about being loved by their workers.

Because there were a few gay activists at Video Ithaca, the fight for a union and contract connected to support from that community. I don't recall anything homophobic about the way Video Ithaca was managed, and I don't believe Richie was in any way discriminatory, but that became one of the undercurrents. I tried to stay in the background, not wanting to personalize the fight between me and Richie and out of sadness for what was being lost personally and politically. But I was clear: Richie had a choice. In fact, he had many choices, and he chose to abandon the values that our coalition held dear. He made a choice that ended our friendship. And he was likely to lose. The workers would have a union and a contract. It was up to him if it had to be an ugly fight for us to get there.

Once or twice, I thought about whether I should have told the workers to go to another union. But I knew there was no other union that was organizing places like this. I knew we were by far the best choice. It was not only Richie who was furious. His wife would glare at my wife at meetings, across streets, you name it. Close friends of Richie's would say to me, "How could you do this to him?" Frankly, it pissed me off. I would come back at folks saying, "Richie made a choice to fight his workers. Are you OK with him being antiunion?" I heard, "But he was your friend . . . " more than once.

The final chapter in the fight was the ugliest. Richie was serving on Common Council. He wasn't a natural politician, always a bit uncomfortable, but he was smart, knew the issues, and was a well-known activist and businessman. He ran in a heavily Democratic ward and had little or no opposition because our coalition was behind him. As the Video Ithaca struggle heated up and Richie kept fighting a contract, I decided we could not let a man who now had become known as antiunion cruise to reelection. A good friend, Roey Thorpe, the chair of the Gay Lesbian Task Force, lived in Richie's district. I went to Roey and said, "You've helped us with this Video Ithaca fight. Would you consider running, or at least pretending to run a primary against Richie? We can't have a union-buster in a liberal seat, and maybe that will push him to settle a contract."

Roey was one of the funniest, gutsiest activists I have ever worked with. I adored her, and we were fast friends. She told me, "What the fuck would I want with being on Common Council? That has got to be the boringest job in town." I told her to throw her hat in the ring, that she wouldn't have to *really* run, and if she did run, she would probably lose to Richie, so just help us and shake Richie up a bit. She reluctantly agreed. Our union's early pro-gay-rights stance at a time of intense struggle for that community was a deep bond.

After Roey announced her candidacy, Richie shocked the local political world. He announced he would not seek reelection, eventually signed the union contract, and pretty much removed himself from public life. We never spoke, and while I know in my head and gut that I did the right thing, in my heart I've always felt some guilt and sadness.

Roey served as one of the most progressive and colorful members of Common Council, and as an officer of the city she officiated at my second marriage with considerable style. She would regularly lambaste me for dragging her into the tedium of public service.

The one other type of organizing we engaged in that grew the union was with Cornell grad student workers. The law on whether grad workers, who do a huge percentage of the actual teaching and lab work at most colleges, can unionize has fluctuated depending on whether a Democrat or a Republican has been president. Presidents get to appoint the National Labor Relations Board, which sorts out eligibility to unionize. There really is no decent rationale to deny these grad workers that right, but that right has bounced back and forth like a ball in a game of ping pong.

Grad students had been important allies and activists in our struggles. They joined our rallies and picket lines and spoke out in our defense. A few of them were among our most radical supporters. Grads who came from other countries with more militant union traditions like Ireland or South Africa or South Korea often offered us ideas that went beyond our imagination or culture. This is when Diarmuid from Ireland lobbied for a "Belfast strategy" during one of our strikes. It was fun watching our rural, gradually radicalizing leadership listen to his proposal to set burning tires in every entranceway to campus. I saw Cindy Doolittle, a wonderful custodian leader and one of our quieter emerging activists, shoot me a look that clearly meant, "Al, are we going to do that?" We never did, but Diarmuid's sincerity, lilting accent, and fierce solidarity had a few heads nodding.

What the grads hadn't done is take on organizing themselves very much. But grad organizing was starting to sweep many campuses, including other Ivies. We worked with them to build an organizing committee. They decided to link with UAW 2300, but at that time we couldn't get the UAW to make a big investment, because the legal right to unionize had been lost once again. The grads were not deterred, so we began a campaign to build a union, legal rights or no legal rights.

It was a low-budget, modest effort. The local was poor and couldn't hire staff, but we did work out a dues system where grads would contribute, and we raised enough money to pay one of their leaders to be a full-time organizer. At its peak there were several hundred dues-paying members. In subsequent years they tried to formally unionize and have come close, but no success yet.

There were times when all this other organizing became difficult for the local, and I took some heat from our Cornell leadership. The truth was that each campaign, whether it was for seven workers or seventy, took a lot of time. Bargaining a first contract could be just as arduous with small shops as big. The small units didn't generate much in dues, so the Cornell folks truly were subsidizing all the other units.

We set a structure to ensure that the small units had representation on our executive board. We would invite the organizing committee leaders from these small shops to come to our membership meetings and share their struggles. Those personal relationships and familiar stories of abuse helped keep most of the Cornell leaders sympathetic to the small-unit campaigns, but more than once I heard that maybe I was spending too much time there.

Despite some grumbling, nobody seriously challenged that we should be in solidarity with any workers who would stand up for their rights. Members felt proud that we had created a movement, an organization that felt like a beacon of hope and possibility to other workers.

I also realized we were building a model of unionism that was different from the progressive analysis whereby you organized by industry to build effective density, sufficient concentration of membership to force an industry to decent standards. Our Noah's Ark approach did have a compelling alternate analysis. I believed that sectoral density (e.g., organizing all nursing home workers in a market) was probably the more important, and larger-scale, approach to building power, but I also believe that specific communities, cities small and large, are sources of real power and influence over many employers. Some employers, especially massive global entities, abandon a community as soon as higher standards are set, or workers start to organize. But many sectors don't allow for that. By building a progressive community that embraced workers' rights, we were creating different forms of local solidarity and power. The fact that no other union in town was doing much organizing meant that we were realistically these workers' only chance.

The other organizing beyond Cornell that we were involved in was the UAW's effort to expand to other colleges and universities. We were part of a set of locals led by young, progressive leaders. Sue Parsons, the District 65 / UAW president at Boston University (where Barbara Rahke got her start) and Julie Kushner and Maida Rosenstein at Columbia University were all leaders in their twenties or thirties dedicated to building dynamic unions. We became good friends and union comrades. There came a time when the UAW decided to commit to a major organizing initiative in Boston. Boston is a college town, and we already had a UAW foothold there. The UAW asked me to take a leave and join the team in Beantown. For six months I worked with wonderful rank-and-file leaders like Harneen Chernow, Ferd Wulkan, and Leslie Lomassan. That Boston office is also where I first met brilliant author-agitator Bill Fletcher, who was doing research out of a tiny space tucked away from the noisy organizers.

Local 2300 had just wrapped up a contract, and I had been reelected to another three-year term, so it seemed like a time I could hand the local off to my fellow leaders and dive into some major organizing. Our Local 2300 leaders were a little wary about my taking off, but they also were excited about building a movement across campuses, and they knew more college organizing would give us more clout inside the UAW.

The campaigns were really tough. Harneen and I brought one to fruition at Berklee College of Music but lost a close vote. It was a fascinating experience tied to our sense of being something more than a one-shop local, but it was good to get home and dive back into building our local future.

Later, the UAW created an internal council of about twenty locals based in colleges and universities. I was elected the first chair of the UAW Academic Council. We tried to use this fledgling, unstaffed caucus to help one another out, parachute in on organizing drives, and to push the UAW for more support.

## Discussion Questions

- Was the UAW's early refusal to take on other, non-Cornell organizing a wise strategy? Why? Why not?
- After the service and maintenance victory, what were the pros and cons of Local 2300 becoming an amalgamated local, and the decision to help all workers organize?
- If you're a union leader and you get calls from people in other workplaces asking for help organizing a union, how do you decide where to say yes? Assuming you don't have unlimited time and resources, what should your criteria be? Size of workplace? Winnability? Relevance to building power in your main sector or in the community?
- Were the small bargaining units worth some distraction of energy from the larger, strategic goal of organizing more of Cornell?
- What kinds of employers are vulnerable to community pressure, and which are less so?
- What do you think of the author's decision to accept the Video Ithaca organizing campaign? Was the loss of a close friendship and the possible damage to the progressive coalition worth supporting those fifteen workers?

Part II

# PUTTING POWER BEHIND OUR TRUTH

# 8

# FIGURING IT OUT

Though often poor, unlettered, and looked down upon by most Cornellians, the blue-collar service and maintenance workers were pretty street smart in 1981 when we organized. As Cathy Valentino once told Cecil Murphy, "Just because we work with our hands, doesn't mean we can't use our heads." Workers had figured out how to raise families on poverty wages. Most workers kept a strong sense of pride and work ethic in spite of being treated with low respect. These formally uneducated locals knew how to navigate around powerful, privileged students, academics, and managers.

A few, including myself, also had a college degree. I had learned some basics about power, or the lack thereof, being a student activist at Cornell. A few of my ILR classes taught me inspiring labor history and some useful technical points about collective bargaining.

What none of us were prepared for or realized, however, was that over the next dozen years we would struggle together to get a PhD in "The Theory and Practice of Winning Worker Power at a Major University." Our coursework would not be based on books, because there were no texts for this. Though we did not realize it at first, we were writing our text. Our source material was our everyday struggle to win a better life for a thousand custodians, food service workers, hotel housekeepers, mechanics, and bus drivers at the largest, richest, and most powerful employer in central New York.

Our union's path to power was a series of trials and errors by fire.

Our initial strategies all relied on the UAW's expertise. We had UAW reps from our region and national headquarters in Detroit helping us. The grizzled, heavy-industry UAW folks were shocked that a buttoned-up, wimpy university would balk at long-established union basics like livable wages and a union shop. Cornell's early hardball tactics included demanding we give up certain benefits we already had and refusing standard practices like binding arbitration of grievances, or even a joint labor-management health and safety committee. This punitive, high-handed behavior insulted the UAW right along with the rest of us and backed our powerhouse parent union into a corner it never expected to be in.

While most of the UAW reps and the regional director projected confidence and provided support, it became increasingly clear they were out of their element here in Ithaca. Striking Cornell was not like shutting down production at a General Motors car factory. Their traditional strategy of picketing twenty-four hours a day, seven days a week at every entrance was almost entirely ineffective at Cornell. The university, spread out over seven square miles (not including a dairy farm that was over sixteen miles from Ithaca), was more like a rural city than a factory. This traditional strike approach meant our members were in small, isolated groups of three to six, picketing endlessly at forty, often obscure, places.

I had four realizations about those first strikes.

First: Our members were tough, but toughness also had its limits. Most members were willing to take the risks of lost income and even job loss and refuse to work, confronting bosses and scabs on picket lines. But the pressures of poverty created limits. Many simply could not sustain a long strike. Plus, we started with 25 percent nonmembers, all too willing to scab. The short duration of withholding of our services created real pressures but was not enough to bring Cornell to its knees.

Second: As historically great and innovative a union as the UAW was, and as dedicated to our success as it was, it really didn't understand our workplace. It didn't understand what made Cornell tick and where it was vulnerable. I didn't have those answers yet, either, but I saw the UAW leadership's surprise that Cornell wasn't budging much. The UAW honchos seemed lost, and that was a frightening revelation.

Third: I knew we needed to do a better job of fighting in ways that made our courageous members feel powerful, not isolated. We were seven hundred strong, but it didn't seem that way when most of what we did during the strike was picket silently with four other people for four to six hours.

Fourth: I realized that students were not the most important constituency at Cornell. I knew from my own days of student activism that Cornell mostly tolerated or patronized "protesters." We hoped, however, that shut-down dining halls and filthy dorms would create enough disgruntlement among the students to get the administration's attention. It was a critical awakening that even the students didn't matter that much.

Maybe we were still stuck in the box of thinking our strike power was our only power. Or that the power of the strike was all about shutting things down.

We needed to ask ourselves more questions to better understand all the levers of power at the university.

Why weren't the students more important? They paid a ton of money, and there were twenty thousand of them. Without students, there was no Cornell. We slowly realized, however, that the demand to go to Cornell was elastic, unending. Cornell already turned away nine out of ten applicants. Once in Ithaca, the students were mostly captive; they had already paid their tuition and fees, so even if they were grumpy because most dining halls were closed and the dorm was getting rank, they weren't going anywhere. Cornell wasn't going to lose any customers.

When *did* Cornell care about students? When enough of them organized in militant or embarrassing ways over a long period of time, the university sometimes sought compromises. It took many years of student and faculty agitation and even arrests for Cornell to make concessions on divesting from South African apartheid. At Cornell's Industrial Labor Relations School, enough students mobilized over a long enough period of time that we were able to win some concessions to our demands for more labor-oriented faculty and classes. That's how we landed UAW's Brendan Sexton as a visiting labor practitioner teaching two three-credit classes.

There were two ways that students could matter politically to Cornell. The first was when they took part in tarnishing Cornell's reputation and became a PR problem for the university. Back to "Image is everything": a faculty supporter once told me that Cornell cares more about one bad article in the *Chronicle of Higher Education* than it cares about dorms stinking or student dining options being compromised during a strike. The second way was their role as future alums. Much more about that later.

What about faculty? If students' support could not be a decisive factor for us, the elite Cornell faculty must be where the power really lies. But there was plenty of evidence that faculty didn't really have much influence either. Many faculty had been deeply involved in a whole range of campus struggles, like divesting from apartheid South Africa, but they only seemed to be taken slightly more seriously than the students. Maybe faculty were like students: plenty of good applicants for every entry-level slot, and not worth a lot of respectful attention unless they could somehow jeopardize Cornell's reputation. Faculty weren't unionized, because bad Labor Board decisions had made that difficult for most faculty at private universities. So they didn't bargain collectively over anything or wield any formal collective power.

What about the Ithaca community? Did Cornell care what the mayor thought? Mayors had always more or less been tools of the university. One of Ithaca's former mayors used to brag that he got invited to sit with the university president at Schoellkopf Stadium at one football game each year. And he was a moderate Democrat. Cornell-community relations were all gown and no town. Big "C" for Cornell, little "c" for the community. The Cornell team name is "the Big Red." The Ithaca High School team name is "the Little Red." Talk about an inferiority complex! Cornell's basic philosophy was "We put this cow town on the map; we accept your total gratitude, cow town."

Still there were big issues lurking in the shadows. What about the poverty? Our low wages not only affected our members and their families but also pushed down wages elsewhere, setting a low standard for everyone else. Didn't Cornell owe the community better? What about the fact that half the land in the city was tax exempt because of Cornell? Even money-making enterprises on campus like private fraternities, the apple cider operation, and the popular Dairy Bar selling delicious ice cream made on location didn't pay any taxes. The city was obligated to provide Cornell services like fire, sewer, and police. They handled permits and repaired roads with only half the usual tax revenues. The Ithaca City School District educated hundreds of children of grad students living on campus without any payments in lieu of normal property taxes.

It took us a few years, but eventually we came to understand there were two big levers of power that the King on the Hill responded to. One was bad publicity. Cornell cherished its reputation among its peer institutions and in the wider world. It also feared that the very best faculty might be less interested in coming to work there, or the superstar professors less interested in staying there, if the university's reputation was beaten down. We came to realize that with the right issues, amplified by student, faculty, and community support and driven by creative worker militancy, we could create a drumbeat of threatening publicity. We needed the right framing, a compelling campaign, and creative mobilization to focus Cornell's attention on our issues.

Our second lever of power took us longer to comprehend. It was related to, but separate from, the issue of image. Over time we came to realize that the most powerful university stakeholder was not workers, not students, not faculty. This part of the community wasn't even *in* the community. It was the alums. Every student becomes one, and that was the students' secret power. Alums love their professors. Alums give money. A lot of money. But not all alums are equal. Rich alums build the endowment, fund academic buildings and sports venues. Got a million? Get a wing of a building named after you. Got ten million? Take the whole building and name it after your mother or your cat. Alums populate the board of trustees and the university's governing body. The university's president spends a lot of time hosting, catering to, and visiting with alums. Every weekly issue of the house organ, the *Cornell Chronicle*, featured at least one article about some important alum.

But while each alum had a special connection to Cornell, so many other institutions also clawed at them and their wealth. Their largesse was in demand. And that connection—and their donations along with it—could fray if their alma mater was making news not for major academic, athletic, or scientific achievements, but for its mistreatment of its workers and community.

So, the theory of power we developed slowly but surely in the 1980s centered on Cornell's vulnerability in respect to its image and on better understanding which stakeholders mattered at Cornell. Going after its Achilles heel required us to be more than self-interested, poor service workers; we had to become the base of a widely supported, righteous movement, one that included students, faculty, alums, and community leaders at local and state levels. It also required us to be willing to be creatively disruptive, to both inconvenience the university in escalating ways and to use that disruption to draw publicity. Finally, it was critical to build not just an effective union, but a healthy union, one where members' leadership and participation were at the center of as many of our activities as humanly possible.

Year after year, contract battle after battle, we honed our internal union-building and external relationship-building strategies. We remained a movement while we also were becoming a formal organization, an institution per se. But there were tensions between institution and movement building, expectations and pressures from the UAW, Cornell, and our own members. The UAW and Cornell looked for us to settle down and mature. To the UAW, reeling from layoffs and concessions in heavy industry, the university seemed an oasis, albeit a low-wage oasis, of economic stability. The UAW was fighting on many other fronts against a tide of foreign car imports and deindustrialization. Cornell just wanted us to go away, to become at most a quiet, negligible entity that rarely infringed on management's superior decision making.

Our members also wanted stability. Many were uncomfortable being recruited into activist, often acrimonious fights every few months. But what the members wanted far more than stability and traditional respectability was to actually *be* respected. This compelled us to aggressively challenge oppressive paternalistic attitudes and our broadly experienced poverty. In order to become a fighting union, we constantly had to calibrate and find ways to resist pressures to conform to a more mature, docile, and ultimately ineffective model of trade unionism.

The story of our union after the organizing drive and first contract battles and strikes is a story of growing our strategic muscle, of figuring out how to put power behind our truth. We knew we had the facts: Cornell paid poverty-level wages. Cornell paid less than peer institutions. We knew we had the moral and emotional high ground. What we hadn't put together was what our theory of change, our path to sufficient power to achieve fair outcomes, actually was. Over several years and multiple contract campaigns we experimented, and we evolved and became powerful enough to make substantial gains and to build an organization members owned, the campus and local community supported, and Cornell and other employers feared.

**FIGURE 14.** Fellow West Campus custodian Leo LaMontain contributed many cartoons and graphics for our fights. This large, multicolor poster was plastered at every bus depot and time clock in over two hundred buildings to launch our 1985 contract campaign. The art projects our growing sense of confidence and swagger. (Photo of Local 2300 poster)

## Discussion Questions

- Was it reasonable for Local 2300 to expect the UAW to provide more strategic assistance given the growing crisis in traditional industries like auto and aerospace where most UAW members worked?
- What lessons from the first strike seem most important to developing better strategies?
- What would have happened if the local's leaders had succumbed to pressures from Cornell, the UAW, and even some members to settle down and work within traditional labor-management boundaries?
- Several levers of power are identified that were important to consider in developing a strategy to take on Cornell—students, trustees, community, embarrassing publicity—that did not necessarily involve striking. Imagine you are a leader at a private enterprise that is not a university. How might the levers of power be the same or different?

9

# "FLOAT LIKE A BUTTERFLY, STING LIKE A BEE"

As the union became increasingly creative and disruptive, we had to understand and balance the attitudes of several key stakeholders. Our leaders and members first and foremost needed to understand and be willing to engage in these activities. Allies, such as students, faculty, and community leaders, had their own ideas of what was an appropriate action, target, or even timing for a creative confrontation. Some actions only required small numbers of our activist core, but that didn't mean we could operate outside the bounds of broad membership consensus and approval. If we got too far ahead of our members, the leaders would become isolated and the union weak. A wise organizer once said, "You can't have revolution in spite of the people." Lucky for us, most members were fully supportive, and many were willing to stick their own necks out when asked. Management invested recurring energy in attempts to persuade us to be less aggressive or ready to involve our members in various meetings and actions. One especially sensitive area was how we chose to respect or disrupt the sacred rituals of higher education.

We were all familiar with the campus calendar. There were big, defining moments every year. Freshman arrival, graduation, board of trustee meetings, alum reunions. Over time we became more adept at synchronizing our activities with such peak-exposure, reputation-defining moments, using these events in creative ways to muddy Cornell's reputation, highlight our struggles and needs, activate other stakeholders, and leverage the power imbalance between us and them. Our theme was very consistent: the brazen gap between the wealth and grandeur of the university and the impoverished daily lives of those who kept it running.

We did have to be careful about the tone and disruptiveness of our actions. It wasn't an easy line to walk. We wanted to make the university brass uncomfortable and get broader publicity for our cause, but we didn't want to alienate our student and faculty allies. We were particularly positive and polite with graduation activities. We understood it was a sacred day of accomplishment and recognition for students and families. We would leaflet, congratulating the students, thanking them for their support, and asking them to remember us as they became alums. In one campaign, we specifically worked with graduating seniors to focus their parting senior gift to supporting the workers who kept their dorms clean and good food flowing in a dozen dining halls.

The university hated what they referred to as our never-ending harassment. But for us, that was pretty much the point. It was another way of getting their attention and being visible. They wanted to hide the poverty, inequality, and everyday abuse: sweep it under the rug or confine it to the negotiating room. We knew that figuring out how to get it out in the open and make people more conscious of it was a step toward pushing it up a notch or two on the crowded university agenda. Public exposure was key to building power.

The HR honchos would tell us over and over, "This is backfiring; you are making it harder for us to nudge Day Hall to do a little more." We pointed out that we *had* brought these issues through the formal channels of collective bargaining and only made small steps forward. We reminded them that we had presented solid evidence of poverty, and equally persuasive evidence that Cornell paid considerably less than peer institutions.

One particularly overbearing and thankfully short-lived HR boss, Marge Sweircz Clark, helped me confirm that our tactics were really working, that we were getting under management's skin, like a mosquito they realized they couldn't just swat away. Whereas our main labor relations contact, Pete Tufford, never went out of his way to make tensions worse, and often tried in vain to get recalcitrant but highly autonomous departments to be a little bit more sensitive to their staff, Marge seemed to relish defending the most inequitable situations. Somehow her being younger and a woman had given me false hopes about her openness to recognizing the harm being caused. She seemed like a true believer in absolutely every management prerogative, and her disdain for having to even discuss our allegations of mistreatment was palpable to workers and stewards, and it really grated on me. Grievance hearings became increasingly acrimonious. I had to remind her that the grievance meetings were where we examined whether management had violated our contract, our rights. Marge would try to turn the session into another round of punishment for the aggrieved worker. Maybe this was her idea of counter-harassment?

I remember her once lecturing me in front of a few stewards, saying I was just a troublemaker and that I was harming the workers' cause that I supposedly cared so much about. "Al, *you* may enjoy it, but *your members* don't want all this fighting, you know." Honestly, I was a little thrown. I was aware that I had the privilege of other options, that while I was living on poverty wages, I could leave and use my degree to make more money. I was also aware that some members doubted our strategies, were tired of fighting, and some were just sick and tired of being sick and tired.

All those thoughts zipped through my head in a five-second pause. Then I remembered what the real, day-to-day dynamic was like between union leadership and members. The vast majority of our members were disgusted with their plight. The vast majority had walked out on multiple strikes.

I came back at HR Marge: "Let me tell you what I hear every day, because really knowing what our members think, that's my job. I hear every day that we aren't winning enough, much less what we deserve, that we need to find ways to fight harder and better because this is about our lives and our family's well-being." I said, "When you talk to me, you are getting the sanitized version of what I hear every day. So, from now on, instead of meeting with me and a couple stewards, let's have a meeting with *all* the members of the department affected. You can hear the raw feelings and then judge for yourself. We represent those feelings. Our members want us to fight harder, not give in more. And by the way, our approach gets tested regularly, because our members elect us."

Marge mocked our tactics. "You think making fun of what the trustees eat is going to win over anybody? You think shouting at people on a picket line helps your so-called cause?"

I said, "You know, each side, management and labor, has a certain amount of power. We wish that logic and empathy were all it took to get our members livable wages. That hasn't worked well enough so far. In fact, you've refused letting a neutral fact-finder make so much as a recommendation. But don't think *you* don't exercise power. You, management, get to exercise power by simply saying no. You said no to our demands, and you said no to a neutral review, so you exercise power by saying no, and then we fail, we don't get what we need. We don't get what we know is fair and right by simply saying yes. So when you say no to us, our only choice is to find ways to persuade and push you to reconsider. Sometimes that means asking other folks, like students and faculty, or the mayor, to amplify our message. And because clearly you personally don't have the authority to move the dollars needed to bring us out of poverty, sometimes we go to more powerful people. You exercise power with a word. Our only choice is to exercise power with our actions, power behind truth."

"How's that working for you, Al?" she smugly concluded.

## Getting More Than We Bargained For

At the bargaining table itself we made many changes in how we involved members and viewed the bargaining sessions. Months before bargaining began, we commenced a rigorous system of surveying the members, asking them what they wanted to see changed. But we pushed for more than a laundry list, asking members to walk a mile in the bargaining team's shoes by clearly prioritizing their issues. We told stewards, "If you can't get a member to take five minutes to fill out a survey, telling us what they want, that member is not going to fight with us." The survey is the first and easiest test. We pushed it till we had at least 90 percent in hand. We then had open-clock meetings and ultimately membership meetings to discuss results and dig in more deeply on the issues with as many members as possible. Our membership then voted on the proposed priorities. Members had a lot on their minds. In one contract survey, sixty issues made it into the collective listing of "top three priorities." Wages always came out on top, but issues of short staffing, health and safety, pensions, and health insurance were regularly in the top ten.

In the first bargaining in 1981, we had a seven-member bargaining committee representing over one thousand workers. We relied heavily on our UAW rep. Initially she, then he, did all the talking during bargaining. This singular professional spokesman role continued, even when some of us got the courage to speak up a bit. We were too afraid we would say something wrong. Even having a degree in labor relations left me feeling underequipped and intimidated to bargain with Cornell's professional negotiators that first time around.

But we were awakening enough to challenge this traditional top-down thinking. Our confidence and willingness to take risks in the name of building power were growing. In subsequent bargaining we made a number of changes based on the belief that the formal bargaining process should be seen as an organizing and leadership development opportunity, not some isolated world where the experts resolved issues.

First, we expanded to a ten-person core bargaining team. Second, I made sure that each member of the bargaining committee spoke, and that happened from the very first session. It was a good way to get the jitters out. Each team member made a short opening statement. They introduced themselves, talked about their pride in their work, their families, and specifically what they had to go without because of the low wages. In addition to their speaking about an issue of particular importance to the workers in departments they represented, I had each bargaining committee member also address a broader issue. We wanted to send a message, that while we all had issues of specific concern, we were more than a collection of parochial self-interests. We were united, one for all, all for all.

We also developed strict, democratic rules about side conversations with management. Employers almost always prefer to avoid the members. Our expectations are too high, and our methods too crude for the elite corporate negotiators. They often tried to pull our UAW reps, whether Tom Natchuras or John Geer, into what management saw as more rational and professional sidebar conversations. As it became clearer over the years that they had to deal with me as chief negotiator and local president, they started trying to pull me aside at critical moments. There were times when we could gain some valuable insight into management's thinking in an off-the-record sidebar, but members could grow suspicious, not exactly sure what was happening, fearing "a deal" would be "cut," or their interests sold out. The key was to create full transparency and accountability. Our policies were clear and endorsed unanimously by the team. I took a second rank-and-file leader into any sidebar. And we never agreed to *anything* in sidebar. Whatever management said was brought back immediately to the group verbatim. We were not interested in shrinking participation; we were determined to expand it.

We constructed a series of bargaining sub-councils so that our eight largest departments had mini-bargaining over issues specific to their work. These issues were both nitty-gritty and wide ranging—health and safety, proper uniforms and safety shoes, shift differential, and even scheduling. Often these issues, while small, were the thorns in those workers' sides, the day-to-day annoyances that needed to be heard. Many of these issues would have been lost at the main table, or most likely never addressed. This allowed stewards and assorted activists to really confront their own bosses about their interests in a formal way. One of the top local leaders would always sit in and assist. It was a ton of work, but we got some issues solved, and grew dozens of more leaders in the process.

Our dining services members were the source of my favorite bargaining sub-council experience. They had a specific issue regarding health and safety. They worked on greasy floors all day long, and their shoes would quickly become damaged and dangerously slippery. Some of them would also carry thirty- to fifty-pound tubs of food or milk dispensers, and the potential to drop something on your foot or to slip and wrench a back was always a risk. Many workers had slipped and fallen, and several had broken toes from dropping heavy objects. We had demanded nonslip safety shoes in previous bargaining, but that got nowhere. There were some 250 dining services workers, and appropriate footwear cost between sixty to ninety dollars. Cornell said that safety footwear was unnecessary and too costly to boot. That pun became a standing joke, often followed with "Let's boot them you know where."

One of the dining workers kept mentioning how much her husband hated her work shoes because the greasy coating made them stink after a while. The grease also made the shoes wear out quickly, so workers were always buying new sneakers to wear at work. I remember several other dining workers commenting on the odors, and at one meeting one said that we ought to make dining management stick their noses right up to one of the old pairs.

Lightbulb! How could we make the problem that real? For the next two months leading up to sub-council bargaining, all our dining members saved their old, beat-up, stinky work shoes. When it came time, they brought them to our office, and we collected about a hundred pairs in big garbage bags. We were all relieved when bargaining came and we could haul them out of our office up to the pristine Cornell conference room. There was a big bargaining table, maybe six feet wide. With the help of twenty dining workers we unloaded the shoes right onto the table. They smelled like deep-fried skunk, and the wear and tear was readily discernible. Cornell's argument that there was no need was blown away. Management was gagging, and immediately developed an understanding beyond what our words alone could have conveyed.

We won on that issue that year. Henceforth, the university would provide a stipend of up to eighty dollars a year for dining workers to obtain a pair of no-slip safety shoes. Every dining worker owned that little victory, and every union member on campus knew how we did it.

Finally, we created "open negotiations," so that any member could attend and sit in with us at a bargaining session. The only requirements were that we needed to know in advance, and we needed to prep them. They would only speak if it was part of a planned strategy. We made efforts to organize certain sessions on particular topics so that the workers most interested, say in health and safety, or night-shift differential, or pension, could witness or participate in the struggle.

Lots of unions and union reps have good reasons not to open up the bargaining process to members in this way. What if we show division? What if someone says something not consistent with our position? Despite the risks, our leadership was fundamentally united around the benefit of this controlled open-bargaining policy. I always felt that if someone misspoke, I could tactfully intervene and clarify or help clean it up a bit. The result was that instead of seven worker leaders seeing firsthand what management was saying, we had over one hundred members cycle through these opportunities. I was our chief spokesperson but was more like an orchestra conductor making sure bargaining itself developed a much wider cadre of leadership and was not primarily some legalistic debate.

Workers who attended became in effect mini-organizers for the union. Initially they were perhaps unsure if local leaders were exaggerating management's bad behavior. After sitting in they would go back to their shops and tell coworkers that management really was trying to keep workers down and the union really was fighting the good fight. In truth, on the days we had the bigger "crowds" we would often ask management questions that forced them to defend their most obnoxious positions. Emily would look at the newbies shaking their heads and say "See, I told you they don't want to give us anything. Aren't they unreal?"

Management hated this and would complain and lecture me about how unprofessional this was and how it was making it impossible to get to a contract. By then I had learned that the best way to comprehend these complaints was to interpret them as management admitting to us this was getting to them and that we were on the right track. I would remind them that the barrier to progress was easily and best removed by getting to a fair offer. We were clear what would make us settle, and they were nowhere close.

I didn't worry much about disrupting the bargaining process because by then I had learned that most bargaining is a waste of time. Ninety percent of progress is made in the final days when priorities are forced forward and the two sides have tested each other's ability to generate or tolerate pressure. Months of tedious bargaining also bottled up some of our best leaders. Instead of organizing and keeping members informed, we would be shut away with management, twiddling our thumbs with no contract in sight. Our leaders needed to remember that they were organizers and not lawyers, and so we all took turns running to time-clock meetings with members or hitting break times.

We also learned the importance of decisions about where to have bargaining sessions. This itself is a subject for bargaining. Neither side can dictate location, dates, or times to the other. Management usually wanted to meet off campus, or at the remote edges of its massive university city. Not having distractions, they said, was important. The UAW officials in our first negotiations went along with this. They were used to "mature" labor relations and couldn't imagine bargaining in the conference room of an auto factory. By the time we had developed our own strategies, we wanted bargaining smack-dab in the middle of campus. We wanted members to have easy access, and we wanted to make it easy for our bargaining team to get into our workplaces when needed. If management would agree to bargain at the fifty-yard line in Schoellkopf, the Big Red football stadium, we would have gladly met them there.

Transparency and inclusion were what our members deserved and were key to building our power. But we went further. We invited our allies, too. At certain bargaining sessions we would include students, grad students, other campus workers, faculty, community leaders, even elected officials from the city and county. They would form a second or third "ring" behind us at the bargaining table. They too knew not to speak unless planned. Cornell hated this even more than having our members present, but the labor law allows each side to select its bargaining team, and the message to our members and to management was that the whole campus and town community was part of our team. These stakeholding members of the "Cornell community" supported us, and we wanted them there. Our whole little world was watching.

## Lifestyles of the Rich and Stingy

Over the years and a few different campaigns, mismatched in power, we continuously sought to find new ways to dramatize and publicize our issues, demonstrate our breadth of support, and engage our members in some strategic mischief. One of our best moments was our "Lifestyles of the Rich and Stingy Tour." This was a parody of the very popular mid-'80s TV show *Lifestyles of the Rich and Famous.* The show's host, Robin Leach, would take poor average slobs like us on tours of the luxury homes of the uber-wealthy, corporate moguls or TV or movie stars.

We decided to organize our own special lifestyles tour in the midst of one of our livable-wage fights. Armed with the salaries and home addresses of the top Cornell administrators, we organized about fifty of our members, rented a Cornell bus, and recruited one of our proud members to drive it. We needed the media to come along, giving up a sunny Saturday morning. For years our fight had been one of the most widely covered local news stories. We had built a lot of trust and even sympathy from local reporters, print and radio, and the one local TV station. Our tactics were blunt, creative, at times inflammatory, and we always tried to frame our issues broadly to hit a resonant chord with the public. When we told the media we needed them to get in their cars, meet us at our union headquarters, and follow us for a great story on a Saturday, they all came, no questions asked. We did not give our well-to-do "targets" any advance warning, and the media trusted that when we said this would be newsworthy, we weren't going to let them down.

We loaded the bus after prepping members in the office. We were going to be polite, but we were looking for an opportunity to meet with, inform, and have a dialogue with the top decision makers at Cornell. Oh, yes, and to highlight the social chasm existing between them and us. At a minimum, if they wouldn't talk, we would present them with a few meaningful artifacts of our members' lives, highlighting the poverty we experienced as a result of low wages. Taking the lead in our delegation were full-time workers who brought blown-up, 11-by-17-inch copies of their food stamps, and two workers who brought bricks of surplus federal cheese that they received. Some members were nervous. What if we get arrested? What if we get shot at? I recall custodian and Local 2300 zone rep Cindy Doolittle, one of our most reliable but quieter leaders, being one of the most anxious. One evening when we were preparing for this action, we ended by holding hands and singing a verse from the famous civil rights song "Keep Your Eyes on the Prize"—not the first time we had sung at our meetings. One verse went, "When they throw your leaders in jail / don't get discouraged if you can't raise bail / keep your eyes on the prize, hold on." Cindy looked at me and just shook her head. But she was there Saturday, early.

Our plan was to follow the law and remain dignified, and with every reporter in town watching we doubted there would be any major hassles.

All four of the administrators we planned to pop in on that Saturday morning—President Rhodes, the provost, and two senior VPs—lived in the same beautiful upscale neighborhood, Cayuga Heights. Cayuga Heights is adjacent to the university, woodsy, with winding streets, great green lawns, and mostly massive, palatial houses. Its residents had certainly never seen fifty slightly ragged service and maintenance workers descend on their world before. In fact, most of them had never seen a bus in the neighborhood.

Our happy but anxious caravan rolled up the hill from our downtown office into Cayuga Heights. What I had not known was that many of these workers, folks whose families had lived in the area for a century, had never been in this secluded neighborhood. Comments on the bus ride ranged from, "Look at that one! They've got three garages bigger than my trailer!" to "How many people *live* in that place?" Folks were getting more nervous the closer we got to our action, but they were also getting more indignant.

At the first house on our list, a delegation of five of us, food stamps and surplus cheese in hand, walked up to the door. The media scrambled behind us, and the rest of our members took over the sidewalk and part of the lawn. Nobody home. Our well-prepped members turned to the media and made a statement. VP so and so makes so much a year and lives in a house valued at such and such. "I've worked at Cornell for eighteen years, and I make $14,000 a year and live in a twenty-year-old trailer. This is a copy of one of my food stamps." Another member made a similar statement and left surplus cheese. We said we don't expect to make what the VP makes, or ever live like this, but we do expect to make enough to feed our families and not have to rely on public assistance.

We moved on, another nobody home, another statement. At the third home we could see older kids peering out the window. The VP came to the door, said something like, "Is this really necessary?" We said yes it was, made our statements, and asked if we could talk. He very nervously said no, and with the cameras rolling ducked back in.

Finally, at our last house we hit pay dirt. The vice president for campus affairs, William Gurowitz, perhaps alerted by his colleague we had just left, came out, absorbed the scene, and on a beautiful sunny morning asked us all if we would like to just sit together on the lawn and talk. Our members shuffled up onto the lawn and formed a big, crowded circle around him and our small delegation. He took the food stamp image, asking the member politely if "this was really yours?" And the member responded, "Yes, I've cooked for thousands of your students for over a decade, and I can't afford to feed *my* family on what you pay me."

The VP—a Cornell grad and chemistry professor—was smooth but not slimy. He listened and asked questions. When he picked up on how disappointed we were with the Cornell administration, he said, "I hope we can feel that the students are all of ours. It's important to keep our service to them in mind." He expressed appreciation for the longevity and hard work of the staff, and he thanked folks for spending a Saturday reaching out.

Then the cops showed up. We had built excellent relations with the also recently unionized campus security guys, but these guys coming up the drive were not them. They were Cayuga Heights officers, sworn to protect the rich and stingy. I could see our members nervously fidgeting, worried that Gurowitz had just played us, and now we were in big trouble. But the VP immediately said, "We are fine, officers. This is my home, and we're just here having a friendly conversation. Thanks for checking." The cops shook their heads and left, and alarmed neighbors went back inside their homes, peering nervously from large windows.

As we continued speaking with Gurowitz, more members began to tell their stories. Most of these folks had never had an opportunity to speak directly with a major boss like this. The bizarreness of the setting, the tensions, and even the media presence seemed to fade a bit. We stayed for an hour. He thanked us, shook each person's hand, and said he would definitely follow up.

Our debrief on the bus ride continued back in the union office. Some folks were a bit charmed and disarmed by the friendly VP, while others said it was all talk and BS. For those members, that day was another step in their development as worker leaders. Five years before, it took a ton of courage just to wear a union button. On this Saturday, five years later, risking being labeled rude or radical, or maybe even being arrested, they brought truth to the front door of where power lived.

The media led with the story and got it right. The food stamps, the surplus cheese, the contrast with Cayuga Heights, all came through. The coverage was so good we simply reproduced it with some added quotes from members and leafleted the campus on Monday.

## Reorienting Orientation

One of our most creative strategies was during a brief livable-wage strike at the beginning of one fall semester. Each year the freshmen arrive en masse, parents in tow, and loaded with trunks full of clothes, music systems, blankets, artwork, you name it. It looked like the opening for *The Beverly Hillbillies*, only it was backward. The Beverly Hillbillies overloaded their ramshackle model T truck with all their poor country belongings and drove into, well . . . Beverly Hills. Freshman arrivals involved mostly wealthy parents driving big fancy cars, exquisite SUVs and high-end minivans, each worth more than double our annual salary, into our hillbilly, Appalachian hills.

This ritual of emptying the nest was stressful for all involved. Kids were eager to have their freedom but also a little terrified. Parents were a combination of all too ready to rid themselves of their all too surly eighteen-year-olds, but also sad and fearful. Unfortunately for them, amid this complex, high-emotion brew, they were arriving during a living-wage "warning" strike. While we felt bad for these nervous families, we reminded ourselves that a thousand service and maintenance workers also had families. And, knowing you never get a second chance to make a first impression, we wanted to use the opportunity to remind Cornell that the best and easiest way to stop our campaigning and "harassment" was just to pay us what every other Ivy League university paid its staff, to pay us a living wage.

Cornell deployed a small army of orientation counselors, or OCs—juniors and seniors who would greet the incoming freshman and generally be all over campus helping them move in, find their way, and acclimate. We had our own powerful army of loyal student activists, ready to rally, protest, or write letters to the editor, and some were up for more radical mischief.

Ten of our most fun-loving and well-informed student supporters infiltrated the orientation counselor program. They learned the OC plan, and they were given the official, bright green OC shirts. As dawn broke over the campus that Friday morning, our OC guerrillas stationed themselves about a quarter mile ahead of the "real" OCs on every major entrance to campus. With beaming faces and big smiles, they welcomed the parents and students and told them that because the campus was on strike, they needed to head to B Lot, a massive parking lot at one end of the campus. In this way, hundreds of parents were diverted from the dorms they were heading for and were funneled instead to B Lot.

Waiting for them in B Lot were more students, a few of our local union leaders, and several key faculty supporters who took the lead. Nothing impresses the parents and freshmen like meeting the faculty. They just expected that to happen in a classroom, not an eight-hundred-space parking lot. Our union-friendly profs then conducted their own orientation, explaining the strike. They pointed out to the anxious families that this strike was about living wages. Since the parents were paying a huge amount of money to send their kids to Cornell, and the university had over a billion dollars in its endowment, was a living wage really too much to ask for those who tenderly care for little August and Kyla for the next four years?

What the professor asked the parents to do, right then and there, was to call Day Hall and let them know they were *not* happy, and that they supported ending the strike by giving the workers a living wage. Were we holding the parents hostage? Well, maybe for a few minutes. Did we tell them they could still move into their dorms? Yes, we did. But first we needed them to make that phone call.

How did the parents and kids react? Most were worried about their big move-in day being ruined but directed their frustration at Cornell. Most made the calls, leaving messages that sounded appropriately irritated with the university. A few argued with us, saying, "If the workers make more, won't that just increase the tuition?" The faculty were great, and none of the families wanted to get on the wrong side of their kid's possible professors. We also had water and fruit for them and gave them plenty of good information about where to get lunch, and how the campus worked. And at the end we did direct them right back to where they were supposed to go in the first place, now "truly oriented."

Was this really a strike? Well, maybe it didn't smell or walk like a strike, but by this time in our strategic development we had learned we couldn't match up against Cornell in a traditional fight. We could not effectively picket forty entrances to the campus 24/7. Nor could we strike indefinitely, costing our members more than they could afford. We needed to be more like the American revolutionary army, or maybe the Vietcong. Creative, quick hits, keeping our adversary off balance, engaging more stakeholders, and letting the Cornell administration know we would never stop.

## Striking for Impact

Building a fighting and effective union always starts with the members. What is their level of commitment to the fight? What risks will they take? What sacrifices are too much? What kinds of engagement have the most strategic impact on the employer? And what builds the members' unity, trust, and ownership of the union for the long haul?

We learned to challenge a number of traditions about how, when, and where to engage members in strike activities. Unions typically seek to prevent operations by withdrawing labor, picketing, and "shutting down" all entrances to the workplace. But trying to do this to an employer the size of a small city meant having just a few pickets at forty mostly isolated locations around the campus. The handful of pickets at each site would become bored and demoralized after a day or two, which outweighed any benefit from being able to turn away a few deliveries.

We targeted the dozen main entrances to campus and deployed ten to twenty strikers, making sure we had feisty activists there to keep chants going, cars honking, and members moving, if not dancing. This way, we let several thousand clerical, technical, and faculty coworkers know that we were loudly and proudly standing up for a better life. Our main focus was the two large dining halls that remained open. We would set up two shifts a day with between 150 and 200 workers, plus at any given time at least that many students, faculty, and community friends. While technically students could weave their way into the building, they had to navigate hundreds of chanting, singing, rallying, sign-wielding members of the campus community.

Our signs became a wonderful source of creativity. "We Can't EAT Ivy" wrote one low-wage animal attendant. "An Ivy League School with Bush-League Wages," came from Gordy the mechanic. He had made a huge sign that included the unfavorable wage comparison with New York's SUNY system as well as Princeton for good measure.

These massive picket line rallies had many advantages. We could communicate with our entire membership continuously throughout the day, beating down rumors ("Everybody from x time clock is crossing the line and scabbing! Not true!") and providing inspiring updates ("We've shut down campus mail delivery!"). It also meant we could have a nonstop array of member leaders speak and gain important leadership skills, plus add to the mix our wide range of allies, student leaders, faculty, and community sympathizers to pledge support and buoy spirits. It also gave the media exciting events to cover where our message was reasonably consistent.

During one strike rally at Willard Straight, the largest dining hall, we ended up notching up the militancy and pressure. A group of union members and student activists there suggested, Why don't we march through Day Hall, the administration building and seat of authority and power for the whole campus? I sent a couple of scouts to case the building. Could we get in? Where could we go? We had rallied in front of Day Hall, and even inside the Day Hall courtyard before. What would happen if we brought our demands to the third floor where the university president and top VPs worked? Would campus security, friendly to our cause, draw the line at protecting the offices of the top brass?

I decided to give it a try. We quickly and quietly organized about 50 of our 250 rally-goers to follow me into Day Hall. To our surprise there was only a single security guard, and he seemed somewhere between amused and overwhelmed as we swarmed into the building. Too late to stop us, he yelled, "Hey, where are you going?" I responded, "We have a meeting."

Chanting "What do we want? A contract! When do we want it? Now!" we marched up three flights of stairs. But the doors had been quickly locked. My claustrophobia started to kick in as we just kept climbing stairs, all jammed in with seemingly no exit. We were now somewhere in an obscure stairwell above the top floor, and there was an even narrower set of unlit stairs ahead leading to a small, shabby metal door. The doorknob didn't turn, so, adrenaline rushing, I just gave the very little door a very big kick, and it burst open wide.

Out we paraded onto the roof of the university president's building. It was a glorious summer day. Fifty of us came out of that dark stairwell into the sunshine and realized that if we moved to one corner of the roof, we were directly facing the rally still going strong at Willard Straight. Word had gotten out to our brothers and sisters that we were bringing the fight to the big bosses at Day Hall, the place where every big decision that affected our lives and our community gets made. When they saw us up on the roof, the rally-goers went nuts. People were cheering and chanting back and forth. We had overrun the Winter Palace.

At that moment, though we knew we had a long way still to go to win respect and dignity, janitors and cooks and bus drivers felt like a liberating union army that had seized control of the university from top to bottom.

Members who went through those experiences tell those stories to their grandchildren. This was very different from the first strike, when we felt wildly courageous to walk out but where our strike tactics seemed to limit and weaken us.

Strikes remained a critical element in our strategy, campaign after campaign. They connected all our strategies in one dramatic period of intense conflict. Worker pressure, campus disruption, campus and local community support, political heat, substantial embarrassing publicity—all these came alongside a formal, legal opportunity to bargain for a resolution of our cause. But strikes meant our members were sacrificing. We could get UAW strike fund benefits, but only if we stayed out eight days or longer. Then we could get $100 a week, retroactive to the first day out, but there was no prorated, daily strike benefit until you were out a full week.

Clearly, our members were willing to walk out. Once we hit more than a few days, however, without pay, it wasn't hard to tell who was under more pressure, us or management. The few hundred scabs, combined with every supervisor being required to work double duty, lessened the impact of our absence. Some of our work's absence caused immediate disruption and impact. For example, hundreds of research animals and thousands of students needed to be fed every day. But the grass could get shaggy and the dorms could get dusty without bringing Big Red

**FIGURE 15.** Our strikes and job actions evolved to become rowdy mass events with dozens and often hundreds of workers together with almost as many campus and community supporters. (Local 2300 newsletter)

**FIGURE 16.** Local 2300 president Al Davidoff revs up the crowd. Radio, local television, and print media followed our fights closely. As our arguments sharpened and our tactics became more creative, the media knew they would get a powerful story. (Local 2300 newsletter)

to its knees. Custodians, our largest group, could inconvenience the university by striking but not impose a crisis situation.

There were various ways we and our supporters tried to turbocharge our strikes. We walked out during critical campus moments, and we massed ourselves in ways that drew maximum attention and maintained high morale. But there was never any incident of strikers behaving violently toward scabs or bosses. In fact, the only serious injury that ever happened during one of our short strikes was when a scab panicked and drove into a group of slow-walking pickets, clipping one of them and sending her to the hospital. While we didn't engage in violence, we did engage in creative mischief during strikes. There were many ways and times workers and supporters took matters into their own hands and tried to add to the disruption. The union knew about, and even tacitly sanctioned, some of these acts, but many stories will probably never surface.

Occasionally, a few of our more industrious and destructive strikers created heavy metal "staple jacks." These sharp, pronged, bent staples could be strewn across driveways in and out of places like the Bus Garage or General Stores, where a lot of campus truck or bus traffic took place. This led to a few flattened tires, but mostly these areas would be swept free of such debris before any damage could be done. And the extent of this form of mischief was also limited because we always had to be careful that we didn't run over our own strikers' staples.

Superglue and skunk oil were a bit further down the hierarchy of sabotage, but probably more effective. I am told that the lock on every custodial closet on campus was superglued shut. One of the leading student activists got caught doing this. She had been seen with me on several occasions and was a major activist ringleader. She and I had also been dating, and that wasn't a secret. When they arrested her, I had to make the awkward decision to distance the union from any destruction of property. Our public stance was that the university had caused this strike by refusing to pay livable wages, and that we had tremendous student and faculty support. Our statement was that the union didn't support destruction of property but that the real issue was the destruction of workers' and families' lives, and that people would fight hard to support us.

This was another "c'mon, Al" moment with Pete Tufford, who suspected she and I were involved. Pete was pissed, saying, "You know how much money we are wasting on locksmiths?" It was always reassuring when management complained about our impact, because mostly their message was "Strike, what strike? We're doing fine." They would undercount how many of our members were out and spread rumors of strike defections. Thankfully, the university didn't want to make a martyr out of my friend, so she ended up with community service and probation. We decided to keep our distance during the strike because she was neither repentant nor her mischief slowed by the university's warnings.

Skunk oil, used by hunters, was also a highly effective tool. It reminded me of the story of organizer Saul Alinsky, who once planned to feed beans to hundreds of supporters and invade the Rochester Philharmonic for an anticorporate "fart-in." Skunk oil was much easier and smelled much worse, I suspect. A single drop in a dorm lounge or a meeting room made the space smell painfully unpleasant. And who was going to thoroughly clean those rooms? Custodians! Oh, but we were on strike. . . .

My favorite act of sabotage during one of our strikes involved an elaborate hijacking of some strange creatures from one of the labs our members maintained. Our lab assistants were never one of our stronger groups of members. They tended to work in isolation from other staff and rarely got involved in the union. But that didn't mean we didn't have a few devoted members there, and their pay was as bad as the janitors'. One of those lab assistants worked with a set of insects, including giant cockroaches. Lord knows what the Cornell scientists fed these creepy beasts or what larger research purpose they served. But a few of them served our purposes in a dramatic way and made the ultimate sacrifice during one strike.

We knew our lab assistant had made off with a small box full of the creatures. She provided them to the union with a mischievous, "I'm sure you can have some fun with these." She was right. We had effectively shut down almost all dining units, but the biggest one, Willard Straight, was being run by scabs and bosses all too effectively. During the lunch rush one courageous student activist let the cockroaches loose on the massive fifteen-foot-long salad bar.

What a lucky coincidence for the health of the student body that our friends in the county health department had been alerted to an extremely troubling issue at Willard Straight Dining. In perfect synchrony, the health department descended just as the steroidal, massive cockroaches were everywhere and the students, some of them our fun-loving supporters, were screaming for their lives.

The health department shut down the dining hall, and it took management two days to get it cleaned up, past inspection, and reopened. Meanwhile students had started a huge petition demanding they get reimbursed for their meal plans. This added up to real money and put some added pressure on Cornell.

One final strike strategy that evolved for us over several years was the idea of not only short, but also targeted, strikes. There were some legal issues about running a "partial" strike, but we never ran into a problem on that front.

An honest power analysis of our strikes underscored our strengths and weaknesses. Some parts of campus were more unified, with 90 to 100 percent strikers and few scabs. Some parts of campus, when struck, felt an almost immediate impact, while others were seriously affected only after weeks. We also knew that having decent numbers out created mass actions that were important for pressure, publicity, and morale. Was there a way to align these factors more effectively than an all-out, albeit short-lived, strike? We came up with the idea of a partial, targeted, short strike of dining units. We had about 80 percent support, the impact was three-meals-a-day immediate, and the over two hundred workers who would participate constituted a big enough group to generate campus support and larger publicity. But there was one big problem. Dining services workers would, in effect, be striking for all of us, not just for their own raises and benefits. This strategy would ask dining workers to make a huge sacrifice—no pay and angry bosses—while others reaped the benefit with no loss of pay. We needed a way to share in the sacrifice of striking; we couldn't ask a fraction of the members to bear all the risk and loss.

To address the equality-of-sacrifice issue, we proposed tithing all nonstriking, working members and creating our own strike fund. If, say, two hundred members went out for two days, at a critical moment on campus, and we could get four to five hundred members to each kick in twenty dollars, maybe we could manage to have maximum impact with the least suffering.

There was a lot of debate about whether we could pull this off. There were always some members who argued we all should just strike indefinitely. It was an inspiring image of us gradually bringing the university to its knees, truly "shutting them down." The problem was most of the campus was still unorganized. Techs had lost a vote by more than two to one, and clericals were still trying, but nowhere near a majority. We had powerful numbers of faculty and students supporting us, but classes went on, and having a few dozen profs holding classes off campus to show solidarity hardly mattered to anyone.

Most of all, we had barely won our union vote, with 55 percent. We had painstakingly grown our membership to around 75–80 percent. On strikes we always lost maybe 5–10 percent of our members to begin with. I had a deep fear that after a week or two on strike, if our numbers gradually dwindled, as they had slightly during our eleven-day strike in 1981, we would face an organizational crisis. We could not lose our own members, coerced by the very poverty we were fighting.

Worse, the psychological impact of becoming a scab would set us back for years with every member who made that awful choice. Our image among our many allies would take a hit if our own members were abandoning the fight. Maybe I just never had the guts to roll those dice, but our leadership team was united in finding ways to fight smarter, not just strike longer.

There were members who thought it would be too divisive to have a strike with only a minority going out. They didn't like the idea. Some thought it wouldn't be effective, while others worried about sending the message to some of our shops that they weren't as relevant to our power as dining services members. Some just wanted to go out too and not miss being part of a powerful and righteous confrontation. We made it clear that this wasn't our last step, that it was part of a strategy of escalating pressure. If we needed to all go out, we had done it before and would do it again.

The deciding factor was that the union leaders in the dining halls were behind the idea. They were militant and well organized at most units, and they knew they had an impact. They were proud that they could lead, and knew that many of their coworkers were among our most impoverished members. We also made it clear that everyone would be part of this fight, joining in after work to picket and march and rally.

There was a big final concern, though. Would our nonstriking members kick in the needed money? We organized the action, and in the days leading up to the short strike we were able to get close to 450 members to hand over a twenty to their shop steward. This was before the internet or cell phones. This meant painstaking, building-by-building organizing. Our philosophy, instilled thanks to Barbara Rahke with our original organizing committee, meant that we had a union with hundreds of leaders. No top-down union with one charismatic leader could have pulled this off. There was not a single allegation or indication that one dollar donated didn't go straight to the local strike fund. We added faculty contributions and got up over $15,000.

The striking dining workers were still making a bigger financial sacrifice, but we were able to pass out about fifty dollars to each worker who went out. We also made it clear that twenty dollars was only half of each working member's obligation. The other responsibility was to show up for two hours of picket or rally duty either before or after a shift.

We pulled off a strong strike and demonstrated the sense of family that we had been building as some workers proudly led while others had their sisters' and brothers' backs.

## Discussion Questions

- Local 2300 made a major change in how it involved members in bargaining after the first contract. Management argued the involvement of so many members and "third parties" like students and community leaders was an impediment to progress. What were the risks of open negotiations and creating a "three ring circus" during bargaining? The advantages?
- The union had to constantly calibrate how far to go with various creative tactics and confrontations. What were the pressures on the union regarding these tactics? With members, allies, management? Did the union go too far, or not far enough?

- The union broke from the traditional strike tactics of the first contract fight. What were the benefits of physically massing members?
- While the union was never directly involved in sabotage, it clearly understood that students and some members were doing more than picketing and chanting. Was the union's tacit support for these activities ethical? Strategic?
- During most strikes, all workers in the same union walk out from a given employer. UAW 2300 tried selective strikes, focusing on strong workplaces where there was an immediate impact. What do you think of this unorthodox approach and the effort to equalize sacrifice?
- How should digital media change internal organizing methods? How are e-mail, Zoom, text, and social media accelerators of unity-building communication, and how might they be less effective than in-person, one-on-one, and small-group organizing?

10

# SUSTAINING STRUGGLE

## Building the Union during the Off-Season

Contract negotiations provided our best opportunity to strengthen our union by building activism, solidarity, and leadership. It was the time when what was just, became possible, and inspiring. Our contract, like almost all US contracts, had a no-strike clause during the life of the agreement. This meant we needed to wait until the contract expired to exercise our membership's most militant power, the simple right to refuse to work without a fair deal. But this only happened periodically, typically every two to four years. What about the rest of the time? How could we avoid reverting to a sleepy "business union" model when we were implementing or enforcing the contract, rather than negotiating a new one? We needed to avoid reinforcing passivity or dependence among the members we "served," by handling their day-to-day problems "for" them, as opposed to mobilizing their power and true ownership of the local.

We came to understand that the imperative of including members in as many fights as possible extended far beyond contract bargaining.

There were many opportunities for us to do this. For example, while most grievances were individualized—someone got a written warning for doing a lousy job or for poor attendance—there were always some grievances and situations that did lend themselves to broader and more creative involvement. We tried to apply the lessons learned from our evolving bargaining strategies to the non-bargaining years.

One opportunity to apply these lessons occurred periodically, every year when the university furloughed most of our dining workers without pay. This happened for a month during winter break, and for as long as two and a half months over the summer. These short-term layoffs impoverished some of our lowest-paid members even further, reducing their already meager earnings by 25 to 30 percent each year. While a few workers preferred the time off to farm, watch their kids, or earn more money at a different job, the vast majority were desperate for every paid working hour. We had negotiated a system based on seniority for who had first opportunities to work, as well as the option of taking the layoff. This still left the majority unemployed.

To make matters much worse, in New York as in other states, school employees who had "a guarantee of re-employment" were not eligible for unemployment insurance to tide them over. At first Cornell's expressed attitude was "This isn't our problem; we follow the law. Should we make up work when there isn't any?" So much for the one-big-family attitude we recalled being lectured about during the antiunion campaign.

Over time we learned that Cornell was self-insured for unemployment insurance with New York State. This made the "who wins, who loses" reality all the more stark. It meant that it wasn't some obscure governmental insurance fund that was saving money from a loophole in the unemployment insurance system. For every dollar of family-sustaining unemployment insurance income our food service workers did not receive, Cornell was saving a dollar. We also realized that if Cornell simply failed to issue a formal declaration of each worker's "guarantee of re-employment," our members would probably be eligible for unemployment insurance. Cornell refused to do this. After years of educating and pushing our parent UAW organization to make amending the state unemployment insurance law a priority, we got other campus unions across New York State to join us and submit a bill. Who lobbied against the amendment? All the universities and a few other seasonal employers that benefited from this omission.

We did the usual political things, writing letters to the editors of our three papers, holding a press conference with workers, and leafleting campus. But we got nowhere. One year, as summer approached, the university announced that several major student and alumni programs were not happening because of construction work. After a few years of frustrating attempts to push management or to change the law, our dining workers had had enough. Due to the construction, fewer workers would have opportunities for any hours, and members came to a membership meeting distraught. We asked HR and dining management to meet with us to discuss what could be done. They booked a room assuming there would be four to five managers, a few dining union stewards, and me. We had a different plan for the meeting.

Pete Tufford, a former All American hockey star at Cornell and the HR guy I dealt with on a near-daily basis, had by now gotten to know us a bit, and he smelled a rat. "So, how many folks are you bringing to the meeting, Al?" Pete was a decent-enough guy, and we had about as reasonable a relationship as you could have during these battle years. He didn't chastise or harangue workers and preferred problem solving to conflict. Our biggest problem with Pete was that he had little power to move the university at the highest levels, and there was a long tradition of departments having autonomy, so Pete couldn't do much to force individual departments, like dining or the Bus Garage, to behave better. Nonetheless, we had solved some issues together as the union relationship became a bit more established. I didn't enjoy misleading him, but I also didn't hesitate. I told him that we'd have a "few" dining leaders there.

We organized every dining worker we could, and about sixty very frustrated, about-to-be-laid-off workers jammed the meeting room. A few of us had arrived early and took the side of the table by the door. This meant management sat across from us facing the door, with a table between us. We asked the dining workers to show up ten minutes later. As they trickled in, awkwardly filling the room, first standing behind us, then, as the space jammed, standing behind management, Pete shot me a nasty look, shaking his head in disbelief. He asked me to talk to him outside for one minute. We walked into the hall, and he was upset.

"You set me up. How can we work out problems if I can't trust you?"

"I'm sorry, Pete," I said, "but we've been asking for this change for years. The layoffs are even worse this year, and folks are really upset. We thought it was important for you all to hear that."

"You lied to me, Al," he replied.

"If I told you sixty dining workers were coming, would you have done the meeting? Let's get back in the room. Today, all you have to do is listen. If you cancel the meeting and walk out, that looks even worse for you." I started moving back toward the room. I didn't want our members waiting on this sidebar.

Pete wasn't a fighter. In hockey he was a skillful skater and scorer, not a bruiser. He sat back down, gathered himself, and said, "Well, if we had known so many of you were coming, we'd have gotten a bigger room."

I took over from there and explained that we had had it with the poverty caused by this system. I said our first choice was work, but if there was no work, these dining workers should be eligible for unemployment insurance. "Cornell is basically profiting from a loophole in the state law. Every dollar you keep is a dollar that should be feeding these folks and their families." The room was getting physically hot. It was severely cramped. Workers, coming off shifts in sweaty uniforms and smelling of grease and food, were standing shoulder to shoulder, hovering behind and looming over their bosses. Management could not have gotten out if they wanted to.

Then I asked the members to speak to the impact. The anger boiled over. Worker after worker talked about what their summer was going to be like. Their kids were not able to go to camps. The shame they felt to not be able to pay for their children's uniforms to join a baseball league. One member glared right at the head of Cornell dining and said, "You don't know what that's like, do you?" It was not a rhetorical question, and he asked again in a loud, agitated, and fast-becoming-intimidating tone, "Do you?"

The director of the university's prestigious dining program, dressed in a suit and tie, a guy we had found arrogant and haughty at grievances and the bargaining table, looked down at his hands and said, "No, I don't."

A couple workers cried as they spoke about how the quality of what their family ate declined during the layoffs, and one gigantic, seething short-order cook shouted, "This just isn't right. Some of us have been here decades. How can Cornell care so goddamn little for us?" Folks were nodding, getting more and more furious. There was something between a French Revolution and *Lord of the Flies* mood brewing. It was not a stretch for management to fear for their safety. Pete tried to settle things down, but the moment was not his to control. It was one of the few times I felt I might not be able to manage the dynamic; the musicians had overrun the orchestra conductor. Then I thought, *So what?*

"What are you going to do about this?" I jumped in after forty-five minutes of nonstop emotional testimony.

"Are you asking us to pay you for doing nothing?" asked Pete. This was a rough ploy for our stoic, self-sustaining, high work-ethic members.

"We aren't asking for a handout. Give us work," yelled one dining janitor, and the room, now an organism coiled around management's bodies like a boa constrictor, seethed, *Yes, give us work*. I didn't like this direction, because I thought it got Cornell off the hook too. They should simply pay the unemployment insurance in one form or another. But the members were proud, and sensitive to the argument that they just "wanted a handout."

At some point I could feel the mood change. It had been emotionally exhausting for everyone in the room. Management looked guilt-ridden and terrified, and the workers were feeling spent. I summed it up, "We need a solution, and we will not stop till something better is done. Either find folks work or stop avoiding unemployment insurance." The meeting ended. Workers needed to head home, and as soon as management had enough space to make a beeline for the door, they got out of there.

There was a rawness and a proximity to physical danger during that confrontation that reminded me that our members' suffering was physical. That as militantly as we expressed ourselves, beneath our strong words were a pain and an anger that were what revolutions actually were made of. I know every manager in the room was shaken. The workers that participated shared two feelings with me afterward: pride for "getting in their face," but also despair that nothing would be done, that management "promised nothing."

We kept fighting over the issue, trying to keep the pressure on. A week later workers and students formed a giant walking circle in front of Day Hall. In between each pair of workers was a large paper doll "holding hands" with the workers to its right and left. The doll had the actual name of one of the children of the dining workers who would suffer that summer. We got good media coverage, and we leafleted the campus with the newspaper article.

We didn't win on every issue, even when we were right and fought creatively. In fact, on most issues we either made small, incremental progress or no progress at all. There was a step forward that summer, and I know it only happened because of the intensity of that meeting. Cornell refused to budge on any approach to providing unemployment insurance or supplemental income for the laid-off workers. They did pledge an ambitious approach to find work for those facing layoff in other departments during the summer. It put us in a bind in that we couldn't argue for prioritizing unemployment insurance "charity" over work. We jumped into this new approach, asking our members in other departments to share with us any opportunities they could imagine to provide work.

This was a test of HR making a centralized commitment but needing each department to deliver. When we told them that one department was already in the process of hiring outside temps for the summer, we could see how weak this new commitment was. "Well, they need to have specialized skills," Pete mumbled. And so it went. We struggled to find more work, and the university did make an effort. Some of our more humane department managers jumped in with short-term opportunities, and even dining came up with significantly more work than originally announced. About half the laid-off workers did significantly better than they would have, and the summer jobs program remained a part of things for years to come.

A second example of our mobilizing instead of just grieving in the non-bargaining-contract years was when our largest department, Care of Buildings, made what they thought was a small policy "adjustment." Care of Buildings was the department that managed three hundred custodians and head custodians who cleaned the academic buildings, basically everything except the dorms and dining halls, which were cleaned by UAW custodians, under different departments. Jean Rogers, one of the more decent and caring big bosses, and one of the few with whom I developed a good relationship, ran COB and had done so for many years. For Jean, this had to be handled discreetly, since I was in constant public warfare with the university. Jean would confide her sympathy for our cause and her pleasure at our creative tactics. She herself lived modestly, and often went the extra mile for her staff when they had personal problems. As she got older, she handed a lot of the day-to-day management over to a young Turk, Rob Osborn. To me, he was a classic know-it-all doofus manager, later exemplified by Steve Carell playing Michael in the popular TV series *The Office*. He was super-eager to "modernize" everything and used lots of corporate jargon. Because he knew that Jean and I got along he tried to befriend me too. Jean had heart and soul; Rob was just a control freak waiting for Jean to retire. Jean needed a high-energy, day-to-day manager over this huge team and figured she could rein in his excesses.

One of Rob's "innovations" was an edict he issued forbidding custodians from carrying a cup of coffee or a can of soda on their custodial carts. The carts held most of their supplies, including cleaning fluids and basics like gloves. The custodian and the cart were together all day, almost like a small rolling office. Most custodians had a magazine tucked in the cart, and pretty much everybody had a beverage to sip on during shifts.

One of the shop stewards called the union office and told me that Rob had just announced they all needed to stop having drinks on their carts. "What the hell does that busy-body care about our fucking drinks?" said the steward. I said I'd call and find out. Well, lo and behold, this was not some misunderstanding; in fact Rob claimed this "loose practice" was a major health and safety violation. He was one of those types that always inserted your name in every sentence for emphasis. "Al, we can't have toxic cleaning fluids and drinks all mixed together. It's dangerous, Al, and how do you think it looks to our customers? Very unprofessional." By customers, Rob meant the students, faculty, and clerical workers who used the buildings. Folks who in many cases had worked for decades with our members and were on first-name bases. It was not likely that the custodians' long-term building "family" was offended by a cart coffee cup.

The safety argument seemed equally far-fetched. I told him, "I don't think our members are going to mistakenly put their toilet cleaner into their coffee."

"Just can't have this, Al—unsafe and unprofessional. Staff get breaks, and that's when they should be drinking." Rob was making a stand.

Strange issue. Did our members care? What were our options? The custodians did care, mostly because it had been a practice forever and because it was Rob stripping away a small piece of their routine, a little bit of comfort from them for no apparent reason. They disliked Rob and saw him as a meddling busybody. We called a meeting of all the COB stewards, around a dozen folks, to brainstorm and discuss options.

There was no specific language in our contract that spoke to this issue directly. There was, as in most contracts, a management rights clause that gave Cornell latitude to make day-to-day decisions on how to operate where not required otherwise by our contract. We could file a grievance based on this being a past practice. In labor relations, a past practice is a customary and long-standing way of doing things in a workplace over which an employer typically must negotiate with the union before ending or changing the practice. But Cornell would likely fight us, we thought, and there was a good chance they would take it all the way to the final stage of the grievance process, a neutral and binding arbitration. The right to binding arbitration of grievances was one of the key victories in our first strike. But there were downsides to this approach. First, it could take many months, and during that time there would be no cups on carts. We also might not win. We knew Rob's reasons were nonsense, cooked up by someone with a little too much time and desire to show authority. But maybe the arbitrator would latch onto his safety argument or see this as such a minimal benefit as to not be a true past practice and therefore be within management's right to change.

One of our best stewards said, "Well, a bunch of the members at my clock are just saying they are going to ignore Rob or hide their drink inside the cart." It got me thinking, and the conversation evolved. "If a few people do that and get caught, they might get disciplined for not following the order. What if everybody, every custodian refused to obey?"

Folks got creative fast. One custodian made a great point. The animals in the Cornell barns and labs had ready access to water. Why should we be treated worse? We got Leo LaMontain, our resident activist artist, to do a biting flyer with a smiling horse drinking from a trough. Our tagline was "Every horse in its stable, every rat in its cage can take a drink, but not COB custodians?" We did time-clock meetings and found custodians thoroughly irritated by this. It wasn't the biggest issue, like wages or benefits, but it was a small, completely unnecessary indignity. Some members who hardly ever engaged with the union seemed to wake up around this issue. Many folks also sensed this was just the beginning with Rob and wanted to put him in his place.

One evening, a bunch of COB custodians came down to the office and prepared three hundred white Styrofoam cups, placing a UAW sticker on every one. We got enough cups for every steward to hand out the next morning at six to every custodian. It was mass defiance. Workers who had voted no against having a union, workers who had scabbed during our first strike, took the UAW cup and proudly gave Rob the middle finger that morning.

We held our breath, waiting for management's move. It came not with a bang but with a whimper. No one was disciplined, and no one ever heard another peep about having a drink. I was hanging out with Jean Rogers the next week dealing with some grievance, and I asked her, "What was Rob thinking with that 'no drinks on carts' BS?"

Jean looked at me and said, "He's an asshole, isn't he?" and then she smiled.

We had another issue with Rob that demonstrated how we could get creative in engaging our members around a different kind of grievance, in this case an individual discipline. I got a call from Tufford saying we had a serious incident where a custodian had threatened Rob's life. The guy had a gun on campus; Campus Safety had taken possession of the weapon, and the worker had been suspended without pay, pending a likely firing. Pete made it sound like swift action had averted a disaster. That is, it sounded like that until I spoke to the member. It took a couple of hours to track down his phone number. Meanwhile, I started wondering: If this was as dangerous as Pete said it was, why was there no arrest?

Rick was a rural working-class dude, in his mid-to-late twenties. He had worked at Cornell for about six years without any problems. He was outgoing, a bit of a tough guy, but there had never before been any incidents of him getting angry, insubordinate, or threatening. "This is totally ridiculous,'" he told me when we spoke. "I was joking with folks in the break room about some stupid damn thing Rob hollered at us about at a meeting and said I'd like to put Rob out there with the other bucks during deer season and see if that would quiet him down. Everyone was laughing. I didn't mean anything. Next thing I know they're dragging me off campus and confiscating my hunting rifle off the back of my truck." It turned out that a head custodian who was present, one who liked to suck up to management, had taken it upon herself to report this break-time impropriety to Rob.

Rob was in a lather about it. "Can't have this, Al. It's a safety issue for me, my family, and the whole campus community."

I called my buddy who was the head of the Campus Safety union. "Jim, what's your take on this? Do you guys view this guy as a threat?"

Jim laughed. "We aren't the break-room police, and we aren't the 'poor taste' police. As far as I can tell he made one dumb joke about Rob. But Rob made a big deal out of it, and even though Rick's gun is licensed, and he had it properly locked and unloaded, we decided we better take it. We're returning it to him tomorrow."

We spoke with the other custodians present, all of whom agreed he was just joking around. I interviewed the likely tattletale, who, when pressed, admitted she didn't think Rick "would ever *do* anything." She just didn't like his cursing and talking rudely about our big boss.

We filed a grievance, and during our executive board meeting we discussed it. Emily Apgar, a fellow COB custodian, made the comment that proved the key to our defense. "Everybody jokes about Rob. Nobody likes him, and we all make fun of him. I remember Bess saying she'd like to throw that little weasel off the suspension bridge."

Bingo! There was one of the most counterintuitive and irreverent defenses we had ever mustered. It was break-room banter, traditional, even sacred free speech to trash your worst boss. And apparently lots of COB custodians fantasized out loud about getting rid of Rob! We had had a first-step grievance meeting already where Rob righteously defended the suspension and possible looming termination. I knew Rob was very sensitive to his reputation. He was ambitious, wanted to climb far and fast, and was new enough to not be sure whose rear end he needed to kiss and whom he should avoid offending. I called Jean and said, "Look, tell me honestly, do you think Rick is dangerous?"

"Nope," she answered.

"Well, let me tell you what we intend to do. At steps two and three, and in our next newsletter, we are going to bring a parade of COB custodians who are going to testify to all the creative ways they've joked about doing Rob in. We've got some very colorful characters with very mischievous minds, you know."

Jean laughed. "Please let Rob know that is what will happen if our guy doesn't go back to work now. We'll live with a written warning but get him his back pay. Campus Safety has already returned his gun. And I'll get our brother to agree in writing to leave the gun at home."

Jean spoke with Rob. Rob concluded it was not a good career move to be known campus-wide as the guy so loathed by his staff that they routinely joked about exterminating him. Rick returned to work, and life went on for all involved. We had engaged our members in humorous defense of a brother. Many were a little let down that they never got to tell their "how to terminate Rob" fantasies.

## Leaders Find Other Leaders

Part of developing an organizing union was to continuously look for new talent and energy from the membership rather than overrely on a few staff or officers. Every one of our participatory events provided opportunities for workers to demonstrate a wide range of leadership qualities. It was my job to be on the lookout, ready to pounce with an ask for them to take a step forward. Each strike, campaign, or event we organized provided opportunities for a member to rise to the occasion and demonstrate leadership qualities. It was not only who could speak up and make a good point. It was who could be counted on, who showed up early and stayed late. Who brought their kids with them and multitasked seamlessly while making posters or debating our strategies.

While every contract, strike or no strike, was ratified by overwhelming majorities, there were always a handful who disagreed and argued, often vociferously and loudly, that we should keep fighting, that we hadn't won enough. A few of those were low-credibility, uninvolved loudmouths. Far more often you could see the same fire in the belly, the same hurt and willingness to call out injustice that had fueled all of us from the beginning. Instead of telling those complainers that they were unappreciative or unrealistic, I would make a point of engaging them right away. I would tell them they were right, we hadn't won enough, and I would tell them we needed folks who felt the way they did in the leadership, at the bargaining table, and organizing the weaker members who were too willing to give in to their fears and be satisfied with minimal, incremental progress. In a way, I was inspired by them, but also wanted to call their bluff. When they weren't "just talk," when they were willing to engage, we found whole new generations of some of our finest leaders that way.

We also found leaders in ordinary grievance meetings, when workers who had grievances met with their manager to air their issue, always along with a steward or union officer. Almost every worker (all but the most self-destructive or terrified) who had a grievance was given a chance to share his or her point of view in the grievance meeting. This was also a good listening ground for finding leaders. How did they handle themselves? Were they clear-headed and strong without being out of control? Could they see how their problems related to others?

The way we trained members to become stewards is an example of this organizing mentality in action. Every union needs to identify or elect and then train stewards. But most treat this training as a technocratic effort to create mini-lawyers, worker experts on contract minutiae and grievance handling, who can face off against and out-debate managers. In truth most workers felt tremendous insecurity facing off against often better-educated bosses. They wanted to be armed with all the ins and outs of contract language. We had to overcome this lack of confidence by providing some technical skills; but more importantly, we emphasized a different analysis. It was that power mattered most. And power came from members uniting and fighting and linking up with the campus and town community. Yes, every steward needed to understand the basics of the contract, the grievance procedure, and progressive discipline. Yes, every steward needed to make sure the initial grievance was filed within ten working days of the issue surfacing. But most of the contract could be treated like a dictionary; you looked up what you didn't know when you needed to.

Yes, it felt good to make a clever point in a meeting with management, but this wasn't an Ivy League debate club, it wasn't *Perry Mason*, and it wasn't *Jeopardy*. The smartest or wittiest person didn't win. We needed our stewards to understand they were first and foremost organizers. Each of them represented between fifteen and thirty members. They needed to provide those members with information and at times inspiration, and they needed to reach out to and listen to what was on the members' minds. When our campaigns, small, medium, or campus-wide, were heating up, the stewards needed to be good at moving their members into participation and action. We expected every steward to regularly organize clock meetings or break-time meetings. I would make the rounds to as many as possible, but so did our other officers and our zone reps, each responsible for overseeing about one-seventh of the campus, with five to seven stewards each.

We recruited stewards who were respected coworkers, folks who generally were seen as being solid workers and also not afraid of the boss. There is an old cliché, "How do you know someone's a leader? They have followers." In some units it was clear who it was people looked up to and listened to, and who was just a blowhard, or too cozy with management. Potential leaders had a feel for injustice but also a nose for BS, whether from management or a fellow worker. They knew who they were, had a solid, authentic core, but could adapt to, respect, and understand others.

We held elections for stewards, but we also felt there was nothing wrong with some of the bigger or more complicated workplaces having multiple stewards. The more leaders, the better. After almost ten years of being local president, I had concluded that my single biggest responsibility was to continuously search for, personally promote, and develop leadership. The true measure of our local's health was the participation and consciousness of our members. That took layers of courageous leadership, workers owning their organization. I still believe it's the labor movement's most essential path to power and rebirth.

Our training strategy was to teach organizing basics. Have a good, updated membership list, and immediately befriend and orient every new hire. Get your members involved. Who can make a sign for the clock meeting? How many members wear UAW buttons on their uniforms? Can a member testify to coworkers about our hardship fund and sign others up? How about a car pool to an important membership meeting? We taught stewards to listen and to learn what people cared about, and then show the connection to collective power and our union.

## Mutual Aid

Cornell's resistance to paying workers a living wage had severe repercussions for our members' lives. Changing this reality was an ongoing struggle for us, and we highlighted it at the bargaining table, during strike actions, and in various other campus or community demonstrations. And with our first few contracts we did make some real gains. But they weren't enough. Hundreds of our members were still poor.

A union should be like an army but also like a family, and while we were doing our best to fight for better contracts, maybe there was more we could do? Indeed there was, so in the mid-'80s we started a member-run hardship fund, and a few years later, a food bank for our members.

These mutual-aid activities served four purposes. First, many of our members truly needed this sort of help to tide them over hard stretches. Second, we made sure that Cornell and the Ithaca community knew we were doing this, and had to do this, because of the poverty wages Cornell paid. Third, running the hardship fund and the food bank were ways a whole new set of members could become involved in building our union and becoming leaders. And fourth, these kind of activities were a way to diversify the role opportunities for participation. Some union-supporting members just didn't want to participate by standing up to their boss in defense of others. Some were not gregarious or self-confident enough to organize their coworkers. My job was to find as many productive opportunities, like involvement in the hardship fund and food bank, as there was interest.

Money for the hardship fund came primarily from our members making voluntary deductions from their paychecks every two weeks. It was something we negotiated into our contract. It could be one, two, five, or ten dollars a paycheck. Cornell collected the money and sent it to the union, and all the money, every cent of it, went into the fund. We did an annual fund-raising drive among faculty that was incredibly successful. We received checks from hundreds of professors for $25 to $200 every year.

Three rank-and-file members administered the hardship fund—all very long-term Cornell workers who were widely respected and trusted. Any member could apply to use the fund. We had a one-page form that just asked what the hardship was. We were clear: it had to be something that had happened, something above the weekly grind of making a living on poverty wages. Our members had no cushion for a rough time. If burned out in a house fire (and most of our members heated with wood), they'd come to the hardship fund. If escaping with their kids from an abusive husband or otherwise in a jam, members could turn to their union hardship fund.

The amounts of money were modest, but the process was fast. Few questions were asked. Members could get help through a quiet, quick, dignified system run by their own people who knew what hard lives they lived. While there were all sorts of worries at the beginning that some folks might lie or somehow abuse the fund, the reality was that our members were not inclined to ask for help. If anything, we needed to encourage folks we knew were in distress to apply. You could only get one contribution per year, so people really weren't going to rip their union family off. Each year a few workers allowed their stories to be put in our union newspaper as testimonials to encourage others. The leaders who ran the fund didn't gravitate toward roles like steward or organizer, but they were union leaders just the same.

Our union also became the operator of the largest food bank in the county. There were already a few solid sources of food for those in need; Catholic Charities in particular did some terrific work. There was a woman, Sara Pines, who was the intermediary for the small food banks around town who had pestered me for several months. She had a reputation as being a little eccentric and intense. I realized that I had probably been described that way a few hundred times, and that I should relax and meet with her. She explained the whole system, how they got the food, what the headaches were, how much labor it took. She was interested in getting our union involved.

It dawned on me that we could do more than volunteer someplace. Our poorer members at Cornell had a huge need for good free food, and by this time, several other low-wage workplaces had organized into our local, places like the Ramada Inn, the *Ithaca Times*, and the Ithaca Housing Authority. We had the ability to generate volunteers, and our members owned trucks to transport the food. Sara loved the idea. We turned out to be kindred spirits, and we began to put all the pieces together.

And so, the Low Wage Workers Food Bank started to provide free high-quality food once a week out of a storefront near our downtown office. Naturally we made a big splash with our office launch, Sara and I. We pointed our finger right at the employers, led by the biggest and wealthiest, who paid such low wages that workers needed to help each other out like this. We had two purposes in branding the food bank as we did. First, it was yet another black eye for Cornell, a little more pressure. Second, it took away a lot of the stigma some of our members might have felt. They were working people. This food bank was not for the homeless, for folks trapped in substance abuse or mental illness (although all those issues existed in our membership). This food bank was for workers and led by workers.

We really didn't know if members would use it. We publicized it widely and loudly and made sure everything from parking to the hours we operated made it easy for our folks. As we talked it up, I remember Pete Tufford scoffing, "C'mon, Al, this is a publicity stunt. Your members don't need a food bank." I reminded him of the food stamps, the hardship fund, the stats, but he saw this as a gimmick, a bridge too far. After a few weeks I got back to Pete. "Oh, by the way, apparently our members *do* need a food bank because they are clocking out from Cornell, coming down the hill, and picking up food every time we are open."

There were two things I loved most about our food bank. First, the friendly, family-like feel of it was evident as soon as you walked in the door. Folks were being welcomed by their peers. Nobody looked ashamed, and everyone was treated like a family member who came to borrow a cup of sugar. Second, I loved that we had another layer of leaders who ran it. It took arms and backs to load and unload the food. Others took the time and volunteered to set it up in our storefront and assist the members. And it took folks to clean up and shut it down. Not particularly steward skills, but every bit as much union leadership. Members who used it would also register to vote there, and many signed up to volunteer or contribute to our hardship fund.

Once we were successful, we realized we needed a coordinator and started paying our best volunteer, Lyn Willwerth, a day of wages a week to manage the whole operation. I remember asking him if he'd like to do that. He said, "Get paid for what I've been doing? Sounds good to me!"

Paying Lyn his day's wages was an example of something else we had learned—that one of the best ways to spend our small treasury was to provide lost-time pay for activists. Instead of buying stuff like fancy jackets to give away, or better furniture in our office, we built up a system of expanding activity based on leadership and voluntarism. If zone reps were putting in a lot of extra after-work time to cover their zone, we would suggest they get a few hours a week off from work, which we would pay them for at their regular wage. Members who proved themselves first, whose dedication and effectiveness were plain to see, were key to our system. We wanted to grow that activism by freeing them up to do even more.

Our secretary treasurer, a position held by a series of exceptional leaders, including Oze Richardson, Gail Fruchey, and Cathy Valentino, would start groaning and cursing my name every year when it was time to do our taxes. Some years we had close to one hundred members who had received some amount of "lost time" payments that had to be accounted for. I used to say, "I know this is a giant pain in the ass, but really, what makes you prouder? We had that many leaders step up!"

Our union was a social animal from the beginning. Our Singing Bears, including banjo and guitar accompanists, performed at community events. We had UAW picnics with over 350 members bringing dishes to pass. We had holiday parties at the Machinists Union headquarters, the Plumbers Hall, or the VFW. Multigenerational gatherings of Cornell staff, kids welcome, would eat, drink, dance, drink some more, laugh, and bond. We commandeered a local bar and restaurant close to campus called the Depot. Hundreds of union conversations and meetings happened there as the unofficial after-hours office for the organizing drive. We sponsored and populated bowling teams and women's slow-pitch softball and showed *Norma Rae* on campus for one dollar.

Our UAW hats, T-shirts, buttons, and stickers were everywhere. One organizing button simply said, "Too Cool to Fool" and showed a man and a woman worker strutting confidently forward with huge grins on their faces. Bus Garage steward Jim Royce Sr.'s son, Jim Jr., was a custodian. Junior got married at the Dryden Town Hall with "the bride wearing her green UAW T-shirt, while the groom wore his in basic white." We ran a full-page photo spread of the whole family wedding party in "Vote Yes UAW" fashion.

Our union could fight like no other organization in town, and we had hard-won, hard-boiled political influence. But we also became a family. We could take care of one another, provide mutual help and support, party and play together, and show our love and humanity to one another.

## The *Bear Facts*

We realized early on—from the day we started organizing the union—that keeping members informed and engaged in informing one another would be challenging. We existed inside a cultural bubble dominated by the university. The university had a full-time PR machine, a weekly, in-house publication for staff called the *Cornell Chronicle*, and was treated as a sacred, benevolent master by the local conservative Gannett chain daily newspaper, the *Ithaca Journal*. The student-run paper, the *Cornell Daily Sun*, was more independent and youthfully willing to criticize the university, but the students initially were largely oblivious to the workers who toiled beneath "the hill."

We needed to communicate an alternative narrative, a story that was widely known but collectively buried, more whispered than shouted. Workers were suffering and deserved much better. But we also needed to educate, persuade, and activate. Many workers were not just afraid; they were also loyal to Cornell, and had accepted the notion that they were "lucky to have a job." Finally, we existed in an impoverished northern tip of Appalachia, a conservative area with limited experience with unions and all the ingrained right-wing fears of Big Labor. Most of our organizing was face to face, in homes, break rooms, car pools, and at clock meetings. We clearly needed a strategy for mass communication if we were going to change the environment on campus.

Logistics of mass communication were daunting. We had members in over two hundred buildings, and to make things even more difficult, some were not easy to find, working various shifts and being mobile throughout the day. We had folks working in vast gardens, labs, on an experimental dairy farm, and as material handlers, mechanics, and groundskeepers who were rarely in one place for more than ten minutes. So we built an elaborate system of hand distribution of flyers. For more dramatic announcements we would also leaflet the massive parking lots where from 4:00 a.m. until 8:00 a.m. many of our members assembled to ride buses onto campus to punch in for work. We held break meetings and clock meetings. But we were always looking for other ways to communicate. During the organizing drive we hosted union meetings at town libraries and VFW halls in some of the small outlying towns like Trumansburg and Groton where many members lived.

We started a small newspaper called the *Bear Facts*. The entire production of a monthly eight-page publication was done by workers and a student intern or two. Planning the stories, interviewing members, writing, editing, design, and layout were all done by amateurs, learning as we went. The UAW had hundreds of locals with publications, and the *Bear Facts* regularly won one of the top national awards. Like our union, our newspaper had heart, humor, and a lot of spunk.

We wanted as many stories directly from workers as possible and rarely ran any canned material. A typical *Bear Facts* issue updated folks on our living-wage campaigns, with quotes from workers and allies. Workers just told it like it was. Yvonne Thomas, a custodian at Balch Hall, was quoted: "You're a peon, and you're made to know it. I am ashamed to tell people what I make." Comstock Hall custodian Hugh Worley added, "We're not greedy, but money becomes important because of the lack of it!" We ran biting articles exposing hard truths, like Vivian Morgan's pension. We reprinted the letter she received on university letterhead from the benefits manager thanking her for ten years of service and letting her know she would receive a retirement check of "$0.38 every two weeks."

We were relentless in making wage comparisons to other Ivy League schools, to the New York State SUNY system, and one of our favorites, Wayne County Community College near Detroit. Custodians there started at wages 53 percent higher than Cornell's and got regular cost-of-living increases.

We had a steady stream of inside information. Secretaries and custodians tend to be ignored, but their very invisibility allows them to see and hear many questionable things. Faculty allies, campus police, and supervisors who secretly sympathized all provided critical stories. That's how we found out about the $8,000 cherrywood desk one university VP had custom made. Not only was that more than my annual salary; it turned out the only way to get it into Day Hall was to use a crane. There was a lot of muck to be raked, and the campus loved our mischievous telling of truth so directly to power.

Faculty allies were regularly quoted. Manning Marable, who later would write a definitive biography of Malcolm X, said, "Unionization will create greater democracy within the life of the Cornell community." Engineering professor Ben Nichols, later to become Ithaca mayor, was an early advocate, saying, "A union would benefit my relationships with employees, in that experienced, qualified people would stay." ILR professor Roger Keeran took direct aim at the way wage increases were handed out, saying he "welcomed unionization" because "it will eliminate the merit system which is as phony and demeaning for the evaluator as it is for the employee being evaluated."

During the effort to organize clerical workers, we printed a powerful "Bill of Rights for Women Office Workers." It included thirteen rights, covering basic concepts of respect and equality when it came to salaries, medical benefits, and opportunities for promotion. The widely circulated document struck some deep cultural chords of class and gender, with, for example, right number five: "The right to choose whether to do the personal work of employers (typing personal letters, serving coffee, running out for lunch)."

We printed a list of every grievance in the *Bear Facts*, including the aggrieved worker's name along with the names of the offending supervisors. We ran a column called "Orchids and Onions," bestowing a literary flower on members, allies, and once or twice a supervisor or manager who had done something kind. But the orchids mainly existed so we could dole out some rotten onions. This is where we really took no prisoners, going after the Rob Osborns or the Bill Crisseys, the supervisors who seemed to go out of their way to belittle and disrespect workers. We also ran "Emily's Helpful Hints," a beloved column that developed a cultlike following. Its author, organizer extraordinaire Emily Apgar, was a font of bizarre cleaning and home maintenance advice. She offered strange organic and at times toxic combos for cleaning, and quirky tips like "If you have a leaky faucet that's driving you insane, tie a string to the faucet and let the drip just run down quietly."

Cornell HR hated the *Bear Facts*. But folks all over campus clamored for it, including secretaries, techs, and faculty. We not only handed them out at every time clock and nook and cranny of our bargaining unit; we also left dozens scattered at more public campus areas, bus kiosks, and employee eateries. Many managers confided that they couldn't wait to get their hands on it. Most supervisors were trapped in very low wages along with us, and knew any breakthroughs we might make would likely trickle up to them. We had many vocal allies, but we also had some off-the-record support from within the belly of the beast.

We did not only rely on the print media to connect with our members and irk management. One approach we took during the organizing drive was running our own radio program. One of our most popular leaders, a Cornell Plantations gardener named Perry Huested, was the voice of "Bear Facts Radio." Perry was a large, handsome, farmer-hippie type. He had a great deal, where he lived rent-free in a tiny Cornell-owned house in the middle of the vast and spectacular Plantations. His obligation was to open and lock the gates to the Plantations and be on duty if there were any problems at night. Perry was a social animal, fun and flirtatious, but also deeply committed to our union. Once or twice, Cornell reminded him of his special benefit, but those threats never put a dent in Perry's activism. He served in many roles, including on multiple bargaining teams and as a trustee monitoring our finances.

Perry's most famous role, though, was as the one and only voice of Bear Facts Radio. Even after the UAW International stopped paying for everything and we were a small, dues-collecting local union, paying for our own priorities, we kept BFR going. Perry used to come on the air very early in the morning, exactly during service worker drive time, between 4:00 and 7:00 a.m. Some 90 percent of our members lived twenty to sixty minutes from campus. Housing costs closer to campus were exorbitant, driven up by the deep pockets of most students and faculty. Our folks were a captive audience, happy to tune in to one of their own dishing out some truth every week.

Perry had a bizarre and, with a couple of decades of hindsight, totally inappropriate signature opening. He would start every show by growling some version of "This is Perry Huested. It's very early in the morning, and I'm your naked Bear. Are you naked out there?" Only Perry could get away with this. It was crude and quirky and a recognition that our folks got up before the sun and were struggling to get dressed and off to work. Perry was so popular because he was the real deal. He'd share some news about the fight with Cornell, a grievance won, or a struggle defended. He made it personal, without ever being egotistical.

Finally, two community and labor activists, Carl Feuer and Robin Whittlesey, helped us create a public access TV program featuring our members and our campaigns. Carl and Robin were part of a movement to democratize media, and to make sure public access TV was used effectively. Candidly, I don't think I had ever watched it. It seemed like the usual combo of local weirdos, except for a Democratic Socialist interview program led by the indomitable Theresa Alt. I just couldn't imagine that our members would tune into public access, and it seemed like a lot to undertake. I was wrong on both fronts.

Thanks to our friends, I learned the basics, and with a small, volunteer production crew ready, we placed our request for a time slot. I learned that thanks to the dearth of original local programming, we not only ran our show, but it could be rerun multiple times each week. There were two keys to making this work. We needed to fill a half hour, and we needed to build an audience.

We did both. We got a steady stream of workers to come share their stories, and sprinkled in with student, faculty, and community supporters, we had plenty to fill the time. Having workers on every show was critical. It turned out that if we could give our members a little notice, they were tremendously interested in tuning in and seeing their coworkers (and even themselves!) on TV. We would put a special flyer out listing the two to four times the show would air and encouraging folks to tune in to see their coworkers talking about what was really going on at Cornell. It was a huge hit. Surveying our members, we found that 50 percent of them said they had watched at least one show.

The show came up at every clock meeting. People were tickled to see each other on television, and the fact that we could take on Cornell so bluntly and so publicly was a blasphemy that proved to be a major draw. We had created very low-tech, unprofessional, "must see" TV. Before YouTube, Facebook, and the internet, being on TV was a big deal. This rough-and-tumble little operation also became must-see TV for management. It cracked me up to picture all the big bosses and Cornell honchos masochistically tuning in to our little renegade program to get their weekly raking over the coals.

We were building a healthy, informed, member-engaged and member-led organization. We were biting the hand that didn't feed us in every creative, provocative, high-visibility way we could find. Finding, and even electing, more and increasingly powerful allies to strengthen our member strategies was our parallel challenge.

**FIGURE 17.** *The Singing Bears* was founded with techs, clericals, and service staff. We showed that we were part of the Ithaca community at local events. Over time we developed many ways for workers to get involved in the union. Social activities from dance parties to bowling teams, a food bank, radio shows, artwork, and a rank-and-file-run hardship fund were all avenues for camaraderie and developing a leadership base beyond the traditional union steward role. (Local 2300 newsletter)

## Discussion Questions

- The union took grievances and mid-contract issues and went beyond the confines of the negotiated grievance procedure by activating members and using community pressure tactics. What issues lend themselves to broader agitation and struggle, and when is that mobilizing approach less likely to succeed?
- The food bank and the hardship fund were embraced by members. How did the union avoid workers feeling stigmatized as poor or in need of "charity"?
- The union used a variety of ways to communicate with members beyond in person: leaflets, a newspaper, radio, and TV, for example. Were there common strategies in how the union communicated that cut across all their platforms? How might a union today use social media for the same purposes that Local 2300 used TV, print, and videos?
- Irreverence, mischief, and fun seem part of many of Local 2300's activities. Yet collective bargaining and representing worker grievances are serious business. How did the union's sense of humor and playfulness contribute to creating a healthy organization? Are there times when this can seem immature, backfire, or send the wrong message?

## 11

# FROM GRASSROOTS UP TO GRASSROOTS OUT

Worker power. Student power. Our union was honing strategy and tactics, learning to "float like a butterfly, sting like a bee." Slowly we developed a strategy and practice for building our power from within the belly of the beast, from the grassroots up. But it soon became clear we needed to do more. How about community power? What about from the grassroots out?

Reaching out to and seeking to mobilize community support made sense on a number of levels. Our issues and history closely dovetailed with those of the Ithaca community. From its home high up on East Hill, Cornell historically dominated both its workers and its town, and both workers and town had long-standing grievances. Cornell had more staff than the next ten largest local employers combined. If the community's dominant employer paid poverty wages, what was the incentive for other employers to pay more? The reduced purchasing power of all these low-paid workers didn't help local businesses, either. We had the facts to show that several hundred Cornell service employees earned below the poverty level and that even after adjusting for cost of living, Cornell paid substantially lower wages than all its peer Ivy League universities.

Cornell tried to hide behind the circular argument that they paid what every other employer paid; it was the market rate, and therefore was appropriate. No one bought this low-road and illogical position. Everyone in the community understood that Cornell, the one and only heavyweight employer, set the market rate. It was clear with a multibillion-dollar endowment (over $7 billion today) and constant expansion that Cornell had the resources. Our message to the community was that Cornell impoverished us because they could get away with it. Help us change that, and we would all benefit.

We had climbed a learning curve on campus to better understand which stakeholders had the most power, the potential to influence Cornell. But which groups and individuals in the community mattered most to our cause? How could we get our message out and mobilize strategic community support? While our analysis of Cornell's poverty wages resonated with average folks and many community leaders, we still needed to access, or create, levers of power within the community.

We realized early in the 1980s that the local labor council was potentially one such source of power, but it hadn't functioned in over a decade, so we committed to rebuild it. I began meeting individually with all the other major unions, the Machinists who represented workers at three major factories and a salt-mining operation under Cayuga Lake, the numerous building trades, teachers, and a couple of sister UAW locals in nearby Cortland, New York. There was unanimous interest in better communications and mutual aid. Local 2300's highly visible organizing victory had elevated the hopes for a stronger union environment. These conversations built and strengthened relationships and led to the birth of the Tompkins-Cortland Labor Coalition representing some twenty thousand public- and private-sector workers. Ironically, a pro-labor grad student, Jay Hoffman, helped us secure resources from the Cornell ILR School for a small dinner on campus. Ostensibly, it was a chance for ILR Extension to pitch their educational offerings to local union leaders. Jay and I understood the main purpose was to pull the twenty most important labor leaders in two counties together to strengthen ties and relaunch our labor council. I was elected TCLC co-president and made sure we always supported the UAW service and maintenance workers on the hill.

Rebuilding labor solidarity was mostly a matter of relationship building, putting one foot in front of the other. Union leaders should by nature have a gut instinct and longing for solidarity, and most do. An injury to one really is an injury to all. Our simple ability to mobilize for each other's rallies and picket lines quickly proved our collective value to one another. We all felt like Davids against corporate Goliaths, with the *Ithaca Journal* unsympathetic and often reinforcing antiunion clichés about "Big Labor" or "labor goons and bosses."

While it's never simple to get union leaders from different cultures and at times conflicting ideologies to unite, labor solidarity is a fairly natural impulse among the working class. But trying to move even a liberal Democratic Party and our local political ecosystem to embrace a feisty workers' movement was a different matter. It sometimes left us feeling like the round peg dealing with a very square hole.

Regular Democratic Party politics in Ithaca were probably not all that different from the politics in a lot of other bucolic college towns. Ithaca was a liberal island in a conservative rural sea. But its liberalism included an obliviousness to working-class issues. Democratic leaders were mostly upper-middle-class professionals, attorneys, and faculty. You could get a crowd to save a historic building, while two miles from that building hundreds of families lived in trailer parks with open sewers running. The Dems were broadly sympathetic to our cause, but we also needed advocates who would make worker issues a priority.

We needed some good people to run for local office.

How about me?

Who?

Me!

In 1985 I decided to run for a seat on the Tompkins County Board of Representatives (the County Legislature). I was twenty-seven years old, and my only claim to fame was striking Cornell and recently attacking, on the front pages of the *Ithaca Journal*, the feared and beloved university for committing "economic apartheid." But some Dems coaxed me into being part of a wave of progressives running to wrest control of the County Board from the grips of rural Republicans who had exerted their hegemony forever. I lived at that time in one of those Republican strongholds, the town of Dryden, about eight miles out of Ithaca.

My opponent, Ken Tillapaugh, was a friendly, moderate Republican who had moved his way through every imaginable local civic duty. Boy Scouts, town and community college boards and committees, neighborhood associations and business groupings, they all knew Ken personally. It was a fool's errand, but I threw myself into it. I registered hundreds of poor workers in the massive trailer parks that dotted the district. I made sure all our own members were registered. But my youth, inexperience in granular town issues, and radical reputation were a losing fit for holding an office that was more about snow removal and zoning than the workers' revolution.

The nature of the position I was running for came into sharp focus while I was going door to door one day. I knocked, and an obviously harried, distracted middle-aged woman came to the door. As I started my enthusiastic introductory rap about who I was and what big ideas I stood for, she blurted out, "The pipe under my sink is leaking like Niagara Falls. I'll vote for whoever can fix it."

I got more votes than any Democrat had ever received in that district, but I also generated a historically high Republican backlash, losing to friendly Ken by a disappointing 57 percent to 43 percent margin. A couple of my progressive wave mates won, and by the next election cycle, the County Board was narrowly in the hands of Democrats for the first time in many decades.

At the same time, in the latter part of the 1980s, we also made inroads with the City of Ithaca Common Council, encouraging and supporting several progressives, including even one UAW member and a few lefty activists, in contests for local office. People like John Efroymson, a Democratic Socialist; Diann Sams, a leader in both the African American and people with disabilities communities; and Neil Golder, one of our own stalwart members and a longtime peace and anti-militarism activist, all got elected to Ithaca's Common Council.

Building power meant building alliances around common values and principles. While we had made progress with local labor and with local officeholders, what about other sectors in the community? We met with leaders from the Black and feminist communities and pointed out what they knew all too well: that Cornell paid everybody poorly, but that Black and female staff were stuck in the lowest pay grades. They were absent entirely from some upper-level service occupations like heavy equipment operator, printer, and bus driver.

In the 1980s the gay community was an unlikely partner for our union, which had a blue-collar, mostly rural and culturally conservative membership. A majority of our members knew how to hunt deer and make a good meal out of the venison but couldn't have told you where our one gay bar was if you put that hunting rifle to their head. We stuck our neck out, way out of the comfort zone for many of our members, and endorsed a highly controversial gay rights county ordinance. All it called for was nondiscrimination in housing and employment. The debate in the county was fierce. Right-wing church groups activated their membership in intense and formidable opposition. Most landlords, a large and vocal force in Ithaca, did too. The County Board appeared evenly divided.

How to get our UAW executive board's support? We were like a family. Most of us had struggled shoulder to shoulder for the better part of a decade. We knew each other's kids, favorite drinks, senses of humor, and our best and worst sides. I knew that a solid majority of them were homophobic, and as far as I knew not a single executive board member was gay. We had only two "out" stewards out of around fifty. Remember, this was the 1980s, in a county with more cows than people. I decided this was a healthy and important issue of principle for us to grapple with. Our executive board relations were strong enough to handle some debate. It was a fascinating process and proved more significant than I imagined at the time. A few leaders were quiet, and a few asked, "Do we really need to get involved with this, Al?" Some made mild homophobic jokes. Two or three leaders joined me to make one simple point: our union existed to fight favoritism. We were born fighting phony merit pay, disrespect, and harassment. Whatever *we*, as individuals, thought about homosexuality shouldn't matter. What mattered was whether we would let bosses, be they employers or landlords, punish somebody because *they* didn't like them.

I knew I was pushing our boundaries some. I knew it would land us in an issue that was very visible, and the most controversial local political issue then. I knew that more than a few of our members would be unhappy, and we needed all the internal unity we could get to fight Cornell. But if we wanted to be a leading progressive organization in the community, if we wanted to lead the rest of the labor movement, we needed to stand for some basic principles. There were few votes we ever took as an executive board that had as much potential to divide us. After two meetings of long, hard discussion and some personal pain for a couple of our most macho leaders, Local 2300's executive board voted unanimously to endorse Local Law C. Only one other union in town, the teachers, took the risk and the heat. In 1991, after a bitter and divisive community fight, the law passed by one vote in the County Legislature.

We did it because it was the right thing to do, because working people, through their unions, should be a voice against all injustice, and because I hoped we were ready. What I didn't understand then was how deeply the gay community was now bonded to us, and how much help they would be in the future.

After a few years of community and political engagement, we had many allies who would stand with us, and they knew we stood with them. Every elected officeholder who thought Cornell should pay a decent wage, or contribute to the community beyond smug benevolence, saw us as a union fighting for both workers and the town. What we did not yet have was a major community-wide leader who was an activist—a champion willing to take on Big Red. That would soon change.

## Before Bernie, There Was Ben

We found our champion in an unlikely place: the Cornell School of Electrical and Computer Engineering.

Ben Nichols was an elderly engineering professor. He could be curmudgeonly and impatient and did not suffer fools lightly, or at all. He was generally hostile to kissing babies and going door to door. Born in New York City to a couple of dedicated communists, he was a lifelong socialist, a World War II vet, and a brilliant, if ornery, community and campus activist. At Cornell he was active during the famous Black student takeover of the campus union building in 1969, and then helped establish the Black studies program and continued as a leader of campus social justice efforts. During our first strike he helped organize faculty support, showed up on picket lines, and donated money. Active in local Democratic Party politics, he won a seat on the Ithaca Common Council in 1987 and rapidly established himself as its most progressive member.

As we became more active politically in the 1980s, we decided to form a coalition with a wide range of activist groups to take on the three-term Democratic mayor John "Gutie" Gutenberger. He was a good guy, the owner of a Collegetown grocery store. He was moderate and personable, but he represented a status quo that would not challenge Cornell's role in the community, neither its employment practices nor its low level of financial support for community needs. Mainstream Dems were freaked out when Ben became our candidate. Ben was a Democratic Socialist and a pain in the ass to many moderate Dems. Why jeopardize Democrats' control of the city and risk handing it over to Republicans? Longtime chair of the local Democratic Party Irene Stein, someone I had a solid friendship with, screamed at me to drop this. She didn't do more than grunt at me for the next six months.

Ben Nichols became one of my best friends, and very close with my family. We constructed what we gleefully but privately called the red-green alliance. Controlled development and environmental issues in general were very popular local liberal causes then. A previous challenge to Mayor Gutenberger had almost resulted in an antidevelopment, green mayor. But the greens had not connected with the red issues of poverty, jobs, or racism in town. We reds had been wary of the often well-off, well-educated, more hippie-ish enviros. We came together, at first tentatively, around a common belief that the current government was mostly serving landlords, developers, and Cornell.

Our coalition also included some key Black, women's movement, housing rights, and LGBTQ leaders. Ben asked me to be his campaign manager, and we met every week in his dining room, on a street named Llenroc, a block from Cornell's campus, to plan and execute our renegade campaign. Llenroc was Cornell spelled backward, a sign that the university's arrogance could encompass a playful sense of community hegemony. But maybe our little band of troublemakers were the ones about to turn things upside down.

Our diverse team of leaders and activists had tremendous energy, humor, and spunk. Miraculously, despite ideological differences and no history of working closely together, we got along, building trust and strong friendships within our coalition. We ran radio ad testimonials from well-known local leaders, like the well-respected director of Ithaca Neighborhood Housing, Doug Dylla. We used all our many networks to reach people with messages geared to the separate constituencies of the coalition. We tried desperately to drag Ben out to do some traditional and effective door-to-door campaigning. He just hated anything he felt was superficial. He did finally agree to some neighborhood door-knocking and ended up in a deeply substantive forty-minute conversation about local childcare needs at the first door.

On primary day, we shocked the political establishment and beat the three-term incumbent by a decent margin. Suddenly the Republican candidate started getting a lot of attention, as a "stop the socialist" backlash began to build. There was even an article in the *New York Times* about our breakthrough. Luckily Ben had been a fixture in the community for decades. Like Bernie Sanders, he was gruff but authentic, no flip-flopping. He also had led a Boy Scout troop and helped design a special science curriculum for elementary school kids. His Republican opponent was Jean Cookingham, a longtime Republican Party fixture. More than a few conservative Dems broke from the party to publicly go with the Republican, but the moderate center held together, and the energy of our progressive movement was relentless. Ben won by only two hundred votes. Our union was seen as the driving force and the convener of a broad progressive coalition.

"Gutie" immediately got hired by Cornell in their PR department. When he retired in 2017, the Cornell Board of Trustees honored him for "27 years of meritorious town-gown service"—that is, seventeen years as a Cornell community relations administrator and ten years as local government official. Like our union, the city, after Ben's tenure as mayor, had become a force to be reckoned with. Cornell's preferred blurring of the lines and sweeter days with Mayor Gutie seemed downright nostalgic.

As mayor, Ben never stopped being a lefty and an activist. There was literally never an ask we made for working people that he refused. He didn't hesitate to pick up the phone to demand a meeting in his office with a recalcitrant employer. He was willing and available to come to the UAW Hall to buoy the morale of struggling workers in organizing drives or strikes. But he went beyond even that. Ben and I began cooking up a strategy to bring Cornell into real negotiations with the city and reset town-gown dynamics forever.

We calculated how much Cornell received in special services from the city. One irrefutable example was the fire station in Collegetown, adjacent to the campus. It existed primarily to serve Cornell's daily false alarms and occasional real fires in labs or dorms. Low-wage city taxpayers essentially paid for Cornell to have this service. Ben asked that the university make a direct payment in lieu of taxes to cover the full cost. Tax-exempt Cornell laughed him out of the room with the old arguments that boiled down to "You need us more than we need you, and there's nothing you can do about it."

The issue was no longer who was right. The community knew Cornell "put us on the map," but that didn't give them the right to rip off workers and the community. Elected political leaders knew it, and major community leaders did too. The issue was leverage: leverage for workers to force Cornell to pay livable wages and leverage to force Cornell into a financially fair and mutually respectful relationship with the community. As we turned up the moral heat, Cornell threw the community some bigger bones. They made splashy donations to a local community group or two, trying to shush up members of our coalition with a few

**FIGURE 18.** Mayor Ben Nichols was comfortable on the back of a truck with a bullhorn. He championed labor and the community and was elected and reelected as a Democratic Socialist. UAW president Al Davidoff coordinated his first campaign. (Local 2300 newsletter)

thousand dollars. This was the same strategy they utilized before we unionized: occasionally toss workers a few crumbs in order to keep a union from gaining traction. For Big Red it was a cheap, sound investment, a preventive strategy to avoid true negotiations and real equity.

What leverage did the city have? Pleading and lobbying with Cornell to contribute fairly for major services went nowhere. We had our seriously mischievous city attorney, Chuck Gutman, research every angle on town-gown relations. He and Mayor Ben started to do some digging into an area Cornell cared deeply about but which required formal agreement with and support from the city: new building construction. Cornell was in the midst of a massive construction boom: $500 million over ten years. It was popular with the community and the building trades because there were lots of construction jobs. But, we realized, Cornell could not lift a hammer without a city building permit. One of those seemingly minor, pro forma services provided by the city now became our cudgel if we dared use it.

But did the mayor dare? Would Cornell budge? Would there be a divisive fight, maybe even a political backlash in the community? Could this be the end of Mayor Ben? What about our labor coalition, which included several building trades unions dependent on Cornell's permanent building boom? Would this be the end of hard-won solidarity?

Denying building permits wasn't a simple issue legally, but the city could deny a permit for many reasons, and the process to overturn that denial could take a long time. Chuck Gutman, the city attorney, was a terrific ally, not averse to exploring every nook and cranny of the mayor's legal authority in service to this larger cause. Cornell was used to local pols rubber-stamping their needs, and major construction projects usually sailed through without a hiccup. Ben made it clear that *all* aspects of town-gown relations needed to be handled in a mutually respectful negotiation going forward. As it became clear that construction permits were being held up, Cornell went through all the stages of grief.

The university felt it had the upper hand because, well, who doesn't like construction? This specific tactic, to deny Cornell building permits, became a hugely public struggle. As so often happens, especially in labor struggles, the "cause" was popular, up and until the tactics required to fight that cause became too radical or inconvenient. The overwhelming majority of local folks knew Cornell was not paying its fair share to the city and was underpaying staff. Most elected officials now also understood and agreed, thanks to years of hard work and our bold politics. But few politicians were willing to play this kind of tactical hardball, risk antagonizing Cornell and losing some popular support. Ben was not a typical politician. When Cornell called his bluff, they found that their construction projects, all on complicated deadlines, were going to grind to a halt. Upstate New York winters don't allow for a twelve-month construction season, and delays could be costly.

We had intense discussions within labor about this. The building trades were getting whipped up by the university. Even those trades leaders who were sympathetic to making Cornell pay more were pissed that their work, their livelihood, was our key leverage. The rest of the unions, especially the public-sector unions who suffered directly from Cornell's tax-exempt status and failure to contribute to fire and police services, were strongly supportive of the fight. The newspaper railed against our extreme tactics. Ben avoided talking directly about the building permit question. He would say the community needed to have a comprehensive relationship with Cornell, including fair contributions and fair wages. He said no jobs had been lost (so far), and the responsibility rested with Cornell to make sure that didn't happen. Our UAW leaders and members loved that the mayor was in essence "striking" Cornell, by potentially shutting down construction.

But even our members were a little torn, as building trades coworkers, all union brothers (and a very few sisters) who had honored our picket lines at least for a day or two, were possibly going to lose work. Many of our members were in extended working-class families with construction workers. We went out of our way to explain and discuss the issues. Ben came to our membership meetings to inform and fire us up, and also to fire himself up as he felt the support from his closest allies in this battle with Cornell.

When Cornell tried to divide UAW members from the community, saying that more money for the community meant less money for worker wages, we called bullshit. Cornell had plenty of money to treat its little town right *and* pay its workers a livable wage. This was a similar argument Cornell tried with student leaders, that better wages would automatically require higher tuition. Our members were sympathetic to the fears expressed by construction workers about job loss, but also felt that if Cornell could spend $500 million on new buildings, they could pay us a decent wage. As much as having to cough up the money, Cornell hated the idea of having to negotiate with the city. It was a perfect parallel to our union experience. It wasn't lost on our members that this was as much about respect as about the money. Cornell was fine with being a dictator, benevolent now and again. But to have to sit down across a table and even pretend to be equals with janitors and cooks, or with the tiny town's elected officials . . . that was abhorrent. Cornell also knew that once you accepted that premise of equal partnership, oppressed workers and communities will almost never go back to accepting crumbs.

The truth is both sides were playing a game of chicken: racing toward a collision and waiting for the other side to give in. Cornell provided time off work for the trades to hold a "save our jobs" rally and march directed at Ben and which ended right in front of City Hall, partially blocking a main artery through town. The firefighters, led by their dynamic young president Lee Marshall, then led a spirited march in favor of fairness for the community. Overall, however, Ben was probably losing support among moderates, and he was facing reelection. The cause was just, but the tactics seemed too radical and confrontational to many. But Ben was stubborn, and never ruled by which way the political winds were blowing. That tenacious attitude and the prospect of real delays in construction scared Cornell. Quietly, Cornell's relatively new senior VP, Hank Dullea, who had a long career in state government, most recently as Governor Mario Cuomo's director of state operations, reached out to me. You know things have changed when the twenty-something, radical strike leader president of the UAW is the guy the university turns to to explore a way out. The custodian they tried to fire for union activity was now their perceived best path to settling a major town-gown rift.

I think they reached out to me for two basic reasons. First, they knew nobody was closer to Ben, apart from his wife, Ethel, herself a county legislator and as feisty and stubborn as Ben. Second, by the early 1990s they had bargained tough contracts and hundreds of grievances with me, and in spite of all the bitterness, strikes, and public jousting, we did eventually come to agreements.

I knew one thing for sure, and then had a simple bright idea that I floated by Ben. First, this had to be a negotiated agreement. Not a promise, not we disarm and they'll quietly throw us a bone. Ben needed a formal, public agreement, and that was as important as the dollar amount. This was a principle, and as Ben's campaign manager, I believed this was key to saving his political hide. My bright idea was almost childishly simple. I told Ben, we needed to get to a million dollars. This was around twenty times Cornell's current voluntary contribution. For a small city, this was a serious amount of money. To me, the symbolism of Cornell agreeing to a million dollars would be political dynamite.

We met late one night, literally in a dark corner of the bar at an upscale restaurant, Old Port Harbor, with nobody near us. Me, Ben, and Cornell senior VP Dullea. After some jostling and jockeying about who this fight was hurting more, and who had the stronger legal case, it became clear that Dullea was not on a mission to harangue or persuade us; he was here to work things out. Ben assured him he saw this as a positive resetting of the town-gown relationship, and he was willing to make a long-term deal so this fight wouldn't happen every year. This checked an important box for Cornell, because they were worried that Ben was a crazy old radical. He had defied all political norms and was clearly taking some political hits but had not flinched or folded. After discussing the idea of an agreement, I laid out the million dollars as our other condition. To my surprise, Dullea didn't flinch. Over a fast-paced week of negotiations, we had our agreement, incrementally raising Cornell's contribution to the city to $1 million over a several-year period. We had a signed document and a triumphal, if respectful, joint press conference with Cornell.

In the end, no trades worker lost a dime, and Cornell had upped its contribution to the city's services to a more appropriate level. At no time before in Cornell's 120-year history had its townsfolk truly stood up to the Ivy behemoth. To do it, we had to build a broad progressive coalition in support of fairness for workers and the community. We replaced a nice, competent but submissive mayor with an irascible Democratic Socialist tiger. We had dug and dug until we found the leverage to prevail in our public campaign.

We should have asked for two million. Ben got reelected, facing no internal Democratic Party opposition and defeating the well-funded Republican, a brash young developer of high-priced student apartments. Ben knocked on maybe three doors that whole campaign.

Our community agreement with Cornell was not only about money or fairness. We also established a principle. Our coalition, our politics, was not transactional, not "you scratch our back and we'll scratch yours." It was based on shared principles and vision. Our union was not a narrow, self-interested force. We lived in the community and were willing to fight for progressive community issues. This shared analysis meant that our non-labor allies understood our UAW fights were their fights too. Power was growing.

## Seeking Friends in High Places

Our hard-won political influence locally did not effectively translate into power in Albany, the seat of New York State government. After all, we were one local union, with two staff, including me, facing off against a massive, deeply connected 150-year-old Ivy League university. Cornell had lobbyists, and many political leaders were loyal, nostalgic alums. But Cornell, deep down in its most basic ancient history, was a radical organization in many ways. While it had become layered over in bureaucratic conservatism and a corporate-dominated board of trustees, Cornell had not always been so staid.

Ezra Cornell founded the school with the motto, "I would found an institution where any person can find instruction in any study." While to our ears today this may seem like a good marketing strategy for the University of Phoenix, for a prestigious university this was a radical origin story in three ways.

First, notice the use of the word "person." Cornell was dedicated to coeducation, a concept very few colleges adopted in the nineteenth century. In fact, most Ivy League campuses and elite schools didn't become coed until the 1960s. Cornell admitted its first woman student in 1870; five years later it admitted forty-nine women students, and growth was rapid thereafter.

Second, Cornell was committed to teaching subjects that included the practical and down to earth, among them agriculture, business, home economics, later human ecology, and industrial labor relations.

Finally, Cornell was a New York State land grant university, established with almost a million acres from the state. Cornell evolved into a hybrid university with seven full colleges. About half were considered private and half state supported. Tuition to go to the state-supported programs like the ILR School was way less than at the private colleges like Engineering or Arts and Sciences. But you could take classes across colleges, and we all lived and played together as one campus.

What did this mean for workers? It meant that about one-third of our members were in departments that were part of the SUNY system, specifically the state-supported colleges. We were all Cornell employees, and we were all on the same miserly pay scale, but if you worked "on the state campus" your pension and health care were connected to the SUNY system.

In fact, one of our strongest living-wage arguments was that custodians and food service workers at SUNY campuses in places like Buffalo, Binghamton, and Albany were paid 15 to 30 percent more than Cornell employees. Those SUNY schools had none of Cornell's advantages. No huge financial endowment, no wealthy corporate trustees, no big majority of students paying a ton of tuition. Somehow, they managed to pay their workers a lot better, and they were often in cities with similar costs of living.

How could we connect to the New York State power structure to engage them and strengthen our hand in battling Cornell here in isolated, rural Ithaca? During our first negotiation, when the strike was dragging on with no end in sight and our members' bellies starting to rumble, the UAW honchos reached out to Governor Hugh Carey. They were able to orchestrate Carey telling both sides to reach a deal. We did it in a way that Cornell knew we had done it, but we decided to keep that quiet, so it didn't look like we were the ones getting desperate. Carey's guy made a few phone calls, but the governor clearly didn't want to get directly involved. It did shake Cornell up a bit to think they were being observed by the governor, and it probably helped move Cornell on some very basic issues like binding arbitration for grievances and accepting our proposal for a joint health and safety committee.

The UAW was not focused on Cornell or university service and maintenance workers, however. Understandably, when you are part of an industrial union at the beginning stages of plant closings via offshoring and deindustrialization, your political priorities are firmly focused on saving jobs, mainly by getting New York State to offer incentives to manufacturers so they remain in the state. Our members had steady jobs, and while the UAW was disgusted by Cornell's arrogance and shocked by our poverty, they had hundreds of thousands of members at risk of unemployment.

Once again, we needed our own strategy. The UAW would help, but we couldn't expect to be their top state legislative priority. Standing in our way was our local New York State assemblyman, Sam MacNeil. He was a tall, older Republican. If the former CEO of General Motors had once famously quipped, "The business of government is business," old Sam would have added, "The business of my district is Cornell's business." We tried talking to him about our problems, but he said that what Cornell paid was none of his business. "That's what negotiations are for. Good luck," he told a group of us once.

The district had been in Republican hands for most of a hundred years and was skewed slightly Republican. Sam was smugly, comfortably, and openly in

Cornell's pocket. He got them special grants, cut ribbons next to the school's president, and could be seen cheering on Big Red sports teams. If Sam had become a full-time lobbyist for Cornell, he wouldn't have had to change a thing about his daily routine.

We knew taking on this longtime incumbent would be a bit of a fool's errand. Everybody knew Sam; he hadn't ever come close to losing, and was well entrenched. It was also a sprawling district that was much harder for us to campaign in than just our city or county. But we decided we had to start somewhere, and that we needed a Democrat who would put our issues front and center even if that meant losing. Some Dems were asking us to support a very moderate candidate as having the best chance. But we went with a brash, progressive young newcomer (of course we did), John Curry, who had moved to the Ithaca area from downstate, where he had been a political activist. Our theory was that the moderate would lose too, but at least John would force our issues into the public debate, further elevating worker rights and poverty.

Nobody gave John a chance, but he had a home with us, literally. His makeshift campaign office was a tiny space in our UAW Hall. He dogged MacNeil about his lack of support for regular working folks and for being so starry-eyed about Cornell that he lost his sense of the realities of his district. John was pugnacious, unafraid, and untethered to local niceties. He was a candidate we were positive would lose, but he was forcing all the right issues forward into the public eye and exposing Sam as the Ivy sycophant he was. Adjacent to the election itself was the fact that publicity on these issues placed Cornell in an exposed and awkward spotlight.

John did lose to the longtime incumbent, but he ran an aggressive race that forced MacNeil to work hard and answer tough questions. MacNeil seemed weakened, surprised that being accused of being in Cornell's pocket had damaged him. Our cause had moved to the center of a bigger stage.

Our opportunity came soon when in 1988 MacNeil chose not to run and was replaced by a weaker, less well-known Republican candidate. Deeply rooted in the Ithaca area, polished, respected, and popular within the Democratic Party, Marty Luster became our candidate. Marty had integrity and was solidly liberal. He wasn't rough around the edges in the ways we loved about John Curry or Mayor Ben, but he was solid about our issues and had a fighting chance to win. We did everything we could to get him elected, and win he did. Now, in addition to having turned the city and county toward working-class issues, we had a powerful ally representing us in Albany.

But Cornell's influence was wide and deep throughout the state. Marty pushed on our behalf, but it was also part of his job to make sure Cornell won a fair share of the state pie. No matter how bad Cornell behaved, we did not want to argue that Cornell should *not* get state resources. Not only would that have been a local PR disaster, but many of our members' jobs were directly tied to state funding. Our efforts at moral suasion and linkage of New York State's Cornell largesse to decent treatment of staff were not powerful enough.

The New York State Assembly was controlled by Democrats, but freshmen like Marty Luster wielded little power. Committee chairs, as senior power brokers, were key. Fortunately for us, Frank Barbaro was the chair of the Labor Committee. Barbaro was a former dockworker, a blue-collar New York City kind of tough guy with a heart of gold. It genuinely pissed him off that this snobby Ivy League college was getting a ton of state money and treating workers so shabbily. We worked with his staff and landed on the idea that Barbaro would come to Ithaca and hold a public hearing into these abuses.

As plans came together, Barbaro's staff and I were in weekly communication. At one point they told me Frank was thinking of inviting his buddy, Edward Sullivan, a fellow downstate Dem who just so happened to chair the Assembly's Higher Ed Committee. They would jointly conduct this hearing.

Cornell was really on the spot now. The hearing was a daylong affair held in City Hall. We lined up several workers to lead off, talking about their lives and living conditions. We presented data comparing Cornell to other Ivies, to SUNY, and to basic measurements of poverty. The emotions were on our side, and so were the facts. Faculty and community leaders also testified on behalf of the workers. Barbaro invited Cornell to attend, but they declined.

By the end of the hearing, Barbaro was livid. He wanted to threaten to cut off funding for Cornell, but we knew that could backfire with the community and many of our members if it became a public strategy. We also doubted Barbaro could enforce the threat at the state capitol. Cornell was too well-connected. Instead, Barbaro went directly and publicly after the university president, still Frank H. T. Rhodes at the time. Rhodes said he was in the midst of a highly touted $1.25 billion fund-raising campaign for Cornell and was "too busy" to participate in the hearing. At the post-hearing press conference, Barbaro led off his remarks to the assembled media by saying what he had heard was "an absolute disgrace, that workers could be working full time and helping make this beautiful campus so spectacular but be left in such dire poverty." He then looked right into the cameras and said, "President Rhodes, you need to find the money. I'm sure it's there. Or I will subpoena you for our next hearing, and we will find the money together."

Having this former New York City longshoreman, now a powerful state legislator, directly and personally confront Rhodes, an above-the-fray, very proper British aristocrat, was shocking to our local ecosystem. Like so many of our tactics, it was not a knockout blow. Cornell had friends in the governor's office and the legislature with more power than Barbaro or Sullivan. Still, the hearing was another brick in the power wall we were building, another frontal blow to Cornell's reputation. And it raised the specter that we might continue to amplify our message and expand our political reach beyond Ithaca.

The hearing also reinforced our standing in the politics of the local community, gave Luster cover to be more aggressive, developed more of our member leaders, and gave our members hope that someday, somehow, we would break through.

## Lifton Lifts All Boats

The final piece of our strategic power puzzle was how to fit the alumni in. Of all of my own Cornell identities, as student, activist, custodian, and union president, at the time being an alumni felt meaningless to me. I had few insights to offer. To Cornell, alums—and their money—mattered. A lot. The overwhelming majority of Cornell's fund-raising dollars came from alums. Frank Rhodes, like every university president, spent hundreds of hours hosting, catering to, and visiting with alums. He traveled to New York City, Los Angeles, China, you name it, because he had announced a $1.25 billion fund-raising campaign. We knew it was the wealthiest alums that mattered most. But Cornell also put enormous efforts into massive communications and outreach to all alums. You never know who might inherit a fortune or invent the internet! Back when I had neared graduation myself, working full time as a custodian, I noticed all the mail I started to receive, wooing me in ways I never got wooed as a lowly student. There was a senior gift, voted on in some strange process, and there was an election among alums for a seat on the board of trustees. Later there were special alum cruises and international trips, with top faculty along to rub elbows and teach about art, history, and culture. And every issue of the *Cornell Chronicle*, the internal university newspaper, seemed to have an article or four about some important alum.

The board of trustees was mostly alums. Despite their power, electing an alumni trustee sympathetic to the workers' plight seemed to be the least likely power-building strategy we could ever adopt. It seemed to have none of the elements that made for a smart strategy. Only alums could vote for alum trustees. Cornell ran the election, declared who was eligible, and how much space they would be given in a mailer. Cornell counted the votes. And what was even at stake here? If we won, we would get one friendly alum in a sea of fat-cat Cornell cheerleaders. Typical alum criteria were fanatical loyalty to Cornell and great wealth. After all, if you couldn't count on your own board of trustees to each kick in a million, who could you count on? Over time diversity came to matter, but not usually diversity of political perspective.

3A

The Ithaca Journal
Saturday, September 5, 1987

# City/Regional

City Editor
Payne Peterson
272-2321, Ext. 30

## LABOR DAY

Here is a list of services and recreational opportunities for the Labor Day weekend.

**TRANSPORTATION**
- Ithaca Transit: Regular schedule.
- Northeast Transit: Regular schedule.
- Tomtran: No service Monday.
- Gadabout: No service Monday.

**GARBAGE**
- City of Ithaca: Pick-up will be a day later.
- Collins Garbage Service: Pick-up will be earlier than usual.
- Superior Disposal Service: All high volume commercial garbage will be picked up. Trucks will pick up as much garbage as possible Monday. Any not picked up will be collected Tuesday.
- Hill's Sanitation Service: Regular service.

**BANKS**
- Norstar Bank: Closed Monday.
- Citizens Savings Bank: Closed today and Monday.
- Tompkins County Trust Company: Closed today and Monday.
- First Federal: Closed Monday.
- Marine Midland: Closed Monday.
- Alternatives Federal Credit Union: Closed Monday.
- Cornell Federal Credit Union: Closed Monday.
- Tioga State Bank: Closed Monday.
- Tompkins Employees Federal Credit Union: Closed Monday.

**GOVERNMENT OFFICES, SCHOOLS AND COLLEGES**
- Tompkins County: Offices closed Monday.
- City of Ithaca: Offices closed Monday.
- Cornell University: Offices closed Monday. Classes as scheduled.
- Ithaca College: Offices closed Monday. No classes.
- TC3: Offices closed Monday. No classes.
- Ithaca School District: Offices and schools closed Monday.
- U.S. Postal Service: Offices closed and no delivery Monday.

**SHOPPING AREAS**
- Downtown Ithaca: Most stores open.
- Pyramid Mall: Regular hours.

**RECREATION**
- Greater Ithaca Activities Center: Closed Monday.
- Southside Community Center: Closed Monday.
- Ithaca Youth Bureau: Offices closed Monday.
- Community School of Music and Art: Offices closed Monday.
- Senior Citizens Center: Office closed. Classes as usual.
- Tompkins County Public Library: Closed Monday.
- Bowl-o-Drome: Regular hours.
- Ide's Bowling Lanes: Regular hours.
- Tri-County Bowling Lanes: Regular hours.
- The City Health Club: Open from noon to 8:30 p.m. Monday.
- Ithaca Fitness Center: Regular hours.
- Courtside Racquet and Fitness Club: Closed Tuesday.

## Workers plan rally on Labor Day

By JAMES AINSWORTH
*Journal Staff*

The Labor Day weekend is here and only a few Ithacans will be toiling Monday.

While all city and county offices, banks and many businesses will be closed Monday, the Tompkins-Cortland Labor Coalition will hold its annual Labor Day picnic and rally from 1 to 5 p.m. in Stewart Park.

The 4-year-old coalition of labor and trade organizations in Tompkins and Cortland counties offers free hot dogs, hamburgers and soft drinks and will make a ceremonious announcement of this year's "Friend of Labor" and "Goat of Labor" winners.

The coalition represents approximately 7,000 workers in the two counties.

**'Labor is taking the offensive again . . . . Locally I think it's been a year of struggle.'**
**—Al Davidoff, UAW Local 2300 president**

UAW Local 2300 President Al Davidoff said the labor movement is once again gaining strength nationally.

"Labor is taking the offensive again. Working people have suffered two major adverse phenomenon in the last seven years — Ronald Reagan and the dismantling of the middle class and loss of decent jobs," Davidoff said.

"Locally I think it's been a year of struggle. We had the toughest labor confrontation we've ever had with the Cargill strike, and now we've got Cornell University and the UAW fighting on broad issues of poverty in the community and what the university's role should be," Davidoff said.

Davidoff said raising wages for Cornell workers would have a "ripple" effect and would benefit the entire economy.

Davidoff said he is pleased with the growth of labor coalition's newspaper, The Working Press, now in its second year of publication.

"The last issue of Working Press is the best ever and now we have local officials quoting it," Davidoff said.

In addition to the labor coalition picnic, Monday will mark the final day of the New York State Fair in Syracuse. Along with carnival rides, agricultural, art and science exhibits, there will be a concert performance tonight by Gary Puckett and the Union Gap, John Cafferty and the Beaver Brown Band Sunday and Monday will bring Micky Gilley and the Urban Cowboy Band to the stage.

Beginning today and continuing through Monday will be the 16th annual "Free Spirit Gliding Festival" in Elmira. More than 100 recreational and professional pilots and hang gliders are expected.

DREW PERINE/Journal Staff

**MAKING A CASE:** *UAW Local 2300 President Al Davidoff concludes an impassioned speech outlining the wage dispute between Cornell University and the union.*

## UAW's Davidoff tells tale of underpaid CU workers

By JOHN YAUKEY
*Journal Staff*

For four hours Friday an aluminum chair facing several TV cameras, a bushel of microphones and a panel of state legislators was occupied by Cornell University employees who took turns fleshing out claims that Cornell pays an "unlivable wage" with accounts of daily life.

They talked about "needing an additional job to get by," "no time for kids and family" and "not being able to save enough for a decent retirement."

The forum was an informal hearing on a six-month-old wage dispute between Cornell and the United Auto Workers Local 2300, which represents about 900 service and maintainence workers at the university.

Both Cornell and union representatives were invited to speak before Assemblyman Frank Barbaro, chairman of the state Assembly Labor Committee, and Edward Sullivan, chairman of the state Assembly Higher Education Committee.

Because Cornell officials declined to attend the session, which was held at City Hall and moderated by Ithaca Mayor John C. Gutenberger, testimony was one-sided.

By her own calculation, Cornell janitor Beverly MacDowell said that she takes home less than $4 per hour for her work after subtracting her taxes, union dues, and money she must pay for her rides to and from the university.

She's been working at Cornell more than three years, she said.

The middle-aged, scratchy-voiced widow lives in a small apartment that a couple in Spencer rents her for $100 per month.

She wants to own a house, but as matters stand she can barely afford to pay her own phone bills, she said.

"The way I see the picture, I'm not even breaking even I'm moving backwards," MacDowell said. "I would like to have enough to do more than just exist and I don't feel it's fair for me to have to go to my children for support. I know owning a home is a dream but that doesn't stop my desire for one."

In addition to union members, several candidates for the city elections in November attended the session.

In a written statement Democratic mayoral contender Daniel L. Hoffman, an alderman who represents the 5th Ward, said, "As our largest employer by far, many of us believe Cornell has a great deal to do with the setting of wage scales throughout the county, and that wage scale is unreasonably low."

According to a master list of union employee wages compiled by the university, about 160 workers earn less than $11,200 annually.

The federal government defines $11,200 as the poverty level for a family of four. Union and university officials have said they have no way of knowing how many on the list are single and how many have families.

"But $11,200 is a lousy wage to pay anybody," union official Cathy Valentino said.

Also according to the list, there are about 40 dining workers who earn less than $11,200, because of seasonal layoffs.

Both Hoffman and Gutenberger said they were "extremely disappointed" Cornell officials decided not to attend the hearing.

In Cornell's refusal, university spokesman John Burness wrote that the wage negotiations are "a matter between the university and its employees" and that a public forum would "undermine the collective bargaining system mandated under federal law."

Barbaro, who spoke briefly before the hearing, didn't agree.

"That's absolutely incorrect," he said. "I'm terribly disappointed that Cornell, a citadel of learning, fails to recognize the fact that a public hearing such as this does not preclude other efforts to solve a labor dispute. Fact finding is one of the best tried and true methods of settling such matters."

During a telephone interview after the hearing, Burness maintained that the press and the public were not "the proper place to settle a labor dispute."

**RAPT LISTENER:** *Frank J. Barbaro, chairman of the Assembly Labor Committee, listens to the union present its case in the Friday hearing in Common Council chambers at City Hall.*

Several weeks ago, UAW Local 2300 President Al Davidoff had proposed an official fact-finding investigation be conducted by a neutral third party. The university refused to participate on the same grounds.

Davidoff opened Friday's hearing with a prepared address laced with literary and political allusions — in his own words "telling a tale of two cities."

The union president, who was applauded by the mostly union audience of about 75, contrasted Cornell as "the gleaming city on the hill" to the "hoovervilles"

See TALE, 5A

## BRIEFLY

### IFD douses small fire

A small fire under a table in a third-story apartment at 105 N. Aurora St. was doused without incident about 9:45 p.m. Friday by the Ithaca Fire Department.

No one was hurt, fire officials said.

The fire trucks and other safety vehicles blocked the 100 block of North Aurora Street for about 45 minutes.

### Police investigate lake incident

The Tompkins County Sheriff's Department is investigating a possi-

**FIGURE 19.** Local 2300 pursued new and higher forms of political leverage in our fight for a livable wage. The chair of the New York State Assembly Labor Committee, Frank Barbaro, *pictured below*, and Assembly Higher Education Committee chair Edward Sullivan came to Ithaca City Hall to hold a hearing to investigate union allegations regarding Cornell's poverty wages. (With permission from the *Ithaca Journal*)

And would running a candidate, and losing, look bad for our cause?

But then along came Don Lifton, who showed that not everything we took on was or needed to be planned from inside the union. Sometimes you just get swept up in someone else's energy and initiative. Elected to the County Board of Representatives in 1983, Lifton became one of the most articulate and vocal critics of Cornell's approach to community and staff. He had a Cornell BA and a Cornell PhD, was married to a Cornell alum, and taught business at Ithaca College. He decided to run for the trustee board with a platform and aggressive campaign focused in part on Cornell's treatment of its workforce. We took an approach of helping Don every way we could, but there was nothing very public about our union's involvement. I was pretty sure Don would lose, and frankly felt that even if he won, Cornell would find a way to nullify the results, or most likely just announce a different winner. There was zero transparency, and we had reason to be cynical.

Our strategy was turnout, turnout, turnout. These elections were typically staid, low-participation affairs, with most alums just anointing whoever was recommended by the existing board. We felt that if we could mobilize votes from the three groups that didn't typically vote but might be counted on to support Don, we had a chance to upend the system with a stealth strategy. It was our only chance. Our strategy relied on three groups turning out to vote. We had contact lists for two groups that might include alums likely to vote for Don, if we could get to them: those who had been supporters of the ongoing effort to get Cornell to divest from apartheid South Africa, and alums of the ILR School. These were not huge lists, but each alum knew others, folks who took a more balanced view of the university.

It is a cliché that folks come to Cornell, fall in love with the beauty, the college town vibe, or with a person they met who didn't want to leave, and then stay for a long time. All those things in one way or another happened to me. I came to go to school. Found my calling, fell in love, had kids, and realized, even embroiled in class warfare for fifteen years, that this was a pretty lovely place to live. I had grown up in a working-class industrial suburb of Buffalo. I had literally never had the concept of "nature" enter my mind until I came to Cornell. Hills, waterfalls, parks all made for a great place to raise a family.

Locals. Turns out there were like a thousand other alums who had also stuck around. The challenge was reaching them. There was no list, but there was a certain amount of networking that could be done. Beyond this, Don and I realized we had to go broad. So he went public with his campaign. It was like he was running for office on a platform focused on Cornell's responsibility to the Ithaca community. Don was the kind of guy who could talk about his love for the university with total sincerity. Because he was sincere. He wrapped his deep criticisms in a flag of warm, glorious rhetoric about Cornell's history and true values. Don's "there's something wrong in paradise" message appealed to the mixed feelings most local alums had. Local alums were not rich corporate types. They were academics and upper-middle-class professionals or their spouses. There were also—and still are—some alternative lifestyle, hippie and activist types, who just loved the pastoral area and were comfortable in a town that seemed so accepting.

At one point Cornell reached out to Don complaining about the "unprofessional" public way he was running the campaign and the irregularity of running a campaign at all. The arrogance that underlay the defense of a system that had simply anointed insiders seemed absurd, but it told me that Cornell was not going to let Don win. I told Don, "They are just going to disqualify you." There were absolutely no rules against anything we did. But the election itself, if we even made it that far, happened in darkness. The counting of mail ballots was an inside job. I told Don that I thought we'd never know how we really did. Plus, I assumed Cornell had its own networks, much bigger than our little troika of targets. Whether it happened honestly or through corruption, I was sure we were going down in flames.

Don was more than a decade older than me, but he was always youthfully ebullient. When I picked up the phone in the UAW office and it was Don, I could tell something was up. He practically giggled. "Al Davidoff, are you sitting down? We won, my brother!" Don, who had been much more hopeful than I during our little campaign, always reassuring me we could win and Cornell wouldn't cheat, added, "Holy shit! I am as shocked as you are, Al. We are going to have some fun with this."

There were some interesting anomalies with the Cornell board, flowing from the New York State land grant history and the university founders' sense of an egalitarian purpose. There was a faculty trustee, a student trustee, and two labor trustees, and the governor and the state legislature each had reps or served themselves but rarely showed. Don immediately began looking for allies on the board. We now had a bona fide, elected leader of alums on the highest decision-making body of the university who could use that platform to support our struggle.

But more than that, what had we learned? If we could reach large numbers of more progressive alums, could we reach large numbers of the most influential graduates? What would it take to move those more corporate or moderate stakeholders to some form of relevant action on our behalf? Could our decade of campus, community, and state alliances also be organized in a way that would influence alums, and therefore Cornell, to care enough to budge?

Our success in targeting progressive alumni in the effort to elect Lifton to the trustee board sowed the seeds of a new idea and a new campaign, our most comprehensive and strategic campaign yet.

## Discussion Questions

- Do you see Local 2300 and the community's interests as being significantly the same? Where might they diverge?
- How do you think the many socially conservative members reacted to the union getting involved in a wide range of internal and external civil rights struggles? Or electoral politics? How did the union handle this possible tension?
- The union attempted to be aligned and integrated with the community, not simply in a "you scratch our back, we will scratch yours" approach. How do these approaches differ, and what might the consequences of each approach be?
- The union pushed the local political envelope, upsetting potential allies by helping lead Ben Nichols's insurgent campaign. What are the advantages and risks of this more assertive and independent strategy?
- The union indicates it lacked sufficient power and will to threaten Cornell with a loss of state funding. Was this a missed opportunity? Might this threat backfire on campus?
- How plausible and strategic a target are Cornell alums likely to be in a living-wage fight? Do you see a theory of greater impact and better outcomes that the union is failing to pursue?
- Is there a more cooperative approach with Cornell that might have led to better outcomes?

12

# IN THE SHADOW OF THE TOWER

All our progress building union power came together in one major, reenergized living-wage campaign. We broadened our message to emphasize the reality that women and people of color were particularly impoverished, but our main theme had been consistent from the first fight back in 1981: No worker should be paid poverty wages. We should be paid comparably to Cornell's peer institutions. In more recent years we had begun to challenge Cornell's role in the community, too, leading a parallel fight to get the university to share its largesse more broadly and fairly with the Ithaca community.

Cornell's counterarguments had evolved some. At first it was, "We just pay the market rate." But that was ludicrous, given that they set the market and could obviously afford so much more. They tried pointing out that it was cheaper to live in Ithaca than places where some peer institutions existed, like Columbia in New York City, or Stanford in California. There were two problems with that. First, Ithaca was not very cheap. Being a college town meant that housing costs were way higher than in nearby rural towns, for example. Second, even after using the US Bureau of Labor Statistics cost-of-living data to adjust to differences across cities, our wages were still way behind. The higher SUNY wage standards were also based in upstate New York cities with similar or even lower costs of living.

Finally, Cornell landed on the "but our benefits are terrific" argument. Yes, compared to the local grocery story or auto repair shop, their benefits were superior. But compared to the SUNY system or other Ivies, they were just average. Then Cornell made a mistake. They talked a lot about their educational benefits, such as the ability for staff and their children to get a free education at Cornell (although years later they reduced this benefit). And, of course, at the time that was a huge benefit, worth many tens of thousands of dollars. It was a benefit that reinforced the special, caring, benevolent identity Cornell had cultivated for decades.

We agreed Cornell should provide decent benefits. But we couldn't pay our bills or feed our families with benefits. We also pointed out that the two most important benefits were regressive in their impact, a fact that is true for most employers. Workers paid a flat amount for health insurance premiums, deductible, and co-pays. That meant a $15,000 a year printing assistant might pay the same $1,000 a year in health care costs as the $80,000 a year professor, or more than five times the percent of his or her income. As for pensions, they were based on a percentage of your salary, so low-wage workers got screwed coming and going.

Regarding the educational benefits, we had always acknowledged that it was a special benefit of working at Cornell, then pivoted to our main point, that you still needed a livable wage. As it turns out, even the tuition benefit was a chimera. We had been slow to ask a fundamental question. How many of our members were actually using the fantastic educational benefits? We submitted a formal information request. The law requires a unionized employer to provide all sorts of info relevant to bargaining. I recall Pete Tufford telling me that he was having a hard time pulling it all together, that it was housed in different departments. We waited and pressed and began to smell a rat the longer it took. Finally, Pete told me that there were two employees who had taken some free classes, but that not one single child of Cornell's one thousand service staff was a full-time student, receiving that amazing free tuition benefit.

A universe lived inside that one data point. Even I was shocked. It reminded me of my own privilege. Growing up in a working-class suburb but with middle-class resources and two parents set me up for the opportunities I had. Maybe 30 percent of the parents in my childhood neighborhood outside of Buffalo had a college degree, but 80 percent of their kids went to college. That was how the working class middle class forged upward mobility. But this was the northern tip of Appalachia, no matter how much Ivy there was. Maybe 10 percent of our members could have been called middle class, and that had as much to do with the teacher or cop they were married to as it did being at the top of the Cornell service pay scale. All the support needed along the way for a kid to end up at Cornell was missing for most members. When we talked about this at a membership meeting, a few of our most bitter members said that even when our kids have the grades, they never get accepted. Cornell doesn't accept them *because* it's free. Cornell was officially out of arguments. But they still wielded power, and that trumped any advantage and support we had from our call to reason and fairness.

We had come a long way since that first traditional bargaining and the UAW International–designed strike in 1981, developing a more nuanced theory and creative exercise of power in the process. We had figured out a wide range of ways to keep our members involved, expanded leadership roles, and provided a menu of opportunities to participate in the life of our union. We had also shown Cornell that we were willing to confront, embarrass, and challenge university leadership at fancy campus dinners or signature campus events, and even at their front doors. Our strikes were brief but widely supported, edgy and creative.

We had come to understand that threats to Cornell's reputation and activating a broad range of critical stakeholders were keys to moving Big Red. We had built local labor solidarity, a broader progressive community coalition, and elected a radical mayor, state rep, alumni trustee, along with key allies on Ithaca Common Council and the County Board.

Along the way we had made important incremental progress. We had an effective grievance procedure and had rooted out a great deal of favoritism, including putting an end to the hated merit-pay system. Supervisors who had sexually harassed or bullied workers were exposed, made to stop, or forced out. Years of service, or seniority, meant something now in case of layoffs and in areas like vacation schedules, and was more of a factor in promotions than before.

Yes, raises had improved, and we negotiated a step system that got more people to livable wages faster. But we were still a good way from parity with peer institutions, and hundreds of Cornell workers still made poverty wages.

Now we had to weave together our power analysis, political resources, and years of experience into a more advanced strategy to get a living wage.

"Share the Wealth" became our slogan and mantra. Soon lots of members and supporters could be seen around town in their new T-shirts and sweatshirts, emblazoned "Share the Wealth," with militant workers, fists upraised and demonstrating in front of a backdrop of the iconic Cornell bell tower, saying it all. These designs, from a small T-shirt silk-screening collective of two radical lesbian friends of the union, sold through the roof. Shops literally called the union asking us if they could carry our line of clothing.

OK, that was good. Sure, if paying workers at Cornell a livable wage could have been put to a public vote, we would have won in a landslide. We were a fashionable and popular local cause, but still searching for a way we could we ratchet up the pressure on Cornell where we now knew it to be most vulnerable—its reputation among key stakeholders.

With the success of our public-access TV show, it dawned on me that perhaps we could make a video to help make our case. I began imagining all that we could pack into it: the mayor, the esteemed professor, the alumni trustee, the impoverished lives of many of our members despite the wealth of their employer. I also knew that our members were more than capable of telling their stories.

Through some friends I contacted a small documentary filmmaker named Pam Kieffer from New York City. She had made a short antiwar video and seemed to have the kind of grassroots, progressive politics that might make her sympathetic to our struggle. I had *no* idea what this would cost, how long it should be, or if the local would even like this idea.

Pam and I hit it off right away. She was a pro, but a pro with deep political commitment to grassroots power and respect for working people. Her passion was political work, but commercial work paid the bills. "That antiwar video I did? The cat food commercial paid for it." Pam understood we were a small union, so I hoped she would make it affordable. In my mind I was developing a strategy that called for distributing this all over campus and beyond, so—pre-internet—we would not only have to foot the production cost but also make hundreds of VHS copies.

During my fifteen years as president of Local 2300 I don't think I ever experienced more skepticism for one of my crazy ideas than around making this video. The total cost was going to run about $7,000, and that seemed like a huge amount of money to us. As local president, I was paid what I made coming out of the shop, a custodian's salary. Given I was a low-seniority, unskilled worker, that meant making less than four dollars an hour at first. After years of paying me that modest wage, plus whatever raises we negotiated with Cornell, the local bumped the president's salary up to the average of the bargaining unit, which moved me to around seven dollars an hour. We were so frugal that when we went to UAW conferences, we would all pile into a single car, double up in rooms, and pack sandwiches for the trip. Once when we visited Solidarity House, the huge UAW headquarters in Detroit, I brought an empty suitcase and loaded it up with everything from free UAW T-shirts to legal pads to Scotch tape so we could save a few bucks on supplies.

Our culture was to do a lot with a little, so forking out seven grand for a video seemed extravagant. The hesitant reaction from the executive board forced me to hone the strategy. What would be on the video, and how would we use it? Why would this work where other approaches hadn't? After a couple months thinking and debating, the executive board went along with the idea. It was a divided vote, and even my supporters were dubious.

Pam Kieffer and I dived in. Emily Drucker, a terrific Cornell student intern, was a huge help, and a half dozen members and other interns pitched in, but mostly it was Pam and I joined at the hip. My original idea was to focus on making an irrefutable case for our raises. That message would not come from the union; it would come from venerable campus and community members. I thought those faculty and elected leaders would be most impressive to the alums and powerful university officials who needed to be moved. We would sprinkle in some footage of workers talking about their lives.

I lined up several union members who I thought might do a good job talking about the hardships they endured trying to live on Cornell wages. We ended up including seven. We could have filmed them sitting in our office, but with Pam teaching me the importance of setting, we decided to ask our members if we could shoot them at home and at work. Pam also roved the neighborhoods where they and other workers lived, rural trailer parks and off-the-beaten-path clusters of small, often structurally unsound homes. She captured the harsh, physical realities of this northern tip of Appalachia in the dead of winter.

After the first few sessions I knew I had been completely wrong about what this video needed to be. Our members were amazing. Simply by telling their stories they laid bare a deeper indictment of the university than any esteemed ally talking head. By having them tell their stories from their homes we were able to include children and the cold physical realities of poverty. Cornell victimized them, but they didn't convey victimhood. They showed their resilience, appreciation of Cornell's beauty, and especially their pride at being able to improve the lives of the students they fed and cleaned for. They expected more from Cornell because they felt a part of the university. The details were what made the portraits real, three dimensional.

Denise, a dorm custodian, shared that she could only afford to heat half her house in the winter, so she and her three children slept in one room together for those months. With her children playing around her in a cramped combined living room–bedroom, Denise said, "We can't have their friends here for a sleepover until the summer. Their friends say, 'We have you at our house, why can't we come to yours?' I just saved enough to replace the outhouse, but we still don't have a water heater. So I carry a big army kettle and heat that for hot water."

Bev, a housekeeper at Cornell's on-campus Statler Hotel, shared photos of her dream home and described how that dream remains out of reach even after decades of service. "Everyone who works should be able to own a home, but my income is way too low to qualify for any loans. I feel the dream slipping away."

Lillie, sitting with her two daughters snuggled against her, spoke about the free school lunch one of them received, and how the other had four teeth that needed to be pulled, but that she didn't have the money for a dentist.

Jeanne spoke about being laid off repeatedly during the year, having to hunt for temp jobs and borrow money. But she also shared how she had two of the law students she cooked for at the small Law School dining unit over for dinner, "So they could have a family meal, get away from the university for a bit."

Henry shared that he couldn't afford to repair the frayed electrical wires in part of his home, so he went without, shutting off the electricity in that part of the house to avoid a fire while he saved ten dollars a month. "What gets me up and going in the morning is knowing I've got a bunch of kids relying on me to do my job."

Jim spoke about his second full-time job, which meant he worked "twelve consecutive days for every two days off." He quoted his exact income from his W2: $13,863.

Bonnie stood in the cold wind outside her trailer with her young son playing in the barren background and spoke about how she didn't see a bright future for him. She didn't imagine he would be able to go to college because she couldn't give him the opportunities he needed. Looking into the camera and glancing into the crook of her empty arm, she said, "and I promised those things to him as a baby."

"He shouldn't have to wear last year's boots to school. I have to wake my two children up at 4:00 a.m., get them in the car, and drop them at a sitter so I can get to work on time. Having a phone is a luxury. If there was an emergency, I couldn't call for help."

Bev ended with a devastating, unedited message. As she spoke with a large cross on the wall behind her, we mixed in images of some of Cornell's most beautiful buildings and then the contrast of the children of the workers from the video, in their austere, poverty-framed homes: "I find Cornell cares very much for their image. But image is not what makes people happy. Image is not what makes people satisfied. They have more than enough money for new buildings. More than enough money to import marble. And in the meantime, the people that work there are being hurt very badly, emotionally, financially, every which way. And it's really a shame because Cornell is one of the most beautiful campuses that you could want to see. And to me, it's a mark against them. I just pray that there's someone in management that will come out of their ivory tower."

The video ends with two statistics. That Cornell had raised $670 million, halfway to their $1.25 billion goal, and that according to the official federal standards, 80 percent of Cornell's 1,075 service workers earned poverty-level wages.

It was completely unscripted. Just responses to a few questions with the camera rolling. It was riveting and heartbreaking.

Pam and I knew we had something explosive, so we flipped our plan on its head. This video would be a portrait of Cornell's workforce. We added plenty of powerful leader experts, but *In the Shadow of the Tower* was a brutally honest window into the impact of Cornell's greed on its loyal and dignified workforce. Neither the union nor I, its president, appear even once in the video. I knew who my target audience was, and I knew they were not pro-union. I wanted every wealthy alum to watch this, and I wanted it to find their heart and wake them up. And I wanted it to scare the crap out of Day Hall.

While they had been demoted to supporting cast, our talking heads were also amazing. A decade of groundwork came together. Mayor Ben Nichols, who had spent a lifetime at Cornell, starting as a student in 1937 and then professor for forty years, and now mayor of Ithaca, spoke about how unconscionable poverty wages were and how that dragged the whole community down. Labor law professor Risa Lieberwitz pointed out the statistics that showed Cornell far below average when compared to other Ivies. Both Risa and Ben hammered one of our strongest points. We had demanded Cornell agree to a neutral fact-finder to offer a recommendation for fair wages, but Cornell had refused. As Ben said, "The willingness to examine the truth is the role of a university. This refusal violates those ideals."

Alum trustee Don Lifton, like Ben elected through our union's efforts, eloquently described the beauty of the university and how these workers were responsible for so much of what made Cornell great but were so mistreated. Don stated emphatically, "We are a one-horse town. Cornell sets the standard for wages for the whole community." He also pointed out that fellow Ivy college Brown had made a public commitment to eliminate poverty in Providence, its much larger host community.

We also had a powerful clip from Assemblyman Frank Barbaro, pointing out that there were full-time workers forced to live as he had during the Depression. Barbaro skewered the contradictory image of the students "with their caps and gowns flowing, and the workers in the shadow of the buildings living in poverty . . . outrageous." He added, "The money I'm sure the workers will need for a decent standard of living is not going to be that much, and the university is just going to have to find it, it's that simple. And if they won't, we'll come in and hold a hearing and subpoena the books, and we'll find for them where the money is."

Cornell might have seen this group of campus and community leaders as "the usual suspects," but they were not sure what to make of our one "cameo" from a major national figure.

Jesse Jackson had run a serious race for president in 1988 and was clearly the leading civil rights leader in America during the 1980s and '90s. Mayor Ben had been a Jackson delegate to the Democratic National Convention. Our local, with an 85 percent white, rural membership, voted to encourage the UAW International to endorse Reverend Jackson. No national leader spoke about workers or poverty as powerfully, and the local's support was another example of our members' rising consciousness about our place in the world.

While we were in the last stages of filming, Ben had learned that Jackson was coming to Cornell to speak on campus. The mayor was a bit irritated, and quickly got through to Jackson's people to say, "You can't come to our community and only visit Cornell." We knew the university was paying a hefty speaking fee, but for Jackson, like many progressive leaders, these gigs helped pay for all the unpaid and underpaid work they did. But the symbolism was all wrong, and Ben pushed hard for a second event to be added.

Ben could be a curmudgeon with grownups, but he had a generous sweet spot with kids. He was like a godfather to my first daughter, Lucy Rose, who was born days before Ben's first inauguration. Ben's big idea for Jackson was to bring him to the downtown community center, GIAC, which was a center for youth programs serving primarily the Black community. The event involved about two hundred children packed into a small gym.

Learning about Ben's initiative in making this second event happen, I realized that maybe, just maybe, there was something else we could ask Jackson to do. We were getting close to wrapping up the filming for our video, and we were in the midst of a campaign with Cornell, so I wanted to try to get Jackson to add his voice. Ben wrote a letter to him laying out our livable-wage fight, but we weren't sure he had even read it. Ben agreed to find a way to get me a few minutes with him so I could make my pitch. The opportunity came in the ten-minute window as Jackson finished his Cornell speech and was being driven downtown.

Jesse Jackson sat in the front seat with the driver, and Ben and I sat in the back. Ben introduced me and referenced his letter about the union fight. Jackson had no idea what he was talking about and seemed exhausted and, I worried, put upon by this last-minute ask. I gave him my best two-minute rap about the struggle, knowing he had been front and center with a similar fight at Yale. I could not tell if he was listening. He barely acknowledged me. I ended, desperate, saying that we had a little film crew at the GIAC event, and if he would please be willing to take just two minutes after, we would love to include him in our campaign video.

He didn't say yes, he didn't say no. He just looked out the window. I felt Ben and I had tried, but this was just not meant to be.

Coming into GIAC with Ben Nichols and Jesse Jackson took me out of my disappointed funk in two seconds flat. As soon as Reverend Jackson entered that gym with Ben, his staffer and me trailing a few feet behind, there was an explosion of cheering and joy the likes of which I have never witnessed before or after. To these young Black kids, this was the most important leader in the country. The energy was so beautiful and intense it felt like waves of hope and pride were echoing everywhere. The contrast with the staid affair on campus was not lost on us. I could see Jackson pull himself out of his fatigue and just light up.

Ben introduced Jesse. I listened but then went to check on our tiny film crew. Filmmaker Pam was back in New York City, and I had two nervous friends with a camera in a small room. I needed to get Ben and his staffer to exit Jackson to this room before he left for the airport. Meanwhile, Jackson was in the midst of a beautiful sermon. He painted a picture of what these young people needed to do: be active, care for one another, stay in school. He also painted a picture of what they should expect from our world: respect, college, a future with good jobs. He ended with rousing inspiration and love, urging them to stand up for what is right and always expect to be treated with dignity.

The speech was over, and I knew Jackson needed to get to the airport. We whisked him through the crowd and into the back corridors of the building. We got him to the room, where he could sit down, catch his breath, and have some water. He saw the camera and said to me, "So what are we doing here?"

I pitched hard, maybe sounding a bit desperate. "Livable wages, poverty fight at Cornell. Largest employer, depresses wages for the whole community." He paused, looked down, smiled at me, and said, "Same fight at Yale." He turned to the camera and said, "Let's go, I got a plane to catch." Jackson then spoke briefly, but he was eloquent as always, ending with, "I stand with you in your drive to organize and demand a livable wage." Fourteen not-so-little words. Our little film now had a nationally renowned civil rights leader and agitator turning up the heat on Cornell.

It cracked me up thinking that Cornell had paid $10,000 for Jackson to spend a couple of hours on campus, while Mayor Ben and the city had the best event for free, and we had Jesse Jackson on video in solidarity with our fight. It was doubly fun knowing that Cornell would have no idea how deeply involved Jackson might be in our plans. They had no idea how tenuous and serendipitous this moment had been.

I worked closely with Pam to edit the video. It felt like we had so much good stuff it was hard to know how to put it all together, how long was too long, and even how to sequence it. Pam was great. She was moved by the workers' stories and had a clear vision that guided us. We finished it up with a running time of about twenty minutes. We showed it to the executive board, and they were impressed. I also wanted to show it to each of the workers filmed. We had obtained releases giving permission, but I wanted to make sure they felt comfortable. I also wanted them to know that they represented hundreds of coworkers, and their honesty was going to help us win better wages. Even though they had each revealed painful truths, and brought us into their homes, none of them flinched about sharing their lives.

We decided to call the video *In the Shadow of the Tower*. The Cornell bell tower, formally called McGraw Tower after the alum who donated the first nine bells, is a beautiful, 173-foot-high structure built in 1891. Student "chimes masters" play the bells throughout the day, and the giant tower clock rings out the time on the hour. It's a classic, iconic, continuous aural and visual manifestation of the beauty of Cornell. To the average custodian, secretary, or food service worker it was a much steeper drop than 173 feet from those Ivy heights to where we worked and lived.

This was not a video about our union or about a campaign per se. Nor did we make it for workers, to show to workers. After all, they lived this story. We made it to energize our allies and to terrify the Cornell administration that the shameful truth was to be widely exposed. And expose it we did, showing *In the Shadow of the Tower* hundreds of times, at faculty meetings, in dorms, and meetings of two dozen different campus organizations, in the community, you name it. Given the primitive state of media, no YouTube or internet, we mass-produced five hundred VHS copies. We hoped this was the added tool we needed to dismantle Cornell's ivory tower, and we meant to use it.

Our contract campaign heated up, pushing Cornell at the bargaining table, but we were still a little over a million dollars apart on wages. That is when we put our alumni strategy into full gear. We had spent a year building a list. From the beginning of our local, we had labor-friendly Cornell student interns working with us, and this project was their baby. We had the interns digging into hundreds of bits of information to build our alumni list. Between the *Cornell Chronicle* and the student-run *Cornell Daily Sun* there was a ton of coverage of major alum donations. We even did some dumpster diving, searching through the stinky garbage dumpster outside Day Hall. The interns did the laborious detective work, pre-internet, of finding phone numbers and addresses for over five hundred major donors.

Our interns were incredibly dedicated. Some got credit, some were being paid for work-study, with us chipping in a small amount. They typically interviewed members for the *Bear Facts*, conducted research, and organized other students. We took them everywhere: bargaining, grievances, clock meetings, you name it. They usually developed a close bond to our struggles, and dozens went on to work in the labor movement after they graduated.

This list was literally a gold mine. One alum actually owned a gold mine. It would cost Cornell $1 million to give each of our members an additional $1,000 raise. Among them, the alums on our list had given Cornell more than fifty times that much.

Alum list in hand, we started writing. First, we sent them a letter outlining the issues and urging them to support paying the workers a livable wage. This letter came to them not from us, but from a couple of Cornell's most prominent faculty, world-famous in their fields, including a Nobel Prize winner, who agreed to sign it. Next, working with trustee Don Lifton, we sent copies of *In the Shadow of the Tower* to another group of fifty powerful alums.

If hearing "ouch" lets you know someone is hurt, the video and what we were doing with it had Cornell squealing. They hated it, and claimed it was inaccurate and misleading. While all the facts cited by Mayor Nichols, Assemblyman Barbaro, Professor Leiberwitz, and Trustee Lifton had long been verified, what really mattered were the workers' stories. How could you refute their lived lives and struggles? The pride they took in their work and in their homes, no matter how poor the visible realities shown, came across with power and eloquence. Once when management challenged the video as false, I said, "So that's not where Bonnie lives? When she says she can't afford to buy new school clothes, she's making that up?"

"That's not Jim's annual income that forces him to work a second job?"

"Denise is lying about not having enough income to heat her house?"

We described to the Cornell administration exactly what we were going to do. I told them we had mass-produced the video, and we had a huge list of alums. I told them about the letter from faculty, and the letter with the video from alum trustee Don Lifton. I told them we were sending fifty videos a week and that Lifton or a faculty member would follow up with a phone call to talk to each wealthy alum. I told them we would stop when we reached a contract with a pay scale that took us out of poverty. Five hundred wealthy alums was a good list, but of course Cornell would never know if we had five thousand within reach.

It was kind of like a threat to kill one hostage each week until our just demands were met, but less violent. We were going after Cornell's most valued commodity, the one thing more important to them than workers, faculty, students, or community: their wealthy alums. Fifty at a time. We didn't need to win a majority and knew we never would with these titans of industry. But we knew and Cornell knew that some of them would be upset by this video, and that all of them had other causes, other charities pleading for their millions. It only took us "getting to" a few out of every batch of fifty for the big $1.25 billion fund-raising push to take a serious hit.

Our other strategies were fully engaged. Sending out the video and letters was only part of our strategy. We continued preparing for a possible strike and building widespread support. We had learned how to build and use our power as a fighting union.

We got Cornell's attention. Once we started sending out the video, Tufford contacted me away from bargaining. He never enjoyed the ugliness of the fight. Whatever his own beliefs were, he never seemed to take any pleasure in keeping us down. He was doing a job within constraints that were set multiple pay grades over his head. Literally, all Pete said was "uncle." The only other time in a decade of struggles with Pete that I ever heard him say that word was when they caved in for Roy Lee Clements. I could feel my pulse quickening. I wasn't sure I heard him. "What did you just say, Pete?"

He laughed, "I think we can work something out, but we need to know this will resolve things, and you have to stop sending the video out immediately."

We had bargaining in a day or two. I told Pete that of course we were interested. I knew that some in management had come to see me as someone they could never trust, someone who would always be in their face no matter how reasonable they were. But my fight—our fight—was always about the issues, and once again that meant a wage increase that brought us out of poverty.

Did I enjoy the fight? Most of the time. I knew it was educating and even radicalizing hundreds of workers, so the fight was important for many reasons. But the truth is the fight was always about respect, dignity, and livable wages and benefits. Give us that and the relationship would mature. I wasn't sure what that would feel like, or where I would fit in with a "mature" relationship. I wasn't sure how you build and sustain a good union without these kinds of struggles. But we had been fighting for a decade, and many, many workers were still on the edge. Ending the poverty was always the priority; embarrassing and threatening the university was a means to an end. And to be honest, some members were tired of perpetual struggle. I was very open to learning what a truly successful contract settlement felt like.

Over the next few sessions, we worked out a contract. We worked it out because Cornell added a million dollars more to the wage pool. We eliminated the lowest pay grade, bumping all those workers into a higher, better-paid, grade. Nobody would get rich. But the added amount, focused on the lower-paid positions, made a difference that provided a small step out of poverty.

And we still had about three hundred videos left . . . a $7,000 video that was the culmination of a decade of lessons learned, strategies developed, and power built. A $7,000 video put our members' pain and dignity in places no one could ignore. A $7,000 video that pushed Cornell to add a million dollars into the pockets of our members. A video backed by a thousand workers readying for another fun and ferocious strike.

## Discussion Questions

- Even ten years after the union's initial victory, many members were still making poverty-level wages. What does this mean? Are employers just too powerful to move more than a marginal amount? If you were starting a union like this, are there shortcuts that could get you further faster? If not, what does that mean about the limits of union power?

- Local 2300 tried many approaches to win better lives for its members. Which strategies and allies seem pivotal to the breakthroughs made?
- Why do you think Cornell added significant financial resources to this round of bargaining?
- How do you feel about Cornell workers sharing painful personal aspects of their lives to push the university? How do you think those workers felt?
- Local 2300 was limited to producing five hundred videocassettes and mailing them. Given huge changes in the ability to communicate more easily to wide audiences, how can unions and social justice organizations magnify powerful messages and create greater leverage for justice?
- When fundamental wages, benefits, and working conditions are fair and decent, how does a union build an engaged membership? Are there some lessons from this book that suggest what a healthy union in a more mature, fairer environment can do to remain vibrant and support other workers and the community?
- What should a mature relationship between labor and management look like? What are its pros and cons?

# Epilogue

I spent my early twenties to my middle thirties building Local 2300. I've spent the rest of my life in the labor movement with the AFL-CIO, 1199 SEIU, AFT, and the global Solidarity Center. It is no exaggeration to say that what I learned at the UAW 2300, and the people I worked alongside with there, have influenced me every single week of my life. What I learned about strategy and authentic empowerment from Barbara Rahke; what I learned about courage and effective organizing from Emily Apgar and Carol Lane/Simon; or what I learned about how the chutzpah and determination of one person like Cathy Valentino can launch a movement are not distant memories. Those experiences more than any others formed me and continue to be my guideposts. Those years centered my sense of values and purpose for a lifetime.

There was a lot of luck and quirky twists of fate that catapulted me into and sustained me in this fifteen-year experience. I'm surprised Cornell hired me. I'm surprised I lasted as a custodian. And I'm surprised that I ended up being the local's president. The UAW and other unions offered me "big" jobs during my time with the local, but I was haunted by my own faulty climb up the learning curve. I could not leave to teach or lead others when I was still learning and testing strategies that would grow and sustain an effective, healthy union. This is the story of that learning curve, personally and organizationally. While there are some good books out there about macro trends and mega challenges for the labor movement, most workers experience their union at the work site or, at most, local union level. I wanted to share one set of union-building stories from the place where most workers reside.

There came a point near the end when I realized I was not the best leader going forward. It seemed like I could become one of those "presidents for life," getting easily reelected every few years. But while I had grown tremendously, I knew the local and I were becoming mutually stuck. I couldn't keep growing without moving on, and the local could benefit from fresh thinking and leadership. It dawned on me that I had become really good at a strategic alphabet from maybe A to G, but that there were other ideas I would never learn and parts of me that couldn't flourish if I didn't take the next step.

Local 2300 wasn't my work world—it was my life. My friendships centered on these labor and political struggles. I couldn't go food shopping in our small town without counting on an extra fifteen minutes to listen to a grievance or plot some political move. My oldest children grew up in Local 2300. They loved the office, and the leaders like Cathy Valentino, Perry Huested, Pam Mackesey, and big Harry Evans were like aunts and uncles they grew up with. They were raised at our rallies and picket lines and at huge Labor Day picnics that I often emceed.

I've been married twice, both union related. My first wife is an amazing teacher and a lifelong labor and community activist. We met at a labor council meeting. She made many sacrifices to support the union, including getting a job at the Ramada as a waitress to help the union win bargaining rights for workers there. My current wife, Meggin, was a worker that led the organizing of her workplace. She was so militant I had to take her aside and say, "You realize, we need to win a majority of your coworkers. Those fence sitters will not vote yes if they think plan B is to burn this motherfucker down." We won that campaign by one vote. She occasionally reminds me that she was that one vote, and I always say, "They all were." Her political fierceness and feminism have helped me keep my politics straight and grow as a man.

Other leaders of Local 2300 went on to many notable achievements. Pam Mackesey served many years on Ithaca's Common Council as well as in the County Legislature; Cathy Valentino was elected the town supervisor of the largest of the towns ringing the city; and Jean McPheeters, a student, clerical worker, and organizer, became chair of the Democratic Party and legislative assistant to two congressmen. My good friend Kurt Edelman had also migrated from being an ILR School student activist into this fight. He was a short-order cook and a great leader within our campaign and then for a lifetime in unions like UNITE and SEIU. Any of these amazing folks could write their own, different version of these stories. This is my story, and I may have been the president, but from the beginning we were a collective, with a never-ending stream of dedicated activists and leaders learning together.

What progress Local 2300 did or did not make after my five terms as president is not in the scope of this story. I've resisted any temptations over the years to be some kind of senior adviser or president emeritus. I've had a few experiences over the decades since that saddened me, like one new Local 2300 president who reached out to tell me that "we were past all that unnecessary fighting, that Cornell was really a partner, and that he had built a comfortable relationship." All I could think about was the line, "He was born on third base and thinks he hit a triple." It also seems true that over the years the university itself became more liberal. There have been university presidents who demonstrated deeper caring and far less arrogance toward staff and community. Regardless, it's important for former leaders to resist too much backward, over-the-shoulder judging. I know the local has both made progress but also lost small units and failed to do much further organizing. I wonder if there were things I could have done to more deeply institutionalize our culture or build stronger leadership, but mostly I accept that a union has a life of its own and the glorious members of 2300 will guide it.

**FIGURE 20.** As our strategies and power became more sophisticated, we never lost the spunk and rebelliousness of our members. Shop steward Helen Patelunas wore her UAW buttons and T-shirts, but she added something extra for one of our strikes. (Local 2300 newsletter)

When I recently met with a few local leaders, I was reminded of what I loved for all those years. They had spunk. They knew they came from a legacy of underdog courage. They were part of a long tradition of local working-class guts, grit, and underestimated capabilities. Just being with them for an hour reminded me exactly why I didn't want to leave for those fifteen years.

Workers not only want to *receive* respect and be *treated* with dignity. Those are important, but passive, words. Those are outcomes of a well-fought struggle. Workers can also enjoy and be transformed by the fight itself, the solidarity, the mischief, the righteous power of standing alongside one thousand Davids, pulling that slingshot back together and letting a thousand pebbles fly.

# Afterword

Watching Donald Trump or one of his many right-wing disciples' rallies today, more than a quarter century after leaving Local 2300, I see a disillusioned white working class that looks a lot like the mostly white, rural, Cornell workforce. Yes, I can see Martha Wiicki gleefully chanting "Lock her up," or "*All* lives matter." But instead, Martha hollered at the top of her failing lungs "Union yes," and "No justice, no peace." She voted for a strong union, organized others, and went on strike four times to condemn and change an unfair system.

Today there are those who have concluded that the white working class is unredeemable. Whether described as white workers, white male workers, or white workers without a college education, have they become so layered in racism, cultural conservatism, anti-immigrant paranoia, religious fundamentalism, and gun worship as to be politically unreachable? I humbly believe that there are lessons imbedded in our granular, workplace-based struggles for justice at Cornell that provide some guidance and hope about building organizations that confront racism and sexism and increase class power.

For hundreds of years the right wing has targeted the struggling white working class with its racist venom, both coded and overt, often finding a receptive home. Our slavery-based economy, Jim Crow, and mass incarceration of Blacks have terrorized and attempted to violently nullify Black participation and power. But for the upper classes and corporate power structure to fully succeed in controlling America's economic and political life, the white working class also needed to be controlled and suppressed. In addition to the brutal crushing of labor organizing, the right wing has long relied on cultivating white working class racism, typically achieving complicity and often outright support. Whether it has to do with the NRA, the Proud Boys, conservative evangelicals, or traditional capitalist myth creation, the white working class has been a broad tipping-point target that can shift political power and keep the rich in near complete control. While the twin evils of racism and class oppression that leaders from Dr. King to Rev. William Barber have powerfully described have kept all workers and all Blacks oppressed, whites of all classes have also been advantaged over Blacks in every sector of social life, including the workplace.

Historically, the white working class has at times been able to see and even fight through the fog of lies and organize. Many white workers joined Blacks and supported socialism and communism in the first half of the twentieth century, organized auto and steel, and elected FDR four times. In thereby creating a few fundamental rights and elements of social democracy, always skewed toward white America, the white working class, linked with people of color, has intermittently been able to be a force for its own class interests and steps toward a more equitable society.

The decline of fighting unions, forces that achieved impressive improvements in the daily lives of millions of workers, has done more than just economic damage to the working class. It has weakened credible sources of information about the world we live in. Labor's decline has also reduced a key arena for the practice of democracy: the local union. This vacuum has been filled with gusto by right-wing forces, by reinforcing social divisions, nativism, and white supremacy, demonizing immigrants, and diverting attention from unmet material needs to abortion, guns, male fragility, and religion. For decades of labor's decline, much national progressive political leadership evaporated. Corporate centrists ruled the Democratic Party, resulting in workers feeling abandoned and leaderless, with their class needs sold out.

For workers like our Local 2300 members, the economic ladder was buried ten feet underground in poverty. But white workers understood they were at least one or two rungs higher on that depressed ladder then their brothers and sisters of color. Building real power, addressing racism while unifying on common economic issues, was a key challenge and learning experience in building Local 2300. The development of Local 2300, described in these pages, is one road map for how the white working class can join in confronting racism, be an ally to all those struggling against oppression and an agent of broad progressive change.

Local 2300 members would show up at fall membership meetings with guns on their pickups. I used to joke with the guys and a few women showing off their rifles that this was going to be a meeting where nobody sat behind the chair. They weren't heading to a Rush Limbaugh rally or to intimidate some oppressed religious or ethnic minority. It was just hunting season.

Local 2300 members were not right-wing activists or consciously ideologically driven. Like most white workers they were socialized into cultures built through centuries of familial and social prejudice against Blacks, Jews, women, and the LGBTQ community. Local 2300 members were also used to accepting that the massive institution they worked for and dominated their community not only held every single card in their lives, but also deserved their loyalty and appreciation.

*In the Shadow of the Tower* is precisely the story of how many of those beliefs changed, and how these workers became activated behind a very different set of beliefs.

There are four lessons I take from my nearly twenty years' experience organizing with rural white workers.

First, ignorance may be a mile wide, but it is only an inch deep for most workers. It is shallow because that ignorance is at odds with self-interest and basic humanity. Our union engaged a thousand workers. Nonstop education came in the form of newsletters, radio, and—by far most important—conversations with increasingly developed activist peers. Self-interest was agitated, and common interest revealed. The union enters the consciousness at narrow but profound points. Merit pay is unfair. Poverty wages are hurting my family. I'd like to have a pension I can retire on. My back is sore from no limits on lifting, and my lungs are bad from all these toxic chemicals. But like a wedge, those narrow points of self-interest open the mind. My problems are the same as others. Our common denominator is we are workers and powerless as individuals. It doesn't have to be that way. Let's get together, learn to fight, and have fun doing it. Imbedded inside each of these awakenings was the reality that in every area of economic hardship, women and Blacks had it even worse. The union consciously played a role in exploring and exposing that reality. We did it because it was an important part of the unfairness that needed to be confronted, and because, while at times controversial, it made us stronger.

Second, agency matters. It wasn't just about education. It was about a clear sense that we were going to *do* something about our plight. This activated a sense of potential and hope. People began to talk about what they deserved and what was possible. They moved through a series of escalating activities, from signing cards to wearing buttons, to voting in the union, to striking for better wages and working conditions. Our mind-set from the organizing committee on was to prioritize participation, collectivize as many decisions as possible, and build activist leaders. We avoided as much as possible the undertow of business unionism, top-down wheeling and dealing, or the cult of a single leader. The workers themselves acted in increasingly effective ways. We did not win every battle; each contract was a mixture of gains and defeats built on high and just expectations. Even in intermittent defeats, workers who participated owned the results and moved forward together. Workers learn most from activity and build loyalty to each other across race and gender and commitment to their organization. They learn about the boss, themselves, other workers, the community, and what more it might take to win greater justice. Local 2300 was a nonstop opportunity for a wide range of participation.

Third, building camaraderie builds empathy. Members got to know each other. The higher-skilled, middle-class workers saw the suffering of the laid-off food service workers. Members learned about gender power dynamics and sexual harassment of their sisters. Members' kids played together across race at union picnics and at our food bank. Socially conservative workers got to know and respect Lesley Finch, an out lesbian maintenance mechanic, a tough-as-nails, smart, and bitingly funny activist leader. Rural white workers imbued with racism from birth and culture got to march and fight side by side with southern-born Blacks.

Finally, you have to win, not all the time, but on a regular basis. You have to win things that matter to your material lives, to your kids and your family, and you have to win things that are about right and wrong. Ending the merit-pay system was more about respect and dignity than more money. It was the most important issue for us to confront in the first negotiations. It was why we struck, and winning the end of that corrupt system was what allowed us to go back to work with our heads held high. Workers will not keep on fighting if we only tilt at windmills. We anchored our progress in every small and medium victory and were not bashful about sharing good news. The experience of winning transforms workers' consciousness by inspiring them with a sense of courage and confidence to change that world. Right-wing populism preys on workers' frustrations, despair, and sense of powerlessness. Success via the union experience gives workers hope and can make them less vulnerable to faux populism. Every fight included people joining together across race and gender. Whites saw that their Black coworkers were solid and stalwart, and men saw women unafraid to confront the boss. Black workers saw that their white coworkers would take on pay inequities and discrimination against people like Roy and Frankie. Systemic unfairness included class, race, and gender. We won because we were together.

The story of UAW Local 2300 is the story of how a union can be a movement for progressive change that brings together white, brown, and Black, straight and gay, hunters and pacifists, and all manner of other differences around a common goal and common strategy of workers as workers fighting for justice, dignity, and better lives for themselves and their families. This was a unified agenda that embraced issues of race and gender not based on transactional accommodation of constituencies, but because a 90 percent white union learned the lessons of struggle and their identity as workers.

Redeemable? Local 2300's predominately white members joined with their siblings of color and elected a Democratic Socialist mayor, endorsed gay rights, supported Jesse Jackson's presidential campaign, built a strong multiracial fighting organization, won major work-site and community victories, aligned with workers throughout our region, and since my departure elected female, Asian, and Black local union presidents. Every worker's struggle within our community found a home with us.

This approach to struggle shriveled the space that hate relies on to manipulate workers' fears and replaced it with unity and fight.

## Acknowledgments

This book would not exist without the collaboration, inspiration, close editing, and "you can do it" encouragement of my longtime friend and comrade Carl Feuer. His wisdom and firsthand, activist experience with this story are present in every chapter. Current leaders and retirees at UAW Local 2300 have encouraged me and provided many of the photos in the book. Author, friend, and agitator Bill Fletcher made time to read an early manuscript. His enthusiasm and political and professional seal of approval provided an inspiring boost. Wonderful "old" friends Joe Alvarez, Jeff Grabelsky, Rudy Porter, and new friend Ellen David Freedman all provided terrific and varied insights that led to dozens of improvements. Academic manuscript readers Risa Leiberwitz (Cornell) and Gordon Lafer (University of Oregon) did more than "green-light" this book. They also let me know that this story had the respectful tone and accessibility that were important priorities, and insecurities, for me. Jim Lance, at Cornell University Press, has moved me deftly through the steps of publication.

My beautiful, loving children, Sam, Addy, Lucy Rose, and Iris, have been with me through every twist and turn these past few years. My wife, Meggin Rose, taught me the value of a comma and shorter sentences and disabused me of my overuse of quotation marks. Through thick and thin she has patiently listened to me ramble about one idea or another. She gave me the support and space to escape into this world of my past, sharing my hope that I could write something useful for the here and now.